Capitalism and the Rule of Law

From deviancy theory to Marxism

Edited by

Bob Fine, Richard Kinsey,
John Lea, Sol Picciotto and Jock Young

for the
National Deviancy Conference
and the
Conference of Socialist Economists
(Law and the State Group)

Hutchinson of London

Hutchinson & Co. (Publishers) Ltd
3 Fitzroy Square, London W1P 6JD

London Melbourne Sydney Auckland
Wellington Johannesburg and agencies
throughout the world

First published 1979

Set in IBM Press Roman

Printed in Great Britain by The Anchor Press Ltd
and bound by Wm Brendon & Son Ltd,
both of Tiptree, Essex

British Library Cataloguing in Publication Data

Capitalism and the rule of law.
1. Deviant behaviour
I. National Deviancy Conference
II. Conference of Socialist Economists
301.6'2 HM291

ISBN 0 09 140330 8 cased
0 09 140331 6 paper

Thi
Book

Capitalism and the Rule of Law

Contents

Acknowledgements

Throughout this project we have received a considerably large amount of help and support. Particularly, we would like to thank Glynis Cousin, Isabel Roberts and Carole Brigden for typing and retyping the manuscript, the CSE Law and the State Group for critically assessing many of the ideas aired in this book, the 1978 Clacton Conference which was its dress rehearsal, Raph Samuel for his enthusiasm which sparked off the project, Victoria Greenwood for ideas and patience with a distraught editorial collective and Dave Cowell for running the Polytechnic of Central London Conference in the first place.

Preface

The subject matter of this book does not fit easily into any single academic category. Its origin lies in the convergence of interests of Marxists working in a wide range of areas. Starting out from the traditional demarcations of sociology of law, jurisprudence, industrial relations, political theory, social history and deviancy theory, the authors are united by a recognition of the need to take an integrated approach to the study of law and discipline in capitalist societies.

This convergence was the basis for the first joint conference of the National Deviancy Conference (NDC) and the Conference of Socialist Economists (CSE) Law and the State Group, held in London in January 1979 under the title, 'Capitalist Discipline and the Rule of Law'. This volume presents a selection of the papers from that conference together with two introductions. Jock Young traces the emergence of a Marxist perspective on law and crime in the NDC from the libertarian and left-oriented currents within Anglo-American deviancy theory of the late 1960s and early 1970s. Bob Fine's starting point is the debates within the CSE Law Group about the class character of the 'rule of law' and its connections with capitalist productive relations, centring around a reappraisal of the work of Eugene Pashukanis.

The common aim of the papers presented here is an attempt to bridge both the 'orthodox' Marxist focus on economic exploitation and the concern of deviancy theory with non-economic control. A particular focus of the book is the intimate relationship between legal control and control in the work place, avoiding both the notion of law as a simple reflection of the economy or as existing in some 'relatively autonomous' realm of its own. John Annette's paper reasserts the tight, though largely forgotten, relationship between classical political economy and legal theory and jurisprudence.

The essays by Richard Kinsey, John Lea and Dario Melossi explore the relationship between the development of capitalist societies and changing forms of discipline and social control. The key work here is that of Melossi who in the pages of the Italian journal *La Questione Criminale* initiated the debate with the elaboration of a series of hypotheses on the changing nature of capitalist social control. His essay appears in English translation here for the first time. Others (particularly Lea) have subsequently formulated replies and expansions.

The following essays, by Phil Cohen, Jeanne Gregory and Roger Matthews, take the discussion into specific areas of social control: those of police work, the role of women at work and the nature of penal and similar 'total institutions' respectively.

From Portugal, Boaventura de Sousa Santos raises the vital question of the nature of alternative socialist legality through a survey of the emergence of institutions of popular justice in Brazil and in Portugal during 1974-5. The book concludes with an attempt by Sol Picciotto to evolve a general theory of law informed by recent work on the nature of the capitalist state (Holloway and Picciotto 1978).

Capitalism and the Rule of Law has been a collective effort involving discussion within and beyond the editorial group. All proceeds from it are to go towards the establishment of a new journal in the area: *Studies in Class and Justice*.

The sphere of circulation or commodity exchange within whose boundaries the sale and purchase of labour-power goes on, is in fact a very Eden of the innate rights of man. It is the exclusive realm of Freedom, Equality, Property, and Bentham. Freedom because both buyer and seller of a commodity, let us say of labour-power, are determined only by their own free will. They contract as free persons, who are equal before the law. . . . When we leave this sphere of simple circulation or the exchange of commodities . . . a certain change takes place, or so it appears, in the physiognomy of our *dramatis personae*. He who was previously the money owner now strides out in front as a capitalist; the possessor of labour-power follows as his worker. The one smirks self-importantly and is intent on business; the other is timid and holds back, like someone who has brought his own hide to market and has nothing to expect but – a tanning.

Karl Marx, *Capital* (1976, p.280)

It is not enough that the conditions of labour are concentrated at one pole of society in the shape of capital, while at the other pole are grouped masses of men who have nothing to sell but their labour-power. Nor is it enough that they are compelled to sell themselves voluntarily. The advance of capitalist production develops a working class which by education, tradition and habit looks upon the requirements of that mode of production as self-evident natural laws. The organization of the capitalist process of production, once it is fully developed, breaks down all resistance. The constant generation of a relative surplus population keeps the law of the supply and demand of labour and therefore wages, within narrow limits which correspond to capital's valorization requirements. The silent compulsion of economic relations sets the seal on the domination of the capitalist over the worker. Direct extra-economic force is still of course used, but only in exceptional cases. In the ordinary run of things the worker can be left to the 'natural laws of production' i.e. it is possible to rely on his dependence on capital which springs from the conditions of production themselves and is guaranteed in perpetuity by them.

Karl Marx, *Capital* (1976, p.899)

1 Left idealism, reformism and beyond: from new criminology to Marxism

Jock Young

> The history of philosophy is the history of forgetting . . . . Problems and ideas once examined fall out of sight and out of mind only to resurface later as novel and new. If anything, the process seems to be intensifying; society remembers less and less faster and faster. The sign of the times is thought that has succumbed to fashion; it scorns the past as antiquated while touting the present as the best . . . . The forgetfulness itself is driven by an unshakable belief in progress: what comes later is necessarily better than what came before. Today, without romanticizing the past, one could almost state the reverse: what is new is worse than what is old. [Jacoby 1975, p.1]

The aim of this article is to put recent developments in Marxist thinking about crime and law in context. Its task is twofold: firstly, it places the recent wave of theory in terms of the left-oriented deviancy theory and new criminology which preceded it; secondly, it looks at the major foci of interest in recent work, noting the striking convergence in concerns between a wide range of writers. It is the central contention of this paper that we are witnessing a major convergence in debate which has the virtue of being both interdisciplinary and international, of embracing social historians, sociologists and lawyers or jurists, of discarding the former American hegemony in the field and considerably widening the forum of discussion. To place this debate in its intellectual and social context is of paramount importance. We suffer from the amnesia which Jacoby speaks of; debates which have been a continuing part of the history of this century are forgotten, hidden away under the rubric of the 'end of ideology' or rediscovered, refurbished and presented as the very latest intellectual achievement – the new model theory, outdating and outclassing last year's model for its steely insight and theoretical grip. So it has been for the two major socialist currents in criminology since the war: reformism and left idealism. Reformism, the major social democratic ideology which in its left and its right wing variants forms the basis of many of the governing and major opposition parties of Western Europe, and which has been disproportionately effective in the spheres of moral and criminal legislation, finds no place in our textbooks of criminology. Students in this country are dispatched with regularity to dissect the Children And Young Persons Act or the Parole Act or the Wolfenden Report, and return crestfallen: all they can discover is eclecticism. Bits of positivism, pieces of classicism, smatterings of labelling theory are all that they can find – but evidence of consistent theory eludes them. For nowhere does reformism occur in their academic bestiary: it is an area where amnesia has set in and where tunnel vision occurs.

As a result, progressive criminology engages in debates which have little credibility outside the academy: it debates with pure positivism, with labelling theory, with structural functionalism. A whole generation of sociology students cut their teeth debating with a consensus theory which is pre-Keynesian in its basis, and allows the most vulgar varieties of conflict theory to be set against it, garnished with the false redolence of innovation.

It is not just a question of learning to look our major political and intellectual adversaries squarely in the eyes. We are looking in the opposite direction – into the academy, and then, the few times we turn our heads to gaze at the outside world, we can see nothing. Reformist theory is a mere mishmash. Conservative thought – despite its extraordinary power and importance – is beyond the pale; we will not even contemplate it.

My colleagues and I have the continuing task of trying to situate, historically and intellectually, the developments in the theory of crime and punishment which have occurred since the war. On one side, this has involved an examination of the official criminology of reformism,[1]* on the other, the plotting of the pendulum of thought within the academy as it swung away from positivism towards the idealism of the new deviancy theory in the mid 1960s.[2] This article, in part, continues the story from there, from the reaction against the libertarian tradition of deviancy theory with its *laissez-faire* approach to social problems, to the emergence of the new criminology committed to a socialist transformation of society. For although the politics changed, the theoretical structures remained in fact scarcely altered. Thus the *laissez-faire* idealism of labelling theory became replaced by a left idealism of the new criminologists in the early 1970s.[3]

Left idealism

There has been around for a decade or more a general rhetoric which passes itself off as a 'Marxism'. Sometimes this is expressed in sophisticated intellectual form, sometimes an old-style Leninism, sometimes just as an unexamined vocabulary co-existing with other vocabularies . . . common elements in this rhetoric are some of the following: first, there is a platonic notion of . . . the ideal capitalist state . . . . This state is inherently profoundly authoritarian, as a direct organ of capitalist exploitation and control, and any inhibitions upon its power are seen as 'masks' or disguises, or as tricks to provide it with ideological legitimation and to enforce its hegemony. It may . . . follow that any symptoms of authoritarianism are seen as disclosing a 'crisis of hegemony' and may even be welcomed as unmasking the 'true' (i.e. platonic) character of the state, and as signalling the 'conjuncture' in which a final class confrontation will take place . . . . And this may . . . consort with a loose rhetoric in which civil rights and democratic practices are discounted as camouflage, or the relics of 'bourgeois liberalism'. And to cut short the list, this very often goes along with a wholesale dismissal of *all* law and *all* police and some-

* Notes to each chapter appear in a section beginning on page 178.

times with the soppy notion that *all* crime is some kind of displaced revolutionary activity.

This is not the place to engage in philosophical wrangle. I will simply say that these are all half-truths which have a continual tendency to degenerate into rubbish. What is more to the point is that this rhetoric can be seen to unbend the springs of action, and to discount the importance of any struggle for civil rights. If *all* law and *all* police are utterly abhorrent, then it cannot matter much what *kind* of law, or what *place* the police are held within; and yet the most immediate and consequent struggles to maintain liberty are exactly about kinds and places, cases and precedents, and the bringing of power to particular account. [Thompson 1978, p.xi]

In the recent period[4] left idealism emerged as a force in the late 1960s and early 1970s chiefly as a radical philosophy of marginalized groups. Black power, the prison movement, the student left, the new Bohemia, women's liberation, gay activism – all have borne strong elements of this position, all carried radical interpretations of crime and deviancy, all worked from the margins (however large these were in reality!) rather than the traditional socialist foci of the work force and the factory. Corresponding to these social movements were profound resonances within the academy: the marginal proletariat found allies in the marginal middle classes.

The key characteristics of left idealism are voluntarism, a coercive conception of order and functionalism. That is, a voluntaristic conception of human nature coupled with a notion that social order is in essence maintained by a series of coercive institutions structured together in a functionalist fashion.

Left idealism is basically a radical version of social contract theory.[5] Man is endowed with reason and free will. Social order and social justice are non-contradictory constructions of man's reason, society hangs together by the voluntary contract of the individual to society. But what if the society is inequitable? If social order itself violates justice? Then, the only *reasonable* course of action is for individuals or groups to detach themselves from commitment to such a body politic. But how then, if it is irrational to conform to an inequitable order, does such an order maintain itself? The distinctive left idealist answer to this question is that order is maintained by coercion. Yet the problem is the plainly consensual nature of social order in advanced capitalist formations. This consensus is viewed by the left idealist as a mere appearance. To start with, it is exaggerated in that there exist, in embryo, contra-cultural forms: but the actual extent of its tenacity is achieved by mystification. The illusion of common interest is fostered by key parts of the control apparatus: for example, education, parliamentary democracy and the mass media. These, on the one hand, deliberately overplay the degree of consensus, whilst on the other hand indoctrinating the individual into consensual values. Whereas certain control institutions are overtly ideological in their role, others represent more openly the 'iron fist' of control. Thus the fundamental left idealist tenet of the coercive nature of reality necessitates a stress on the totalitarian and mystifying nature of the control apparatus. Without the latter it would be difficult to explain how the intransigent rational citizen could not immediately see through the transparent inequity of the system.

The law itself represents a universalistic patina thinly covering the interests of the powerful, whereas the police and the prisons represent the direct coercion in which the state is based. All control institutions, whether overtly coercive or apparently ideological, are part of a single control apparatus which has its basis in coercion. Indeed, there is a tendency towards the conflation of all institutions into the unitary concept of 'social control' which is seen to utilize a strikingly similar mode of discipline, controlling and coercing the individual from cradle to grave. The school, the factory, the prison are the same.[6] Not only are the various institutions of civil society conflated together but so are the institutions of the state and of civil society. The institutional order becomes an extension of the state, involving the same disciplines, the same form of power for an identical purpose.

This institutional structure is seen to be a seamless web of institutions which are unambiguously supportive of capitalism. Each institution is 'explained' by being related teleologically to the total society. Contradictions, whether between or within institutions, are ignored. Most importantly, the development of such institutions (parliamentary democracy, the welfare state, etc.) as a result of class struggle is ignored in this functionalist analysis. We have a peculiar Marxism which allows the class struggle only in permitted areas (for example, work, grass-roots politics, etc.).

The control institutions are seen to gear together as a series of cumulative layers acting on the biography of the individual to produce a miasma of misperception and irrationality backed continuously by thinly disguised coercion. But, paradoxically, despite their extraordinary power and homogeneity of purpose, human voluntarism breaks through everywhere: crime and deviance are the visible signs of the triumph of the human spirit over conditioning.

If law is the direct expression of ruling class interests, then working-class behaviour, being a direct and spontaneous expression of proletarian interests, inevitably contradicts it. Where the two trajectories cross is crime. Research reports, whether they are self-report studies of high-school delinquency or exposés of crime at the top – which point to the widespread nature of crime – add fuel to this simple conflict theory. Crime is endemic throughout society; it is, in fact, scarcely differentiated from normal behaviour. The hidden figure, the grey zone of undetected crime, becomes so huge that it has swamped and encompassed all normality. Events as diverse as the Watts Insurrection and the Watergate trials all show the underlife of the consensus and, what is more, the reality which mere appearances attempt to mask.[7] Crime, in this theoretical structure, scarcely needs an explanation: it is obvious that capitalism – the inequitable social order – causes crime. The unwavering line of causality stretches from capitalism to crime – independent of historical specificity and comparative analysis.[8]

Just as crime becomes conflated with normal behaviour, crime and deviancy become less and less distinguishable. The interests of the ruling class express themselves as a series of pragmatic strategies against the underclass whether this involves the deployment of the label 'criminal', 'mentally ill', 'inadequate' or 'subnormal' etc. But there is a strategic pattern in their deployment. The positivist label 'mentally ill' is more often used to defuse voluntaristic criminality just as the supposedly demeaning label 'common criminal' is used to defuse the political dissident. Thus when ruling-class strategies change, because of economic crisis or because of a political offensive, the repercussions are experienced fairly homogeneously throughout the control structure (for example, Scull 1977). That is, the categorization which is used by the authorities is seen as largely irrelevant, basically a smokescreen for a unitary system of social control and, in reality, a false categorization anyway. It is vital that we move away from their categories and definitions of crime, to the construction of our own definitions which are both morally and conceptually superior (see Schwendinger and Schwendinger 1975).

Crime, then, is a first flicker of consciousness, a proto-revolutionary event which challenges property relations, reappropriates value, or counterposes a violent defiance against the power of the state. The empirical focus of left idealists is directed to those forms of crime closely related – either historically or contemporaneously – to the class struggle over property rights or to large-scale theft or looting, but rarely to minor violence, petty theft and alcoholism; although soccer hooliganism and vandalism have been interpreted as inarticulate forms of class struggle. A key feature of left idealism emerges here: it *plays down* the impact of working-class crime against the working class; it *maximizes* the anti-working class effects of ruling-class crime whilst at the same time stressing its endemic nature.

The real criminals are in power; the poor are pilloried for their crime and used to discipline the masses. The very inefficiency of the prison system is its efficiency: the palpable warning to the rest of the population that criminal infractions lead to a near irrevocable stigmatization. The prison is depicted as the central control institution of capitalism and the police as its agency; it is the fist of coercion which is poised over the population and the clearest indication of the true nature of the social order. But even within the penitentiary, mystification has set in; positivism acts as an ideology which, under the rubric of treatment, occludes and indeed extends the rigours of punishment. The indeterminate sentence, the use of psychotropic drugs ('the liquid cosh'), of sensory deprivation and isolation techniques, all augment the panoply of coercion whilst invoking the rhetoric of humanitarianism and medicine.

Positivism, in all its manifestations, inside and outside prison, is seen as the main ideological enemy and thus the prime target of left idealism. It is the major ideology directed at the criminal in an effort to mystify his presence and defuse his actions. Periodically and with greater and greater insistence sightings of further incursions of positivism are made: we are on the brink of a scientifically manipulated society where all resistance is obliterated.

The strategy of left idealism is *exposé*, it is to reveal the iron fist within the velvet glove, and then the final task, if we list the parts of the apparatus of social control – the prison, the police, the school, the mass media and even the nuclear family – is their systematic abolition. Both the form and the content of these institutions are inimicable to working-class interests; their form is undemocratic, manipulative and coercive, their content an illusion which pacifies the masses. As they are functional to capitalism, they must be removed: in its most invidious form, reform itself is seen to be functional and great lengths are gone to to avoid the siren-like embraces of reformism.[9] For it is necessary that the existing institutional order be smashed and replaced by proletarian institutions.

Given the nature of law and the police, it is the traditional lumpenproletariat who are in the front line and who are often the front-runners of consciousness. The lower-class contraculture with its antagonism to work, to law and the police and with its immediate experience of the callous reality of social order is the group most likely to reach out and seize the desiderata which have been denied them and in the process be most ready to conflict with the capitalist forces set against them. The necessary prerequisite in this struggle is the forging of popular alliances across the ranks of, first of all, the various marginal groups: prisoners, mental patients, claimants, clients, students, and then to move on from the margins to the centre where the indoctrination has been greatest.

The central theme of left idealism is its stress on the illusory nature of appearances: the consensus masks coercion; the crime statistics are sheer fiction, hiding the criminality of the rich; treatment is a cloak for punishment; the universalism of law is a rhetoric which hides particularism; 'normality' and 'deviance' are concepts of ideology; the differentials between various parts of the social control apparatus merely conceal an identity of purpose and a unity of form and discipline. In its most extreme form idealism is unable to distinguish the factory from the prison, education from brainwashing, the anti-social from the social, fascism from democracy.

Left idealism and reformism on law

I want to turn now to reformism and to introduce this section by contrasting the left idealist and reformist understanding of bourgeois rights. For it is here that the most crucial discussion occurs.

Both positions start from stressing the gap between the ideals of law and their actual practice. For the left idealists such a gap is an unbridgeable chasm: furthermore, it is scarcely a surprise, for it is a further revelation of the illusory world of appearances. It is precisely out of such a disparity that the 'revolutionary' cynicism, by which Thompson aptly characterizes left idealism, arises. Thus the central strategy as far as law is concerned is to debunk it. That is, to expose the unequal reality underneath the rhetoric of equality and to thus cast doubt on the legitimacy of the system. For the reformist, likewise, it is the gap between bourgeois reality and ideals which can be used to prise open capitalism, but this is part of a piecemeal process of reconstructing the social order. Ellen Wood (1978, pp.227-8) captures this well when she contrasts the two:

Social Democratic revisionism [had as its basis] 'patchwork reform' and passive faith in some 'peaceful process of dissolution' which would eventually and more or less automatically transform capitalism into socialism. This strategy seems to have been based on the assumption that the liberty and equality of bourgeois democracy were so antithetical to capitalism that the mere maintenance of bourgeois juridical and political institutions, assisted by reform, would produce a tension between freedom and equality at this level and unfreedom and inequality at other levels of society. This tension would in a sense replace class struggle as the motor of social transformation. At the other extreme might be a position that regards liberal democracy as so completely a mere reflection of capitalism that it must be regarded as simply a deception, a mystification. This is roughly the position of various ultra-left groups. Liberal democratic capitalist states, according to this view, are not substantially different from authoritarian or even fascist forms of capitalism.

The keynote of reformism is the interventionist state, on the one hand, and the bifurcation of human behaviour on the other. The state can, and must, be wrested from ruling-class control and set to the process of realizing socialism. It is not the form but rather the content of the institutional order which is inimical to working-class interests. Thus it is not the police force but the control of the police which is the problem, not the prisons but their size and 'lawlessness', not the educational system *per se* but its limited degree of opportunities, not parliamentary democracy but political awareness, not the form of the law but its content and targets. Furthermore, reformists would differentiate between the various institutions of society and would ascertain certain areas as relatively innocuous and others as in more desperate need of reform. Thus Company Law may need to be radically changed to swing the balance in favour of the working class, whereas criminal law itself – for instance, the laws against personal violence, rape, burglary, etc. – are a problem more in the degree to which they are implemented and the public protected rather than in their present form or content.

As Ellen Wood points out, the mainspring of such a programme involves the taking of bourgeois ideals seriously; for the supposition is that they can never be realized until socialism is achieved. The friction between bourgeois ideals and reality, between equality and property is the generating force of advancing legislation in the interests of the vast majority of the population.

For the reformists there are two sorts of people: the normal and the determined. Normal people – the vast majority – are free and voluntaristic; free, that is, in a given social order whose market laws like laws of gravity put limitations on the individual. Socialism involves the collective control of such a market, a means by which the powerful do not dominate it and where production is for the universal good. Capitalism interferes with the freedom and equality of the individual, it perverts the market and it brings elements of particularism and inequality into the legal system. By means of legal intervention, reformism restricts the egoism of the powerful which constantly threatens the freedom and equality of the less powerful; for example, educational opportunities, anti-discriminatory measures in the occupational spheres, egalitarian medical facilities, etc. It opens up opportunities, on the one hand, whilst it protects on the other. The law can, thus, create a world where individuals compete on equal terms and where all its subjects' property and personal safety are protected against excesses of power and wealth.

In contrast to the voluntaristic majority, there is a small minority of individuals who are, in essence, determined and who by dint of biological, psychological or social reasons are unable to exert free choice. They exist at the margins of the social order, they are a different order of humanity, the product of a separate and marginal aetiology.[10] The role of the reformist state is simultaneously to intervene in the realms of normality to maintain and increase freedom whilst protecting, treating and attempting to reintegrate the deviant into the body politic. Crime in these terms is a product of such a bifurcation: on the one hand, one confronts egoism – a product of the individualistic ethos of capitalism – which leads to voluntaristic crime; on the other, one finds pathology – a product of marginal problems of capitalism giving rise to a deterministic criminality. The contrast here is between the egoistic property speculator or professional burglar, voluntaristically embracing the cupidity of capitalism, and the alcoholic and petty thief, mere artefacts of their wretched social environment and faulty individual natures.

Whereas left idealism conflates the various institutions of social control, reformism sees them as distinct and separate; whereas idealism sees the state as an artefact of civil society, reformism argues for the autonomy of law from the influence of particular interests; whereas left idealism conflates, reformism differentiates and *demands* clear demarcations.[11] The deviant must be differentiated correctly and scientifically from the normal, the criminal separated out by due process from the mentally ill, treatment must not occur in places of punishment (for that is the insidious face of positivism) but neither must punishment masquerade as treatment (for that is a violation of basic rights).[12]

In left idealism, crime was ahistorically and abstractly linked to capitalism, and, thus, with its overthrow crime would disappear for the inequitable society which gave rise to it would no longer exist. With reformism, crime in essence is seen as a natural phenomenon, an inevitable product of any social order, although its present excessive rate is attributable to capitalism. The advent of socialism will drastically reduce the prison population for, on the one hand, it will remove the ethos of egoism which causes much voluntaristic crime, whereas, on the other hand, it will ameliorate the conditions in the margins which cause deterministic crime. But there will always remain a minority of people, particularly in a complex industrial society, who will have to be controlled by penal sanctions. Individual variations in human egoism and pathology will always give rise to rule-breakers, to a contradiction between the highly co-ordinated discipline of the modern industrial order and human freedom.

Now, whereas left idealism sees crime as a crude yet protorevolutionary action and the possibility of building up a movement from alliances of the marginal groups, reformism takes the opposite course. Crime on the streets and the control of crime in the corporations are an important justification of reformist politics and the reformist state. Crime is the universal enemy which unites all sections of the population. From the German SPD to the Italian PCI, law and order are the stock in trade of reformism.

Yet even if it is a major part of electoral strategy, the control of crime is not viewed by reformism as a central locus of social control. Indeed, the central tenet of reformism is that the working class is capable of controlling the state and that the means of doing this are already legitimately available. Social control is made legitimate by the provision of economic justice backed up by political democracy. It is in the work place and the voting booth that the citizens may either grant or withhold their consensual support for the state – direct coercion is a minor part of social democratic forms of government, and is applied only against criminals and terrorists, marginal social categories against which coercive reaction is not a subject of dispute.

In conclusion, let it be clear that in contrasting left idealism and reformism one is referring to typologies within which few authors achieve the maximum consistency. Furthermore, many writers will show differing tendencies at differing times. This being said, it will be no revelation that the left idealist position is not a million miles away from the work of the new criminologists whether they be Taylor, Walton and Young, Richard Quinney or Carol Smart; nor for that matter from the work of Michel Foucault. If it should be protested that such 'instrumentalist' Marxism is long since intellectually transcended (cf. Balbus 1977), let me point to the palpable vigour of left idealism within a wide range of fields and hazard the suggestion that its reluctance to disappear reflects its having a relationship to reality which is of more significance than being a 'mistake' in thought.

The continued attraction and prevalence of idealist and reformist notions of crime and law reflect a recurrent tendency of social thought to reduce itself either to the view that the world of appearances is merely an illusion occluding the real world, or that the concepts of everyday life are an approximation of reality which have been biased by the influence of particular interests. Thus, left idealism informs us that the image of the social universe as a consensus of free men and women confronted by a minority of determined deviants is an illusion, that consensus is a sham, and that determinism is a pseudonym for coercion and mystification. And that the gap between bourgeois ideals and practice is direct evidence of this sham, as is the 'class bias' in the criminal statistics. Reformism, in contrast, instructs us that the bifurcated image of society is more or less accurate. It would debate the degree of freedom at present possible, it will challenge the accuracy of existing categories and insist on the possibility of large reductions in the ranks of the deviant, but criminals and 'normals' will always be with us. Following this line of reasoning, the gap between statute and reality is simply the result of the perversion of justice. This must, and can, be eradicated. Thus, the greater weighting of working-class people in the official statistics is a product of bias – although in the lower reaches of society one will always find a leavening of misfits, inadequates and ne'er-do-wells.

The criminal statistics as a product of class struggle

For reformism, most crime is the product of a separate aetiology, and is committed by marginal people with atypical biological makeup or psychological disposition or social environment. For the left idealist, since crime is ubiquitous there is no need for a separate aetiology, rather the problem is to explain the way in which the poor are scapegoated and vastly over-represented in the official statistics.

To an extent the left idealists are correct, for there is a consensus among criminologists, based on the analysis of self-report and victimization studies, that crime is a ubiquitous phenomenon (see Pearce 1976; Wright 1973). Thus we have a concentration of state coercion at a particular point of the class structure and this despite the well nigh ubiquity of crime. Given this, the reformist notion of the marginal causation of crime is obviously at fault.

But for the idealists there is also little comfort in these statistics, for they usually fuel their polemic by contrasting crimes of the working class with the considerably more costly crimes of the powerful. And indeed the cost of corporate crime is greater than that of professional crime which, in turn, is greater than street crime. But one group is nearly always forgotten: a significant contribution to the cost of crime is that of working-class people in their work place (part of the 'hidden economy' phenomenon: see Outer Circle Policy Unit 1978). This costly problem of crime has a very low arrest rate and contributes comparatively little to the official statistics. Thus a significant section of the working class are *not* scapegoats of the criminal justice system. It is 'street crime', crime amongst the lower working class, which is the major component, numerically, of the statistics. Furthermore, when one looks at the official criminal one finds that far from the Robin Hood version of criminality preferred by the idealists, the victims of street crimes are usually working class (see Platt 1978).

Why then do the crimes of the powerful or of the organized working class go relatively undetected? I want to suggest that the criminal statistics are a product of class struggle. Laws are passed, themselves a result of struggle, which aim to control for example: pricefixing, pilfering at work, industrial relations, supplying goods to Her Majesty's enemies, etc. The existence of such laws allows sociologists to talk of 'undetected crime rates' but the actual degree to which they are implemented is dependent on the balance of class forces at a particular time and place.

With this in mind we may hypothesize that street crime is massively over-represented in the statistics because:

Universality It is the common enemy; all sections of the population (except perhaps left idealist criminologists) are united in their opposition to street crime.

Vulnerability The lower-working-class criminal is the most vulnerable of all the population which engage in crime. There is extreme disorganization.

Transparency Street crime is more transparent than crime of the other sections of the population. Interpersonal violence is more apparent than the violence accruing from 'bending' the rules as to factory safety legislation; 'mugging' is a more obvious theft than the alteration of accounts or the secret fixing of prices between oligopolies.

Qualitative difference Street crime is the only form of serious crime where the victim is overwhelmingly in the same social category as the offender. It is lower-working class against lower-working class, black against black, neighbour against neighbour. Much of it represents the ultimate in anti-social behaviour and unites all sections of the population against a common enemy.

On the level of aetiology, the subjective degree of desparation and individualism needed to commit crimes which are both comparatively likely to be apprehended and anti-social endows such activities with a qualitatively differing meaning. Yet the cause of crime is intimately linked to the aspirations of the employed worker. For it is the denial of citizenship, of access to the wider consumer society, which is at its roots, otherwise the dole and the welfare benefits alone might serve to pacify them (cf. Piven and Cloward 1972).

The spiral of functions and dysfunctions

To summarize briefly the place of crime and crime control in the capitalist social formation, one might see it as a series of processes which are in a contradictory fashion both functional and dysfunctional.[13]

The contradiction of employment

Capitalism produces a relative surplus population which does not have a stake in work and work discipline (see Spitzer, 1975),[14] but this alone explains only their potential for crime and not their actual criminality.

The aetiology of crime

The ever-present disparity between effort and reward, the emphasis on equal opportunities yet the unequal reality of a class society, the stress on individual competition yet the handicapped nature of the race – all militate to create a criminogenic milieu. Such contradictions are particularly hard on the marginalized groups who are denied full access to the consumer society. Thus, the very process which binds the worker to his bench, turns the mind of the unemployed to forms of crime which have, in fact, a high rate of surveillance and apprehension.

Legitimation and the control of crime

The state intervenes in the control of lower-working-class crime to protect the 'honest' citizen. This has a real basis (crime is a threat) and involves an element of popular justice (street crime is unjust to the worker). Crime control is a central part of the legitimation of the state, and the element of reality contained in such control underlies the process of *ideological inversion*. That is, to the question, 'why does capitalism have severe problems?', the answer is 'because of problems such as crime' and not that capitalism is the cause of such problems.[15]

Criminalization, discipline and the prison

The prison, on one level, given its high recidivism rate, is a dysfunctional institution: it hardens and well nigh irrevocably stigmatizes its inmates. But this feature is, of course, all the more effective in the control of those who have not been prisonized – particularly those in work who have most to lose from such a stigma. Thus the dysfunctional becomes *in part* the functional.

We see, then, how the worlds of work and crime control are intimately related, both in terms of the pragmatics of control and the ethos of legitimation.

The contradictory nature of appearances

Ideology arises from the opacity of reality, where the opacity of reality is in fact the forms in which reality 'presents itself' to men, or the forms of its appearance conceal those real relations which themselves produce the appearances. [Mepham 1974, p.103]

Social reality . . . produces *appearances* which are sometimes more than mere illusions . . . . They have far greater consistency, let alone coherence, than mere illusions or ordinary lies. Appearances have reality, and reality involves appearances. [Lefebvre 1968, p.62]

It is the contradictory nature of reality which denies the assertion of left idealism that appearances are only illusions; it is this and their opaque nature which allows reformism its credibility. Let us examine the image of crime and of the law-abiding citizen in this light. I have argued that the conventional image of the criminal is on one level a mystification (crime is ubiquitous, there is no separate aetiology of the criminal individual, the cost of street crime is lower than other forms of crime), whilst on another it has a reality (street crime is a product of the marginalized, the nature of their crime is qualitatively different, the criminal is determined compared to the labourer, the criminal poses a real danger and an injustice to the working class). Thus, the images used by reformism, tied as they are to the world of appearances, are not mere illusions. It is their cognitive fit with reality that explains their credibility, it is their real sense of justice that generates support for them among the people. This will be made clear if we return once again to the two spheres (see the quote in the introduction to this book) and examine the world of the worker in contrast to that of the criminal.

On the level of the sphere of circulation the worker freely sells his labour, he obtains the market equivalent for it, he is an equal before the law, he is not cheated by the individual capitalist. But, if we leave 'the noisy sphere' of human rights and enter 'the hidden abode of production', we find a different story: instead of freedom we have coercion and necessity; instead of formal equality, substantive inequality; instead of equivalence, exploitation – the extraction of surplus value. Yet, of course, the adult male worker has a qualitatively greater freedom than, for example, under feudalism, or in a fascist state with the direction of labour, or – most appositely in this context – than those of his contemporaries who are excluded or marginalized from the labour market (for example, the unemployed, women, old people, adolescents, racial minorities). The market economy creates, indeed needs, real freedom, rationality and individualism, at least in *certain sections* of the population.

Bourgeois rights and capitalist production

For the left idealist, the illusions of freedom and equality in the market place give rise directly to the illusions of civil liberties. For the reformists, civil liberties exist independently of the market and indeed can be used as a fulcrum to change the inequalities therein.

In fact, the extent to which bourgeois rights occur varies widely within capitalist social formations. For example, when we compare the absolute monarchy and the democratic republic, or the fact that in some capitalist societies women are fully enfranchised whereas in others they are excluded from the electorate (see Luxemburg 1969, p.56; Therborn 1977, pp.3-41). Ellen Wood (1978, pp.229-39) sums up the relationship well:

> . . . liberal democracy, while grounded in the juridical principles of capitalist productive relations, cannot be reduced to them . . . . If equality and freedom of a very limited and ambiguous kind are essential and common to *all* capitalist social formations, liberal-democratic political institutions have *not* been equally common and are certainly not essential.
>
> One must go beyond the function of juridical and political freedom and equality in sustaining capitalist relations of production and the position of the dominant class, take account of [their] value for subordinate classes, indeed, the degree to which these political and legal forms are the legacy of struggles by subordinate classes.

Let us see how such an analysis will aid our understanding of the use of law in the struggle for justice.

Anatole France and sleeping under bridges in Paris

I want to argue that the nature of law is contradictory: that formal equality is a gain to be struggled for, not a sham (compare with left idealism), but that formal equality obfuscates and legitimates substantive inequalities (compare with reformism). Similarly, progressive law can make a real impact on the world, although its aims are always undermined by the class society of which it is a part. That is, law in the present period, both in its form and its content, can embody progressive if contradictory moments. Left idealism would deny this assertion both in terms of form and content; reformism would argue that the content of law can be progressive and uncritically accept the form of law. I want now to briefly examine the position that Isaac Balbus (1977) has adopted. For this is considerably more sophisticated than left idealism, yet represents a tendency in recent work which is constantly in danger of reverting to a politics which is scarcely distinguishable.

Balbus's stance is that the debate centring on the possibility of law being autonomous from the interests of the powerful is fundamentally misplaced. For the degree to which law can be proven to be autonomous of individual interests is the degree to which it articulates with the needs of the capitalist system. That is, it is precisely in its autonomy and its abstractness that the legal form corresponds to the very cell of capitalism: the commodity form. This is a fascinating interpretation of the separateness of the state and civil society. For it argues that it is precisely their separation that guarantees their domination by the commodity form. The fetishistic form of law will always undermine its possible progressive content. What immediately makes one suspicious of this argument is that Balbus avoids the problem of spelling out how progressive pieces of legislation, gained through working-class struggle, are rendered counterproductive by virtue of their legal format.

At base, his problem is the absence of any substantive link between commodity fetishism and legal fetishism. Their coexistence is argued on the level of metaphor with the invocation of notions of homology and functionality.[16] Such an argument becomes problematic when confronted with the variety of legalistic devices (juvenile courts, tribunals, etc.) which are not discernibly homologous with the commodity form. Thus, rather than an attempt being made to ground these forms materially and substantively, they are merely noted as a unitary homogenous deviation from strict legal fetishism and then baldly linked to the occurrence of 'decommodification' (cf. ibid., p.586). Thus the functionalism of his approach denies the role of subordinate classes in their struggle, for example, for legislation with a progressive content, for the imposition of bourgeois standards of law against conservative attack, or for the evolution of new forms of law in the areas of juvenile justice. The absence of any element of class struggle in Balbus' structuralism leads to a position which would suggest that the very achievement of legal equality would in fact reinforce present inequalities, conceal their existence and further serve to legitimize the system. Thus Balbus writes:

> The 'quality' established and protected by the legal form is thus purely formal insofar as it is established in and through an abstraction from the real social inequalities of capitalist class society, which nevertheless continue to exist, of course, even if denied 'political' recognition . . . . The formality of legal equality, however, does not prevent it from having substantive consequences which are anything but equal and are in fact *repressive*. On the one hand, the systematic application of an equal scale to systemically unequal individuals necessarily tends to reinforce systemic inequalities; this, of course, was the force of Anatole France's famous, ironic praise of 'the majestic equality of the French law, which forbids both rich

and poor from sleeping under the bridges of the Seine'. Thus Marx argues that the right of 'equality' guaranteed by the legal form is 'a right of inequality, in its content, like every other right'. On the other hand, and probably even more importantly, legal equality functions to mask and occlude class differences and social inequalities . . . which militates against the formation of the class consciousness necessary to the creation of a substantively more equal society. [ibid., pp.577-8]

I believe this position, with its ritual invocation of Anatole France, is profoundly mistaken.

1 It ignores the fact that the rich are treated more leniently than the poor for equal offences (see Trubeck 1977) and that this is a systematic disparity occurring at each stage of the legal process: apprehension, trial, sentencing and scale and type of penalties.
2 It ignores the fundamental bourgeois category of proportionality, putting all its stress on formal equality alone. If penalties were applied proportionally to social harm, first of all the sanction against sleeping under bridges would remain what it is – trivial, while the bourgeoisie who commit extremely costly offences on any *comparative* measure would be very heavily penalized.
3 Further, implicit in the Anatole France assertion is, of course, that the majority of crime is the determined result of poverty, which is simply incorrect.
4 Balbus, once again, grossly over-simplifies the nature of legal categorization, much of which has in fact strong substantive elements (for example, race relations, equal opportunities, juvenile justice).
5 He takes out of context Marx's argument in the 'Critique of the Gotha Programme'. True, the right of equality is the right of inequality like any other right, but Marx did not foresee the disappearance of bourgeois rights until the material basis of such rights had itself disappeared. Thus:

   to avoid these defects [of inequality] right instead of being equal would have to be unequal. But these defects are inevitable in the first phase of communist society as it is when it has just emerged after prolonged birth pangs from capitalist society. Right can never be higher than the economic structure of society and its cultural development conditioned thereby. [Marx 1968, p.320]

   Thus even communism in its first phase retains what Lenin termed 'the narrow horizon of bourgeois right'. Indeed law in this transition period, as Pashukanis argued, would remain essentially bourgeois. All this is a far cry from Balbus's diatribe against the use of law in contemporary American capitalism.
6 To turn one's back on the law leaves one in a position where one would deny oneself its protection, where we would be in danger of making the blunder of conflating bourgeois democracy with fascism, and would, as Edward Thompson has so forcefully argued, allow us scarcely any purchase on the political controversies of our time. For the conservatives and the social democrats in their repeated law and order campaigns would be met by a left idealist denial of the problem of crime or of the possibility of legal justice.

Conclusions

If democracy has become superfluous or annoying to the bourgeoisie, it is on the contrary necessary and indispensable to the working class. It is necessary to the working class because it creates the political forms (autonomous administration, electoral rights, etc.) which will serve the proletariat as fulcrums in its task of transforming bourgeois society. Democracy is indispensable to the working class, because only through the exercise of its democratic rights, in the struggle for democracy, can the proletariat become aware of its class interests and its historic task.

In a word, democracy is indispensable not because it renders superfluous the conquest of political power by the proletariat, but because it renders this conquest of power both *necessary* and *possible*. [Luxemburg 1969, p.63]

The legal struggle at the formal level

I wish to reject the left idealist position which sees bourgeois rights as a sham, and legality as the insidious basis of co-optation. Rather I would suggest that the achievement of formal equalities in the field of criminal law in equality of protection from crime, apprehension and sentencing, coupled with penalties proportional to social harm, would result in:

(*a*) an immediate reduction in the size of the prison population;
(*b*) a reconstitution of its population;
(*c*) the transformation of the prison itself from a 'lawless' to a lawful institution.[17]

Such a programme would give rise to severe problems of control and have important repercussions within the social order.

The legal struggle at the substantive level

I wish to reject the reformist position which sees the formal struggle as easily realizable and as an end in itself. What is necessary is neither the outright rejection of bourgeois norms nor their blanket acceptance, but their transcendence. For instance, we must move from the bourgeois concept of mitigating circumstances (i.e. random, individualist, accidental excuses) to a class-based conception. Boaventura de Sousa Santos (1976 and chapter 10 below) has provided examples of this from the Portuguese revolution involving the criteria used to judge individuals in the People's Courts. Similarly, we must involve ourselves in legislation which moves from individual to collective responsibility for crimes and we must make much of the 'excuse' of unemployment as mitigation for crime, for this denial of citizenship is a fundamental contradiction under capitalism.

The key position of crime control in the legitimation of the state

I have argued that the control of crime is an important way in which ruling class legitimation occurs. This resolves around the real yet contradictory depiction of street crime. People are in part protected against crime and the control of crime is presented as a major *raison d'être* of the system. This ideological inversion which depicts the problems which capitalism gives rise to as the justification for the status quo is of central importance. It is important, therefore, to directly confront law and order campaigns, as well as defending and extending basic civil liberties.

The control aspects of work and the prison are not separate areas but intimately linked, both in terms of their impact and of the ethos behind them. The equation of effort and reward is made positively in the work place and negatively in the prison. It has a hold on the population because it stands from the same premises of justice: thus the struggle for economic justice and penal reform is one and the same thing.

Non-linear nature of the control structures

In terms of strategy, it is vital to recognize the diversity of the different control structures. Some areas, such as juvenile justice and anti-discriminatory measures, already involve recognition of substantive inequalities. It is important to reflect on the contradictions of a position which all too frequently leads the radical criminologist simultaneously to demand formal equality in the field of juvenile justice and substantive equality for adults. Each social category involves strategically different problems which have scarcely been mapped out, let alone properly analysed. Likewise, over time, it is necessary to be aware of contradictory processes, non-linear changes in the control structure, such as the phenomenon of bifurcation, wherein both a hardening and softening of state reaction can occur towards different segments of a problem population.

Contradictory nature of reforms

There is no such thing as a reform which is without contradictions. For example, elsewhere we have shown (Greenwood and Young 1976) how the right to abortion as a formal demand conceals the substantial inequalities which force some women to have abortions. Progressive abortion legislation involves gain on the level of women's rights but is simultaneously a control measure on the part of population controllers. Reforms, because they emerge from a class-divided society, will always display such a two-sided nature. The search then for the 'pure' reform is a chimera which we can well do without.

The strategic use of law at different historical periods

There is a simple yet frequent confusion about the strategic use of law in different historical periods. It is necessary to make the distinction between law used as a means of defence for the working class at the ebb of struggle (for example de Sousa Santos's work on the courts in Rio [1977]), law used as part of a working-class offensive, law in a revolutionary situation (for example, de Sousa Santos's work on popular justice during the Portuguese revolution [1976]) and law in the transition to communism (for example, the problematic of Pashukanis).

The contradictory nature of appearances

Our quarrel with bourgeois theorists is not one of maintaining that their depiction of crime and law is an illusion but rather that, however inadequate their premises, the tenacity of their theory is because of its intimate if contradictory relationship with the real world. For if left idealism believes criminological theory to be illusion, reformism believes that if we were to examine enough facts and develop a sufficiently correct theory, we could produce a programme which would solve the riddle of crime. Against this, one must note that the contradictions of theory are not resolvable without fundamental change, for they are generated by the contradictions of reality itself. As Pashukanis (1978, p.184) put it:

> At the Hamburg Congress of Criminologists in 1905, van Hamel, a reputable representative of the sociological school, declared that the main obstacles to modern criminology were the three concepts of guilt, crime and punishment. If we freed ourselves of these concepts, he added, everything would be better. One might respond to this that the forms of bourgeois consciousness cannot be eliminated by a critique in terms of ideas alone, for they form a united whole with the material relations of which they are the expression. The only way to dissipate these appearances which have become reality is by overcoming the corresponding relations in practice, that is by realising socialism through the revolutionary struggle of the proletariat.

Postscript

Recently David Downes has accused radical criminologists of writing:

> as if imperialism was monopolized by capitalist societies, as if the tanks had never rolled into Prague or Budapest, as if people in capitalist societies were utterly dehumanized . . . .

It seems that we are unaware of 'such a record as *The Gulag Archipelago*' on the one hand and 'the humanistic achievements of Western societies "under capitalism" ' on the other (Downes and Rock 1979, p.9)

I hope this volume disabuses our critics; there must be neither amnesia regarding the past nor a detente of the senses with regard to the horrors of the present. As a matter of fact, it is liberals and reformists who are most forgetful of the past and most willing to compromise with the present. As socialists we have more to lose from a failure of democracy and more to gain by its transcendence. It is on this principle that we face the future.

2 Law and class

Bob Fine

The political context

From many quarters there has arisen within Marxist debates on law and the state a renewed concern with the social and historical character of the forms of regulation expressed by these categories. What is it about bourgeois legal and state power which differentiates them from other ways of exercising power? What is the historical basis of these forms of domination? Are they present in all societies, as a natural product of social order in the abstract? Are they the product of the increasing 'complexity' of society, as the social division of labour and forces of production grow beyond the confines of more informal and personal modes of control? Are they the product of societies based on independent producers, whose connections with each other are mediated through the exchange of commodities? Are they the product of any society divided into mutually antagonistic classes, due to wither away with the abolition of class society? Or are they the specified product of capitalist relations of production?

These questions concern the class character of bourgeois law, punishment, and the state: their claim to represent the general interests of society over against the private and class interests pervading economic relations; their claim to embody a democratic principle, at least in potential, if not in their present actuality; and their claim to be the necessary foundation of democratic organization, whichever class rules and whatever form of production and distribution is dominant. And they concern counterclaims that their democratic appearance is no more than a mask, obscuring the fundamentally dictatorial character of all class rule and state regulation.

It is this latter tendency, for example, which Edward Thompson has recently castigated as a source of cynicism toward the whole question of democracy, and for its debilitating effect on the left in countering the intensification of class oppression. He writes:

> there has been around, for a decade or more, on the unofficial Left a general rhetoric which passes itself off as a 'Marxism' . . . first there is a platonic notion of the true ideal capitalist state, to which any actual case is only an approximation, but to which all cases must inevitably tend. This state is inherently profoundly authoritarian, as a direct organ of capitalist exploitation and control, and any inhibitions upon its powers are seen as 'masks' or disguises, or as tricks to provide it with ideological legitimation and to enforce its hegemony. It may (but need not)

> follow that any symptoms of authoritarianism are seen as disclosing a 'crisis of hegemony' and they may even be welcomed as unmasking the 'true' (i.e. platonic) character of the State, and as signalling the 'conjuncture' in which a final class confrontation will take place. This may easily consort with a profoundly pessimistic determinism, in which that kind of authoritarian state can be seen as the necessary concomitant 'structure' of the 'capitalist formation'. And this may, and often does, consort with a loose rhetoric in which civil rights and democratic practices are discounted as camouflages, or as relics of 'bourgeois liberalism'. And to cut short the list, this very often goes along with a wholesale dismissal of *all* law and *all* police, and sometimes with a soppy notion that *all* crime is some kind of displaced revolutionary activity. [Thompson 1978, p.xi]

The target of Thompson's assault is not clear, but it corresponds with some diverse tendencies within the left, including those who see a manifestation of 'fascism' in every court case, and certain 'libertarian' positions which attack without differentiation all forms of 'social control' (a posture not unknown to critical deviancy theory). My concern, however, is not so much over the undoubted limitations of this political stance (a target over the years of numerous Marxists), but with the particular assumptions underlying the kind of critique, illustrated here by Thompson, but currently gaining a much wider currency within the left.

For the basis of Thompson's critique consists in an unflinching belief in the democratic character of the legal side of state power. He writes that law seems to him to be 'an unqualified human good', in that it 'imposes effective inhibitions upon power' and defends the citizen 'from power's all-intrusive claims'. No problem is raised over the form of bourgeois law itself, the only issue concerns the struggle against the intrusion of 'class-bound procedures' into the legal mechanism. Even the rise of a working-class power, based on egalitarian productive relations, will require 'the negative restrictions of bourgeois legalism', and Thompson declares any belief to the contrary to be a 'utopian projection' (Thompson 1977, pp.264-6). So it is that Thompson's critique of the official left is directed against a 'bureaucratic statism', in which 'the state, in *all* its aspects, was seen as a public good, a defence of working people, or of the little man, against private vested interests' (Thompson 1978, p.xi). It is bureaucracy, waxing fat on the narrow line between welfare state and police state, which is the dark side of democratic rule. Law itself appears unproblematically, from this viewpoint, in the light, as do its 'dogged' defenders in, for example, the National Council for Civil Liberties.

It is clear that the 'rule of law' does impose effective inhibitions on power. What remains at issue, however, is what kind of inhibitions, what are its limits, what is its base? For law is not the *only* way in which restrictions on power can be instituted; for example, whatever the strengths and weaknesses of soviets, they too provide a model for the inhibition of centralized power. And in the present context, organization of the working class inhibits the power of capital and the bourgeois state no less than law. What must be resolved is the relation between inhibitions enforced by the form of law and by forms of extra-legal political organization. We should inquire, for example, why it is that Engels, by contrast to both

Thompson and his 'left' adversaries, takes the position that under communism law will disappear 'in its entirety'; and that under capitalism the rule of law, in its most egalitarian form, complements the class domination of capital:

> the specific character of economic oppression which weighs down the proletariat stands out in all its sharpness only after all the special privileges of the capitalist class have been set aside and the complete juridical equality of both classes is established. [Engels 1968a, p.501]

Engels emphasizes that the working class 'cannot fully express their conditions of life in the juridical illusion of the bourgeoisie'; that the victory of the working class cannot be attuned with a 'juridical attitude' in which 'the basic rights of workers to the full proceeds of their labour' is secured. On this basis, however, Engels insists on the necessity of putting forward 'specific legal claims', without which 'an active socialist party and indeed any political party at all, is impossible' (quoted in Korsch's appendix to Pashukanis 1978, p.192).

The issue which these passages from Engels raise is that the bourgeois form of law is contradictory. Between two polar positions, between its dimissal as a mask and its elevation as an unqualified good, we need to understand the way in which law acts as a form of domination, the social basis upon which this form of power emerges and sustains itself, and thence the contradictory functions which it performs both for the rulers and the ruled, capital and labour.

The contemporary significance of the class character of the form of law derives from two major sources. On the one hand, events in Europe (the persecution of Mehdvedev, Bahro, Charter 77, etc.) continue to raise the question of the character and causes of the repression associated with Stalinism: whether they should be connected with a de facto *disregard* of legal form by the ruling bureaucracies; or alternatively with the development of the notion of 'proletarian law' by jurists faithful to Stalin, and the introduction of an essentially bourgeois legal constitution and code in 1936, just before the peak of the terror trials. On the other hand, the issue comes up in the West in the context of serious incursions by bourgeois states into democratic freedoms and rights, the development of state and corporate bureaucracies scarcely touched by legal regulation or any other form of public accountability, and, not least, in the context of the growth of neo-fascist parties. Behind the enforcement of the Official Secrets Act in state trials (for example, the 'ABC' trial), D-notices censoring the press, long-term 'emergency' legislation (the Prevention of Terrorism Act), the deportation of aliens (Agee, Hosenball), the restriction of legal and political rights of immigrants, the growth of special security forces (SPG, Special Branch, etc.), the constant clamour for increased police powers – behind these 'gradual' invasions of legal and democratic rights, most blatant perhaps in the *Berufsverbote* practised by the West German state against dissidents on the left, there lies a deeper problem: whether the 'restructuring' of the state which accompanies every crisis of capital accumulation is in the present situation leading it even further beyond the bounds of the rule of law, and how the left should respond to these political developments.

It is in this context, when the imperatives of capital accumulation and the class struggle have put into question the viability of the 'rule of law', and when we witness a movement toward the substitution of bureaucratic–police rule for social-democratic forms of power, centred around legality and parliamentary representation, that the issue of forms of bourgeois domination has emerged again with particular sharpness. The question of law is brought into close connection with that of the state, and the distinction between a Marxism, which addresses the political significance of law, and a sociology, which directs attention to the connections between law and the 'moral order', become most marked. At the same time, within Marxism, it becomes imperative to differentiate between the forms of power through which the domination of capital is mediated and secured. It is this which has led some sections of the left into an unqualified defence of 'legality' against 'arbitrary power'. On the other hand, this emphasis on *form* poses its own dangers: that of neglecting the class *content* behind the forms of law; and of neglecting the significance of the erosion of legality for the imposition of new conditions of exploitation and accumulation.

Without making any mechanical parallels, there are some general lessons which we can draw from the rise of fascism in Germany. On the one hand, the position of the Comintern and the German Communist Party (KPD) (in the 'third period' of 'adventurism') was precisely one of ignoring the differences between 'social democratic', 'fascist' and what Trotsky called 'Bonapartist' forms of bourgeois domination. Since all of these represented the interests of monopoly capital, since all were instruments in the hands of the bourgeoisie and functioned for the reproduction of capitalist social relations, the KPD was able to come to the absurd conclusion that there was no essential difference between these forms. This theory of 'social fascism' had the disastrous political consequence of disarming the working class at each stage of fascist growth; for if social democracy is already fascism, then the transition from one to the other appears as a matter of no consequence. Further, the possibility of a 'united front' between social-democratic and communist workers in the face of a common threat was severely impeded, since social democracy appeared as no more than a 'left-mask' for fascism. On the other side, the 'constitutionalism' of the German Social Democratic Party (SPD) led them either to support or to offer no fight against the growing acquisition of power by the bureaucracy, police and military, increasingly dispensing with democratic ties to the judiciary and parliament, and increasingly resorting to rule by 'emergency decree'.

In that context, in which the social-democratic left justified the erosion within the state of legal and political rights under the rubric of 'stability' and the fight against fascism, and the communist left dismissed legality as one face of 'social fascism' in their general equation of all forms of bourgeois rule, the defence of law had as much, or more, importance then as it does today. But the significance of the form of law could not be separated from its *content*: namely, the class relations which constituted the foundation of the legal form; and the transformation of these class relations hidden behind the move first to 'Bonapartism', which relegated legality and parliamentarism to shadows of their former selves, and then to fascism which substituted for them brute force and police terror. The strength of Trotsky's analysis was precisely to probe the links between these distinct forms of state power and the class relations which provide their substance. Trotsky, in the course of his extended critique both of those who identified social democracy with either Bonapartism or fascism, and of those who defended the spirit of the constitution as it elevated the bureaucracy above society, constantly searches for the class basis of these historical developments. Thus he writes of fascism:

> Fascism is not merely a system of reprisals, of brutal force and police terror. Fascism is a particular governmental system based on the uprooting of all elements of proletarian democracy within bourgeois society. The task of Fascism lies . . . in demolishing all the defensive bulwarks of the proletariat . . . when a state turns fascist, it doesn't only mean that the forms and methods of government are changed . . . but it means that workers' organisations are annihilated . . . and that a system of administration is created which penetrates deeply into the masses and which serves to frustrate the independent crystallisation of the proletariat. [1969, pp.17, 21]

Trotsky was well aware of the political significance of different forms of bourgeois rule and in particular of the significance of the 'rule of law'; for this, he was dubbed an abettor of social democracy by the Stalinists. But he did not dislocate bourgeois legality from the class relations to which it gives expression; he did not elevate the forms above its content. For instance, in reply to the KPD's assertion that there are no 'class distinctions' between democracy and fascism, both being bourgeois in character, Trotsky replies:

> The ruling class, however, does not exist in a vacuum. It stands in definite relations to other classes. In a developed capitalist society, during a democratic regime, the bourgeoisie leans for support primarily on the working classes which are held in check by the reformists . . . . In a fascist regime . . . capital leans on the petty bourgeoisie which destroys the organisations of the proletariat. Is there a difference in the 'class content' of these two regimes? If the question is posed only as regards the ruling class, then there is no difference. If one takes into account the position and the inter-relations of *all* classes, from the angle of the proletariat, then the difference appears to be quite enormous. [ibid., p.23]

For Trotsky, the defence of the form of law could not be isolated from its content. Bourgeois law was not an absolute elevated above the conditions of civil society which gave it birth; but the expression of capital mediated by the independent organization of the working class. It was for this reason that it had to be defended against attack from the right and against indifference from the left as the political form necessary for the exercise of 'proletarian democracy' and for the transition to socialism.

Form and content of law

I have dwelt upon the political context in which the relation between the *forms* taken by state and legal domination and the *content* of their activity should be analysed in order to demonstrate that attention to these questions has not merely been a quirk of an academic Marxism, but has been one of fundamental significance in the history of Marxist movements. It is, however, a history that has been suppressed, in some measure as a result of the heritage of Stalinism. The works of the Bolshevik legal theorist, Evgeny Pashukanis, have been particularly influential in the recovery of these issues; but it is also the fact of his somewhat scholastic style which has given credence to the notion that concern over the connections between form and content of power is an over-subtle and esoteric luxury. In fact, the works of Pashukanis himself must be seen in the light of his political intervention against currents of belief, later closely associated with Stalinism, which held that the maintenance of legal forms in the Soviet Union was not a necessary hang-over of bourgeois forms of regulation, destined eventually to disappear with the growth of communism, but the first expression of the development of 'proletarian law'. Pashukanis saw in such a position an implicit conservatism which failed to uncover the social roots of the legal form, and which was consequently caught in the idealization of law itself as a supra-historical force. The theoretical achievement of Pashukanis, however, has been to steer a course between the fetishism of form and the fetishism of content. It is this theoretical issue which I wish to comment on briefly.

Pashukanis criticizes those normative theorists who present law as the expression and condition of all order. A familiar illustration of this position within sociology, perhaps, is to be found in the approach of Émile Durkheim (1964), who presented law and punishment as the expression of the 'collective conscience' of society and as the functional prerequisite of social order. Thus Durkheim idealizes the form of punishment, as a 'public power' acting in the name of society, and distinguished from the private will of any individual or group within it. Similarly, crime is presented as a violation of this collective conscience, closely associated with egoism and lack of normative control by society. Not only is there no investigation of the social content behind this form of appearance; but not the slightest attempt is made to analyse the historical character of the legal or penal forms. It is assumed that they are necessary characteristics of any social order. Pashukanis sees this kind of approach as a 'formalism', which entirely ignores the question of content. We might add that attempts by reformers to give a Marxist gloss to such theories, does little to improve their value. For example, the Dutch criminologist, Willem Bonger (1969), continued to see in punishment the expression of a 'public power' acting on behalf of society, only to criticize existing penality in terms of the intrusion of class distortions into its practice; for example, by the confinement of political prisoners. Criminality still appeared as the egoistic violation of the general norms of society, located however in the individualized character of economic relations. There is still no investigation into the historical or social character of punishment: only a desire to bring the actuality up to the ideal.[1]

In contrast, a sociological approach which looks to the economic and political interests behind specific legal and penal measures appears as a significant advance over the high-sounding phrases of formalism. But here again there is a disappointment. For exclusive attention is directed towards the class interests served or the economic functions performed by one or other measure of law or punishment; in other words, exclusive to the question of content. Why these interests or functions should have been served by the *legal* form of regulation or by *penal* repression remains a question unaddressed. So that, while a more or less adequate political or economic history may be gleaned, there is no concern with law and punishment themselves as historical forms of domination. For example, it is not sufficient to explain the proliferation of confinement in the seventeenth and eighteenth centuries by its functionality for the growth of capitalism, through its provision and disciplining of forced labour. Whether or not this is true, it does not explain why forced labour was provided through the forms of punishment, and not say slavery, indentured labour, press gangs, direct dependence on the manufacturer, and so on.

This exclusive focus on the content of law leaves the social and historical character of its form unexamined (and thus open to any dogmatic interpretation). The tendency then exists to reduce these specific categories to the general categories of control, repression, imperative co-ordination, sanction, power, regulation and so on. The form that power takes is entirely ignored; or when it is addressed, it is only to declare the attributes of these forms (their claim to be egalitarian, to protect the freedom of the individual, and so on) as ideological fictions, or as masks obscuring the unitary and timeless reality of power as such. Since the question of form is neglected, the limits which particular forms impose on the performance of a particular content cannot be conceptualized, and a very strong impression of the uncontradictory rationality of the law as an instrument wielded by the ruling class results, or alternatively an uncontradictory assessment of the functions law provides for the reproduction of economic relations and for the reproduction of class dominance.

It is a failure to pursue the question of form that flaws some of the most productive analyses by Marxists of penal law and punishment. The consequence is that the forms of law and punishment are eternized in ways similar to those of formalism. For example, Rusche and Kirchheimer (1964, p.5) fail to address the specific forms of power expressed in the category of punishment, when they state: 'Punishment as such does not exist; only concrete systems of punishment . . . . Every system of production tends to discover punishments which correspond to its productive relationships.' Punishment itself appears as a natural and timeless form of power.

There exist similar problems in otherwise adventurous attempts[2] to develop a Marxist analysis of penal law directly from the treatment which Marx gives this question in *Capital*. In discussing the emergence of a 'proletariat, Marx emphasizes the role played by law in expropriating and disciplining the available labour force. But Marx is not concerned with law as such, only with its effects on political economy. One cannot jump from a position which analyses the important functions performed by, for instance, penal statutes on vagrancy for primitive accumulation to an analysis of these laws in terms of their functionality for the development of capital. What is legitimate for a study of political economy is not legitimate for a study of legality; in the latter case, what has to be explained is not only the reasons for the bloody repression of vagabondage, but also why this repression took the form of legislation that 'treated them as "voluntary" criminals, and assumed that it depended on their own good will to go on working under the old conditions that no longer existed' (Marx 1976, p.896). It is not sufficient to discover beneath the form of punishment in the sixteenth century a class repression; it is also necessary to work back synthetically and ask why repression should take the form of law and penality. Marx was aware of the problem, that he dealt with 'the state, law, morality, civil life . . . *only in so far* as political economy itself professes to deal with these subjects', and Engels in turn commented that he and Marx 'neglected the formal side of political, juridical and other ideological notions – the way in which these notions came about – for the sake of their content' (quoted in Thompson 1978a, p. 259).[3]

A closely connected tendency which Pashukanis also criticized is one which conceives of legality as an ideological fiction, imposed on a social reality to which it has no correspondence by some organ of centralized authority (the state), and usually serving some particular function for the ruling class or for the reproduction of economic relations. All these elements are to be found in Poulantzas's structuralist account of law:

> Judicial structures (determined in the last instance by the structure of the labour process) which sets up at their level agents of production distributed in social classes as juridico-ideological subjects, produce the following effect on the economic class struggle: the effect of concealing from those agents in a particular way the fact that their relations are class relations . . . . This effect of isolation is terrifyingly real: it has a name, competition between the wage earning workers and between capitalist owners of private property. It is in fact only an ideological conception of the capitalist relations of production . . . . [1973, p.130]

Against this kind of extraordinary reasoning (not, of course, against Poulantzas himself) Pashukanis responds, firstly, that it makes no sense to say that 'the norm (judicial superstructure) generates the legal relation'; for, in order to assert that law has an objective existence, it is not sufficient to know the content or even the form of its commands. Rather one must know in addition whether 'this normative content materialises in life, that is, in social relations'. It is the position of the 'legal dogmatist' not to look at whether the legal form is 'valid', i.e. has an objective social basis, but only at its logical connections:

> If a law has merely been promulgated without any corresponding relation having arisen in practice, then an attempt to create a law has indeed been made, but without success. [1978, p.88]

Secondly, to explain the advantages of juridical ideology for the rulers (in terms of its 'isolation effect' on the working class) does not explain how this ideology came into being: 'the conscious exploitation of ideological forms is not the same as their emergence' (ibid., p.140). Lastly, Pashukanis is able to locate legality as an 'objective social relation' with its own real and determined history as the other side of the coin of the relation of commodity exchange; the same exchange which fetishizes the product as a commodity fetishizes the owner as a 'juridic subject'. There is thus no need to take the circuitous route from bourgeois exchange relations to legality via the state and its functions. What these criticisms boil down to is the necessity to see law as 'an objective social relation'. Thus Pashukanis raises directly the relation of the 'form' of law with its 'content', that is, with the social relation which it hides and which in turn must express itself in the legal form. In this respect, he follows the *method* adopted by Marx in his analysis of *economic* 'forms of appearance' and the *social* and *historical* relations which constitute that 'content' or 'substance'. The specific problems with Pashukanis's derivation of law from commodity exchange rather than from production relations I shall discuss later. For the moment, let us take up the way in which Marx discussed the relation between form and content of power in general and of law in particular.

Marx's analysis of law

For Marx, attention to forms of power and to their relation with the content of their activity became a fundamental issue when the proletarian revolution came on the agenda. Marx's own position, based primarily on an analysis of Bonapartism and the Paris Commune, and shared for the most part by Engels, was that it was not sufficient for the working class 'simply to lay hold of the ready-made state machinery and wield it for its own purpose'. It was also necessary to 'smash' the existing state and replace it with a new form of power and a new type of democracy. The revolution, in other words, consisted not merely in the transfer of power from one class to another; but in the *transition from one form of power to another*. This was a necessity, since the failure to do so would lead to the defeat of the workers' movement and the restoration of bourgeois rule:

> The disarming of the workers was the first commandment for the bourgeois, who were at the helm of the state. Hence, after every revolution won by the workers, a new struggle, ending with defeat. [Engels 1968b, p.249]

Alternatively it would lead to a new dependence of the working class on their own leaders; the transformation was necessary in order to

> safeguard the working-class against its own deputies and officials, by declaring them all without exception subject to recall at any moment. [ibid.]

But if historical experience demanded the transformation of forms of power alongside forms of economic organization, and alongside the simple seizure of the state as a means to secure these economic changes, the question remains: what is it about the form of the bourgeois state which need be dismantled and replaced? What, to put the matter in another way, is bourgeois about the bourgeois state? What is the real content of this process of transformation?

The basic answer given by Marx and Engels was that the transition consisted in a move from a 'special power', existing 'above society and alienated from society' to a power exercised directly by the people; from a power based on entrenched bureaucrats, a standing army, professional police, an independent judiciary, and on the limited confines of parliamentary 'talking-shops' within which representation took place, to one in which all officials were to be elected by universal suffrage, revocable, compensated at 'workmen's wages', in which the 'people armed' would become the sole force of repression, and in which representation was to extend to all 'working bodies, executive and legislative at the same time' (Engels 1968a, p.576).

Now, this conception is skeletal and has been subjected to numerous criticisms. But one thing is clear: the 'bourgeois' character of the state is acquired in the first place by virtue of its very form, and not only by virtue of the class which controls it or the uses to which it is put. From which it follows that the first necessity of critique is to connect the form of the state itself with its functions and content once it exists, not to reduce one to the other: to analyse the form of power 'appropriate for the economic emancipation of labour' (Marx 1968a, p.290).

This is a familiar story for Marxists. I recall it because much of contemporary Marxist theory of power, law and the state appears to neglect the problems of form, as if it were a great mystery. Lenin was right in his day to criticize those who 'examine only the content of power' to the neglect of 'its form'. Indeed, it was over the question of the historical and social character of the form of the state that Lenin (1973, p.54) attempted polemically to distinguish 'revolutionary' Marxism:

> The utopians buried themselves with 'discovering' political forms under which the socialist transformation of society was to take place. The anarchists dismissed the question of political forms altogether. The opportunists of present-day Social-Democracy accepted the bourgeois political forms of the parliamentary democratic state as the limit which should not be overstepped . . . and denounced as anarchism every desire to *break* these forms . . . Marx did not set out to *discover* the political *forms* of this future stage . . . . He limited himself to observing French history . . . and to drawing the conclusion that matters were moving towards the *destruction* of the bourgeois state machine . . . and to studying the *forms* the mass revolutionary movement of the proletariat (in the Commune) had discovered.

It is in the spirit of this study that we today analyse the legacy of Stalinism, which by no means neglects the state 'as an exceedingly active force', but does neglect the *social* character of the state form in favour of its *technical* necessity for class rule: 'the seizure of power', says Stalin, 'is only the beginning'. For Marx, it was also necessary to transform it into a 'fuller democracy'. For Stalin 'the whole point is to retain it, to consolidate it, to make it invincible' (1973, p.121).

Five years after the fall of the Paris Commune, Marx took up again the question of power in his critique of the draft programme of the German Social Democratic Party, the Gotha programme. This critique is of particular interest, since it was specifically concerned with the question of law and the centrality of this issue for the character of the socialist movements. It was aimed against reformism for its failure to examine bourgeois concepts of law and right and their place in the transition to socialism. It was inadequate, Marx argued, to demand a '*fair* distribution of the proceeds of labour', for such 'legal conceptions' as 'fairness' derive from economic relations inherent to capital. Marx unambiguously identifies the concept of 'equal right' with 'bourgeois right', and derives this principle from relations of commodity exchange, characteristic of a society in which 'individual labour exists in an indirect fashion . . . as a component part of the total labour of society'. The very form of law and right contains as its 'content' an inequality, based on the fact that formal rights abstract from the concrete social existence of individuals:

It (equal right) . . . is a right of inequality in its *content* like every right. Right by its very nature can consist only in the application of an equal standard; but unequal individuals . . . are measurable only by an equal standard in so far as they are brought under an equal point of view, are taken from one definite side only . . . . To avoid all these defects, right instead of being equal would have to be unequal. [1968, p.320]

Further, Marx equally unambiguously saw, with the elimination of all forms of exchange (that is, with individual labour becoming *directly* a component part of total social labour), the complete transcendence of the 'narrow horizon of bourgeois right'. In other words, the 'form' of law, that is, equal right, cannot be isolated from its 'content', namely, substantive inequality. But this dialectic between form and content of law in Marx's analysis cannot be transposed into a simple denunciation of all law as a bourgeois mystification of underlying inequalities.

Firstly, Marx insists, even in the advanced state of socialist transition when the means of production are communally owned, on the necessity of bourgeois right. It is required, so long as distribution is organized around the principle prevailing in the exchange of commodities: namely that each individual shall receive back from society the equivalent of the labour which he or she has put into it. In other words, the abolition of bourgeois law cannot precede the abolition of the objective social relation which is its content and from which the legal form derives. Law is not just a mask; it has an objective social basis. It follows that the abolition of an egalitarian legal superstructure without that of the objective commodity relation, which is its substance, can only lead to arbitrary determinations.

Secondly, it is as a direct consequence of this analysis that Marx lays great importance on the posing of *specific* legal demands by working-class movements, depending on the character of the state within which those movements are operating. Marx is highly critical of the posing of general political and legal claims – to universal suffrage, direct legislation, popular rights, a people's militia, etc. – which 'contain nothing beyond the old democratic litany familiar to all. They are all demands which, in so far as they are not exaggerated in fantastic presentation, have already been *realized*'. What are required are specific demands, not for a 'normal' working-day, but for ten or eight hours; not for state supervision of factories, but for inspectors to be removable only by a court of law and for workers to have the right to prosecute them for neglect of duty; not for 'regulation of prison labour', but for the right of prisoners to engage in productive labour. The characterization of law as 'bourgeois law' in no way entails, as Marx and Engels repeatedly asserted, what they called the 'abstentionist' position, that the securing and defence of specific rights – to assembly, association, freedom of the press – are of illusory significance. 'Those are our weapons', Engels said, 'are we to sit back and abstain while somebody tried to rob them from us?' (Engels 1968c, p.310).

Thirdly, in order to understand the specific character of *bourgeois* law, that is, of law under capitalism, it is not sufficient merely to see the legal form as expressing the exchange of equivalents in general. There is a distinction to be made already between a society based on the general exchange of commodities and a socialist society in which labour and individual means of consumption are the *only commodities* which can be exchanged:

> Here (under socialism) obviously the same principle prevails as that which regulates the exchange of commodities, as far as this is exchange of equal values. *Content and form are changed*, because under the altered circumstances no one can give anything except his labour and because, on the other hand, nothing can pass to the ownership of individuals except individual means of consumption. [Marx 1968b, p.319]

This, I believe, is a point of great importance and one missed by those who attempt abstractly to derive law from the exchange of commodities as such. There is an even larger distinction to be made between a capitalist society in which exchange is *subordinated* to the production of surplus value and to the circuits of capital, on the one hand, and the exchange of equivalents under socialism, where 'principle and practice are no longer at logger-heads'. In order to understand the specific form and content of capitalist law, we need to investigate this matter further.

The *starting point* of Marx's analysis of the legal form in *Capital* is to be found in the sphere of circulation. The emergence of juridical relations is derived as the immediate effect of the exchange of commodities:

> In order that these objects may enter into relations with each other as commodities, their guardians must place themselves in relation to one another as persons whose will resides in these objects and must behave in such a way that each does not appropriate the commodity of the other, and alienate his own, except through an act to which both parties consent. The guardians must therefore recognise each other as owners of private property. This juridical relation, whose form is the contract, whether as part of a developed legal system or not, is a relation between two wills which mirrors the economic relation. The *content* of this juridical relation (or relation of two wills) is itself determined by the economic relation. [1976, p.178]

Later Marx pursues this theme when examining the purchase and sale of labour-power, in so far as it is merely part of the sphere of circulation:

> The sphere of circulation or commodity exchange, within whose boundaries the sale and purchase of labour-power goes on, is in fact a very Eden of the innate rights of man. It is the exclusive realm of Freedom, Equality, Property and Bentham. Freedom because both buyer and seller of a commodity, let us say labour-

power, are determined only by their own free will. They contract as free persons, who are equal before the law . . . . Equality, because each enters into relations with the other, as with a simple owner of commodities, and they exchange equivalent for equivalent. Property because each disposes only what is his own. And Bentham, because each looks only to his own advantage. The only force bringing them together is the selfishness, the gain and the private interest of each. [ibid., p.280]

For many Marxist commentaries, including that of Pashukanis, it is this competition of atomized private interests and the fetishism of the 'juridical subject' immediately accompanying the fetishism of the commodity, which provides the basis of his analysis and critique of the bourgeois legal form. However, for Marx this analysis only holds true while we remain within the sphere of simple circulation or the exchange of commodities. When we leave this 'noisy sphere, where everything takes place on the surface' and enter into 'the hidden abode of production, on whose threshold there hangs the notice "No admittance except on business" ', a certain change takes place 'in the physiognomy of our dramatis personae':

He who was previously the money-owner now strides out as a capitalist: the possesor of labour-power follows as his worker. The one smirks self-importantly and is intent on business; the other is timid and holds back, like someone who has brought his own hide to market and now has nothing to expect but – a tanning. [ibid.]

We cannot leave Marx's analysis of bourgeois legality at the doorway; we must follow him through the doors of the hidden abode of production.

What we find there is that the exchange relation between capital and labour is subordinated to the self-valorization of capital, as one moment of its circuit. What comes back to the workers in the form of wages is nothing more than a portion of the product which they themselves continuously reproduce. The form of exchange becomes a 'mere semblance':

The capitalist, it is true, pays him the value of the commodity (labour-power) in money, but this money is merely the transmuted form of the product of his labour . . . . The capitalist class is constantly giving to the working class drafts, in the form of money, on a portion of the product produced by the latter and appropriated by the former. [ibid., p.712]

The emergence of the class relation between labour and capital is in no way equivalent to the simple exchange of money for labour-power. For money to transform itself into capital, it has to be able to be exchanged for living labour. For this to happen, what is required is a social and historical process in which workers are made free in the double sense: free from the bondage relations which fetter the worker to 'the lord of land and soil' and free from the possession of the means of production or subsistence:

A division between the product of labour and labour itself, between the objective conditions of labour and subjective labour-power, was therefore the real foundation and the starting point of the process of capitalist production.

Under these circumstances, the content of the exchange relation, that Eden of innate rights, is utterly transformed. Beneath the surface form of equal exchange, apparent in the relation between individual workers and their employers, we now find, when we view the matter from the perspective of capital as a whole and labour as a whole, an inversion of the exchange of equivalents: the appropriation of the product of one 'owner' by another without equivalent. The move from petty commodity production to capitalism does not merely entail the generalization of commodity exchange and its entry into the sphere of production; but the transformation of the exchange relation itself and of its content into its opposite. The following passage crucially modifies the analysis Marx offered when he considered exchange in abstraction from production:

Each individual transaction continues to conform to the laws of commodity exchange, with the capitalist always buying labour-power and the worker always selling it at what we shall assume is its real value. It is quite evident from this that the laws of appropriation of private property, laws based on the production and circulation of commodities, become changed *into their direct opposite* through their own internal and inexorable dialectic. The exchange equivalents, the original operation with which we started, is now turned round in such a way that there is only an *apparent exchange*, since, firstly, the capital which is exchanged for labour-power is itself merely a portion of the product of the labour of others which has been appropriated without an equivalent; and secondly, this capital must not only be replaced by its producer, the worker, but replaced together with an added surplus. *The relation of exchange between capitalist and worker becomes a mere semblance belonging only to the process of circulation, it becomes a mere form, which is alien to the content of the transaction itself, and merely mystifies it.* The constant sale and purchase of labour-power is the form; the content is the constant appropriation by the capitalist, without equivalent, of a portion of the labour of others .... Originally the rights of property seemed to us to be grounded in man's own labour. Some such assumption was at least necessary, since only commodity owners with equal rights confronted each other, and the sole means of appropriating the commodities of others was the alienation of a man's own commodities, commodities which however could only be produced by labour. Now, however, *property turns out to be the right, on the part of the capitalist to appropriate the unpaid labour of others or its product, and the impossibility on the part of the worker, of appropriating his own product.* The separation of property from labour thus becomes the necessary consequence of a law that apparently originated in their identity. [ibid., p.730]

If the relation of exchange under these circumstances becomes a 'mere semblance belonging only to the process of circulation', 'a mere form alien to the content of the transaction itself', we must in this light reconsider our analysis of law as the form of equal right expressing the exchange relation of two 'owners' of commodities. In this regard, Korsch's criticism of Pashukanis for his 'extremely strange – for a Marxist' over-estimation of circulation as the basic determinant of the bourgeois form of law takes on a particular relevance. For if we consider the exchange relation and the legal form from the point of view of its derivation from social relations of *production*, we see the entirely different content it has in a society of petty-commodity production, based on independent producers whose interconnections are established through the exchange of the products of their labour, from that which it has in a capitalist society, based on the expropriation of the working class. For in the former case, the fetishism and the competitive antagonism which lay hidden behind the form of law do not erase the real character of the exchange and its real equality in terms of a flow back in one form of what flowed out in another. But in the capital-labour relation, the exchange is illusory in that what flows back to the worker is not an equivalent in another form (money) of what he or she has put in in the form of labour; nor is it merely an 'unequal exchange' in which the labourer gets back less than he or she puts in. Rather, the content of the exchange is quite illusory, since what the worker gets back is only what he/she puts in in an earlier period. The bourgeois class character of law, as opposed to its fetishized and atomistic character, only becomes apparent when we analyse its determination by relations of production, and not by circulation alone.

It is not only that 'concrete individuals' possessing particular personal characteristics and embedded in particular social relations appear in the form of abstract 'juridical subjects' – though this is certainly the case; not only, as Trotsky put it, that 'the landlord, the labourer, the capitalist, the proletarian, the minister, the bootblack are all equal as "citizens" and as "legislators" ' (1972, p.39), which gives to bourgeois law its class character. It is rather that the very 'substance' of the exchange to which bourgeois legality gives expression and from which it is derived is an exchange only in form. Behind the form lies the constant reproduction of expropriation without return. To analyse the form of law, without relating it to its content within social relations of production, will allow us to see the commodity relation which it conceals within itself and beneath its idealization of the 'free subject'. But it will not allow us to discover the specifically *class* character of bourgeois legality. This is not hidden in the form itself; only in the inner connection between bourgeois legality and the relations of production founded on the expropriation of labour.

If this analysis of law is correct – and it is only intimated in the passages from Marx which I have cited – we see the real basis of Marx's critique of bourgeois legality. Not that legality is a mere 'mask' for class exploitation, for, though circulation is subordinate to production, it does remain the *form* through which social relations of production are mediated and it does remain as the necessary mediation in the perpetual movement of capital through its circuit from money to productive capital (means of production and labour power) to commodities to more money. As Pashukanis has clearly demonstrated, legal relations do have an objective basis in relations of exchange. It is only in that peculiar exchange between capital and labour that this objective basis of equivalence breaks down, when the anatomy of that relation is revealed. But it is still crucial that the relation between capital and labour takes the form – spuriously – of relations of equivalence governing other transactions between commodity producers. There is an objective basis for bourgeois legal 'right' and the 'freedom' and 'equality' posited with it. But the limits of this 'right' under capitalism lie not only in the 'abstraction' of its real content (the 'real, sensuous human being'); but also in that these 'rights', however much extended and democratized, cannot *in themselves* erase the class relation between labour and capital. For this 'exchange', however much it is 'equalized' and however much the 'freedom' of the 'contractors' is guaranteed by law, remains a 'mere semblance'. This is why the statement I cited earlier from Engels – that 'the specific character of economic oppression which weighs down the proletariat stands out in all its sharpness only . . . when the complete juridical equality of both classes is established' – seems to me to be a particularly wise one. And this is why Marx attacks those 'socialist jurists' who defend bourgeois right and law – however uncompromising the defence and however radical the content which is given them – for their failure to penetrate the class character of bourgeois law.

And yet a paradox remains which has puzzled commentators on Marx and Lenin and which has led to one-sided resolutions. On the one hand, Marx calls for the 'smashing' of bourgeois state and legality; on the other hand, he insists on the necessity of 'bourgeois right' even in advanced stages of transition and therefore, as Lenin pointed out, on the necessity of a bourgeois state capable of regulating observance of these rights. How can the necessity both of immediately smashing the bourgeois state and legal forms, and that of their preservation as forms of regulation under socialism, be simultaneously proffered? Resolution of this paradox can be found by denying one or other of the elements. Either the question of 'smashing' is dropped and illusions are generated concerning the mere extension of bourgeois into socialist 'right'. Or the question of 'socialist right' is dropped and the protection of objectively legal relations by a superstructure of formal legal equality yields to 'arbitrary' class power. This paradox is, I believe, resolved when we relate the 'bourgeois form of law' to its real and changing social content. As Marx put it, between law regulating capitalist relations of production and law regulating the exchange of labour with portions of the total social product under socialism, there is 'a change in form and content', over and above the fact that they both embody the fetishism derived from the general characteristics of commodity exchange.

I shall sum up these tentative conclusions. Legal relations are objective social relations, not merely an instrument of state domination or an ideology useful to the ruling class by virtue of its 'isolation effect' or whatever. The legal form is one immediately taken by social relations of production under given historical conditions, whether or not this form is expressed in a systematic legal system. Of course, it is a matter of considerable importance whether such a system exists and how legal relations are regulated (by force of arms, by an impersonal judiciary, by a bureaucratic-administrative apparatus, etc.). The real 'content' or 'substance' of the form of law consist in particular relations of *production* and not the exchange relation of the sphere of circulation itself, as Pashukanis and others have concluded. The changing historical content of these relations of production is directly interconnected with the changing forms and functions of bourgeois law. The *class* character of the bourgeois form of law derives from the illusory character of the exchange relation between capital and labour, seen from the perspective of the productive relations which underpin it.

It is only when we view the connections between the form and the content of bourgeois law that its *class* character becomes apparent. At the same time, however, we also see the contradictions inherent in the legal form as a mode of bourgeois domination. The form of law restricts its efficacy as a means of regulating capitalist relations of production, just as the fact that circuits of capital must be mediated by exchange poses constant difficulties (contradictions) for the reproduction of capital. It would seem that legal institutions are, on the whole, well adapted to regulating relations between commodity owners, but in order to regulate *other* social relations of capitalist society it has to treat them *as if* they were commodity relations. This creates considerable problems, as when the fiction of the legal subject as owner of his or her body is created, and violation of the person is assimilated to violation of property. These problems emerge with particular sharpness, however, in the regulation of relations between capitalists and workers within the immediate productive process. Functionaries within the enterprise, industrial syndicates 'with their fighting funds, their black-lists, their lockouts and their regiments of strike-breakers' (Pashukanis 1978) are undoubtedly organs of power outside the mandate of legal regulation. This raises also the problem of the relation between state power and the forms of law. The legal form is not the only one through which the state regulates relations between capital and labour. The difficulties that it has in so doing are clear enough from the recent history of attempts to legislate industrial relations and the resistance which they have provoked; and even clearer in the examples of transition from social-democratic legality to bureaucratic police rule and to fascism. The contemporary problem is to assess the significance of tendencies in these directions and to work out an adequate political basis for resisting them.

3 Despotism and legality

Richard Kinsey

If the control of the capitalist is in substance twofold by reason of the twofold nature of production itself – which on the one hand is a social process for producing use-values, on the other a process for producing surplus-value, in form that process is despotic. As co-operation extends its scale this despotism takes forms peculiar to itself. [Marx 1970, p.314]

My question in this essay – what form does the despotic control of capital assume at different periods in the development of the capitalist production process? – seems relatively straightforward. An initial response can be stated quite simply: as changes in the production process occur – in technology, in the composition of labour, in the extension of the division of labour – so the control of capital over labour assumes different characteristics. Thus, just as the development of production is itself dependent upon and is set within a matrix of historically given social relations, so despotism in the production process and the particular forms that control and organization of labour assume at different times depend upon social relations as they are realized within production itself.

The distinction between organization and control of production must be handled with some care. In the passage cited above, Marx argues that the despotism of capitalist production is characterized by its twofold nature. On the one hand the capitalist labour process requires the organization and co-ordination of labour – specifically in the division of labour in the work place. On the other hand capitalist production rests upon the exploitation of labour and the appropriation of surplus-value which entail the subordination of the class of labour to capital in production relations. As such capital asserts its dominance in the labour process in two necessary yet antagonistic dimensions. The capitalist (the personification of capital) must at once ensure the organization of labour within the workshop or factory, and yet at the same time exercise control or 'dominium' over the use of the means of production in order to guarantee the continued production of exchange values. In the organization of production we may say that capital seeks to unify the labour process whilst in control we may say that capital divides and separates labour from the means of production. In other words capital must both organize and control labour in order to exploit it, whilst the tendency of the one is to negate the other. Thus Marx writes:

All combined labour on a large scale requires, more or less, a directing authority, in order to secure the harmonious working of the individual activities, and to perform the general functions that have their origin in the action of the combined organism, as distinguished from the action of its separate organs. A single violin player is his own conductor; an orchestra requires a separate one. The work of directing, superintending and adjusting, becomes one of the functions of capital, from the moment that labour under the control of capital becomes co-operative. Once a function of capital it acquires special characteristics. [ibid., p.313]

As this passage suggests, however, the picture becomes more complicated. The constant drive to increase the production of (relative) surplus-value permanently impels capital to raise the productivity of labour, and to revolutionize the social relations of production from within. This involves the continual development of more sophisticated techniques both for the organization and for the control of labour within the labour process. So, Marx continues:

The directing motive, the end and aim of capitalist production, is to extract the greatest possible amount of surplus-value, and consequently to exploit labour-power to the greatest possible extent. As the number of co-operating labourers increases so too does their resistance to the domination of capital, and with it, the necessity for capital to overcome this resistance by counterpressure. The control exercised by the capitalist is not only a special function, due to the nature of the social labour process, and peculiar to that process, but it is, at the same time, a function of the exploitation of a social labour process, and is consequently rooted in the unavoidable antagonism between the exploiter and the living and labouring raw material he exploits. [ibid.]

Thus, Marx argues that as productivity and the division of labour within the labour process increase – that is, as 'co-operation extends its scale' – so the despotism of capital in the labour process – in both its dimensions – assumes different shape. So, while capitalist production is always despotic in form – that is, it always involves the appropriation of surplus labour in the form of surplus-value – that despotism is mediated in different ways depending upon the state and development of production relations.

Now while it is important to recognize the distinction which obtains between the organization and control of labour, it is equally important to note that in practice both may (or may not) be realized simultaneously and through the same instrumentality. Thus it is all too easy to subsume within the undifferentiated notion of discipline, for example, either one or both dimensions, thus failing to penetrate beneath the surface of immediate experience. In fact, as we shall see, control and organization in the labour process have been achieved in radically different ways and through very different modalities. For that reason, and also because it seems to me to be more in accord with common usage, I propose to restrict use of the term 'discipline' – as opposed for example to terms such as 'coercion' or 'economic compulsion' – to those moments when control and organization are realized simultaneously and through the same medium.

The development of the capitalist production process and the extension of co-operation thus produces qualitative changes in the form of despotism. Too often however it seems that, while it is widely recognized that the material conditions of the labour process undergo quite fundamental and dramatic transformation, it is assumed – quite wrongly – that the form of the despotic control of capital remains constant and invariable. This failure is particularly evident in the work of two important but very different writers, Karl Renner (1949) and Harry Braverman (1974). Both in different ways recognize the centrality of legal institutions in the control and organization of the labour process but both fail to specify with any rigour the conditions within which such institutions develop and hold.

Thus Renner argues that the primary and virtually sole site of the despotic power of capital is to be found in the universal form of the property norm enforced at law. Now, although it is indisputable that private property relations are crucial to capitalist appropriation the problem is far more complex than Renner suggests. While private property rights and their legal protection may be sufficient under certain conditions to secure and guarantee the production of surplus-value, the redefinition of private property and private property rights has continued throughout the history of capitalist production in a manner which should spell caution to any attempt to derive a 'general rule' pertaining to private property and capitalist production relations.

In a similar manner, although with vastly different emphasis, Braverman has asserted the universality of the contractual relation to the capitalist labour process. Again, under certain conditions, this argument may hold good; however, it is necessary to specify very carefully what those conditions are and what exactly is meant by the term 'contract' before generalizing to capitalist production as a whole. Thus in opposition to Braverman I shall argue that the extension of control and organization of labour through the contractual relation is dependent upon the realization in practice of relatively advanced social relations of capitalist production and that as such the contract of employment can in no way be seen as a universal and necessary condition of capitalist appropriation. Indeed, it is doubly important to realize just how recent this form of control is, in order to pierce through its apparent timeless and universal quality.

Both Renner and Braverman accord a direct and central role to law and legal institutions in the control and organization of the labour process. Although, as will be apparent, I am in broad sympathy with this project, in Renner's analysis especially this argument provides the explicit basis to a reformist theory of law and socialization of the means of production. Therefore in criticizing Renner's conception of the labour process and capitalist property relations I shall deliberately, indeed I must, take up the critique of the social-democratic analysis of legality and the rule of law, of which Renner's work is the best and probably the most rigorous example.

The principal object of the essay however is to argue that three periods in the development of capitalist production are broadly identifiable within which qualitative changes in the control and organization of the labour process are visible. These are: the period of manufacture which is identified with simple co-operation, and the exploitation of skilled labour; the early period of modern industry which is identified with the rapid introduction of the machine and the abstraction or deskilling of labour; and later modern industry or advanced capitalist production which is to be identified with the high organic composition of capital and the intensification of scientific 'man' management. Within each period I shall seek to establish the 'peculiar form of despotism' as it is assumed within the material conditions of the labour process; respectively these are: the despotism of property, the despotism of the factory and the despotism of legality.

The despotism of property: the social-democratic analysis

There is nothing that so generally strikes the imagination and engages the affections of mankind as the right of property; or that sole and despotic dominium which one man claims and exercises over the external things of the world, in total exclusion of the rights of any other person in the universe. [Blackstone 1973-5, p.2]

Renner's *Institutions of Private Law and their Social Functions* (1949) provides one of the most sophisticated analyses of the despotism of private property in the capitalist labour process.[1] Unfortunately, however, the analysis is crucially vitiated in certain dimensions which render Renner's political conclusions false.

The major difficulty with Renner's work stems from his conflation of the despotism of property in the period of manufacture, and the forms of despotism in the period of modern industry. Throughout his work he ignores the qualitative differences existing in control and organization as practised in manufacture and factory production. In consequence the despotic form of property is treated as the universal form of control throughout the development of the capitalist production process. In subsequent sections I shall examine in more detail the forms of despotism assumed in the course of this development. It will then be apparent that these qualitative differences must severely limit the social-democratic theory of law which Renner derives from his conception of production relations. The preliminary task however must be to explain that theory.

At the time he wrote, the political thrust of Renner's work within the politics of Austria and the Second International was to legitimate social-democratic intervention and to discredit the Bolshevik programme of vanguardism and proletarian dictatorship. Thus Renner adopted a position conventional to social democracy which emphasized 'the socialization of capital from within', which he argued was to be seen as an evolutionary process in terms of which the efficacy of law as an instrument of political and social change was fundamentally restricted to that allowed by 'the evolution of the economic substratum'. The economic order knows of evolution only, not revolution, he argued (see Kinsey [forthcoming]).

It is important to note however that at the same time the historical-social process was conceived by Renner, as by the Austro-Marxists generally, as actively set in motion by the agency of individual subjects, in other words, by individual men, rather than as in some sense self-generating. There was no reduction of history to iron laws of development and catastrophic negation. Man was at once the subject and object of an historical process in which he or she could intervene and yet which set the limits to that intervention. In this way the political programme of the

Austro-Marxists was at once gradualist and interventionist. As such it opposed directly both the revolutionary theory and practice of Bolshevism (termed by Renner 'the idolatry of the decree') and the pessimistic passivity and determinism of the older German tradition within the Second International.[2]

Predictably the social democratic programme of the Austro-Marxists in 1919 included the 'planned and systematic socialization of all the branches of the national economy (which today) are ripe for this purpose' (cited in Gulick 1948, p.155). It is notable but not surprising that the social democrats were not alone in this demand. The Christian Social and Catholic Parties had formulated similar proposals. But for the Social Democratic Party 'socialization' had, in 1919, an additional ring to it, for, according to one commentator: 'The historical importance of socialization attempts in Austria lies chiefly and almost solely in their relation to the struggle against Bolshevism' (Gulick 1948, p. 143). The post-war working class of Vienna was already predisposed toward the revolutionary example of Bolshevism set in neighbouring Hungary and Bavaria and the democratic socialization of the means of production was thus a minimum demand. The working class would accept nothing less. None the less it was accepted, and the beneficiaries of the singular failure of Bolshevism in these circumstances could only be the socialists.

Of course in reality the ensuing socialization of the economy in no way amounted to revolutionary expropriation. 'One cannot socialize debts', Renner frequently commented in relation to the bankruptcy and inadequacy of key industries in the immediate post-war crisis. Socialization – whether as a necessary good or as a necessary evil – was accepted as necessary by all sides: the picture is familiar.[3]

In Renner's theoretical work, however, the process of socialization has a particular significance for his theory of law and the state. For, in the socialization of private property, Renner argues that the despotic power of control of the factory owner is assumed by the state: in socialization, the private legislator (the property owner) becomes public legislator. The state, by taking the despotic power of property out of the hands of the capitalist, Renner argues, thereby takes control of the labour process. But this is true if, and only if, the ownership of private property provides the sole basis for the despotism of modern industry. It does not, but it is a necessary assumption of social democratic theory that it should be so. By examining in outline Renner's position we can see why this is the case, and why analysis of the labour process is crucial to the politics of legality.

The interventionist politics of Austro-Marxist social democracy had led the party theorists to invert the orthodox Marxist conception of the base-superstructure metaphor and to assert the priority of the individual subject and thought in history.[4] Thus Renner argues that the existence of human society in any time and place presupposes four 'ideal' or *a priori* categories of social order through which are mediated four universal economic functions which taken together amount to the material basis of the social division of labour (co-operation). These are an order of labour (production), an order of goods (consumption), an order of power (distribution of goods and labour) and devolution (continuity in production). It is no more possible to 'think' society outside the 'idea' of order than it is to exist as a material being in a society where these four economic functions are not fulfilled. The fulfilling of the universal economic functions presupposes the 'ordering' of society in terms of the ideal categories (cf. Renner 1949, ch. 1, p.ii).

In capitalist society the universal economic functions (co-operative labour) are fulfilled by means of the legal institutions of private property, the contract and succession, the latter two being complementary to the first. At first sight, Renner notes, these institutions suggest that the capitalist economy knows only an order of goods and their possession, exchange and devolution through testamentary succession. But Renner argues this is only a 'sophisticated illusion': 'Bourgeois society has successfully developed the illusion that labour is not a social duty but a private affair for which no regulation of labour is required' (1949, p.72). Nothing could be further from reality, says Renner. Put simply, private property vests in its owner the power not only to appropriate the social product for individual use, but also to determine who produces what, where and under what conditions that production is to take place. By virtue of his ownership of private property the capitalist has an unlimited power of command over the worker who surrenders his autonomy to the capitalist in the contract of employment.

The social function of the institutions of private law is, according to Renner, to effect co-operative labour. Throughout his analysis Renner constantly emphasizes the role of law in the organization of the labour process and underplays its importance in appropriation, so personifying society or 'the community' in the person of the property owner. Reference to the exploitation of labour, to class and class struggle, or revolution is always marginal to his analysis. By emphasizing the co-operative aspect of the labour process the possibility of socialization from within becomes so much greater in theory. As such the institutions of private law are merely class-neutral means to the universal end – the regulation and ordering of social production – at a particular moment of economic evolution. Throughout capitalist production then, for Renner, co-operative labour is realized at the despotic command of a property-owner who exercises that command on behalf of society. It is this power which is socialized by the state.

In so far as Renner seeks to establish universal categories of social production, however, there remains the problem of agency in society in general in that regulation in all societies presupposes a subject of power. It is here that we see the specifically idealist character of the analysis for, Renner tells us,

> Whenever the community has the power of command as it has in every society, it exercises this power by means of the individual acting as its organs. There is no society without the regulation of power [ibid., p.71].

Two immediate consequences follow from this. First, according to Renner's analysis, society in all epochs is to be conceptualized as the aggregate of individually willed activity through which social regulation obtains. Secondly, and as such, all societies and co-operative labour presuppose relations of power obtaining between individual wills. These relations must necessarily take the form of commands – the universal form of law in Renner's analysis – since, on the one hand 'Whatever the stage of evolution, where men establish relations with one another, society as the common will must always subjugate the individual' (ibid., p.70), and, on the other hand, 'The community exists only through its individual members' (ibid., p.73). Thus co-operative labour in all societies can only be realized through the form of an individual power of command. Yet the universal subject of social order is society itself acting through the commands of its individual agents, for the individual power of command is exercised 'on behalf of the community', the individual is the 'trustee' of social power expressed as individual power. It is in these terms that Renner conceived of the social function of the owner of private property in general and the factory owner in particular. Thus, 'The right of the capitalist is delegated public authority conferred indiscriminately upon the person who will use it for his own benefit' (ibid., p.115). Increasingly however the evolution of the economic substratum dictates that the despotic power of private property becomes insufficient to fulfil the economic functions of labour organizations, the sheer scale of production necessitates centralization and planning, and the market is inadequate to secure the distribution of the social product. The delegated right of public authority should be rescinded and vested in the state as the more rational agency of social regulation. The development of public law institutions regulating labour, housing, education, etc. represent the 'first unavoidable step to nationalization' (ibid., p. 121).

Three aspects of Renner's analysis are central to his social-democratic platform of reform through legality. First, by stressing power relations as obtaining between individual wills and as fundamental to the very 'idea' of society Renner succeeds in writing out of his work any immediate concern with class relations and the appropriation of surplus labour. The bearer of social power is and always must be the individual. Social relations are never more than willed relations, obtaining within history certainly, but between individual men and women rather than classes. The idea, for Renner, of the power of capital as opposed to capitalist is 'unthinkable', as is the idea that a social relation might be embodied in a machine or the form of law. Both the machine of factory production and the law are merely instruments in the hands of the individual 'agent'.

Secondly, and in consequence of this first point, Renner's work tends to centre upon the efficient use and abuse of political power. Thus in relation to law we find he is principally concerned with the ends to which the law is put, rather than with the form of law itself. Throughout his work we find consistent references to the imperative form of law as being an 'empty frame' which is as 'neutral as an algebraic formula'. Law is the most efficacious means to bring about the rationalization of co-operation and as such the 'development of law gradually works out what is socially reasonable' (ibid., p.122). Note in addition that in so far as law takes the universal form of command, presupposed in all social orders, so too are property relations, in so far as the community must hold and distribute the social product through the exercise of social power by individual men and women. This must be within legal or juridical institutions whereby possession is secured to the individual agents of society. The criteria of individuation may change within a given social order so that legal capacity may devolve upon the state, the capitalist, the joint stock company, the child, who or whatever, but the formal structure of the property norm remains unchanged. Thus one of Renner's best-known aphorisms relates to the functional transformation of the property norms where the norm itself remains constant. Renner writes:

Fundamentally the norms which made up the law have remained absolutely constant, and yet an enormous revolution has occurred without any transformation of norms. [ibid., p.89]

Renner was then to argue that the socialization of private property and the transition to socialism involved the negation of neither the property norm nor the imperative form of law in general, and indeed presupposed the continuation of both. Furthermore the construction of socialist society would occur within the neutral framework of legality or the rule of law, upon which would be devolved the social functions of a 'Socialist commonwealth'. That possibility was immediate:

nearly all the legal forms which would be applicable in the socialist commonwealth are already now in existence, though their functions have not been fully developed. [ibid., p.83]

In a socialist society property ownership would devolve upon the state and with it the sovereign power of property to command and regulate labour and goods. The socialization of property is however possible according to Renner only when the 'economic substratum' has evolved to such a point that the institutions of private law are no longer sufficient to the task of the regulation of co-operative labour. Apparently this point had been reached in the aftermath of the 1914-18 war. The private legislator was to go public. As I noted earlier this whole argument rests upon the apparent 'fact' that the despotism of property is the sole mechanism of capital's control. It is not.

The despotism of the factory: Marx on the transition from manufacture to modern industry

It is [machines] that sweep away the handicraftsman's work as the regulating principle of social production. Thus on the one hand the technical reason for the life-long subordination of the workman to a detail function is removed. On the other hand the fetters that this same principle laid on the dominium of capital fall away. [Marx 1970, p.347]

In this section we must question Renner's assumption that the capitalist's control of the labour process derives simply from the despotic power of property. A close reading of Renner's work would show how he conflates the control of manufacture and that of factory production, but it is more useful in the present context to subject Renner's analysis to criticism from outside rather than from within the text.

The manufacturing labour process of the initial period of capitalist production existed primarily by employing as wage labour the artisans and craftsmen of the pre-capitalist period. The division of labour within the workshop took the form of the simple co-operation of skilled workmen who, although they were increasingly tied to the 'detail function', were nonetheless of *singular* importance within the total labour process. Thus in Marx's words 'the whole body is paralysed if one of its members is missing'. The worker thus retains his skill as a fundamental quality of his labour-power which under such conditions is a scarce resource. Indeed the worker knows this and may combine with others to protect his technical skills and 'tricks of the trade', thus using his specialized 'guild' knowledge against the capitalist. As Marx writes:

> Since handicraft skill is the foundation of manufacture and since the mechanism of manufacture as a whole possesses no framework apart from the labourers themselves, capital is constantly compelled to wrestle with the insubordination of the workers . . . throughout the whole manufacturing period there runs the complaint of want of discipline amongst the workers. [ibid., pp.346-7]

In stark terms, under the conditions of manufacture, the problems of organization and control were present to capital on the one hand in the need to orchestrate simple co-operation within the workshop, and on the other hand in the need to subjugate skilled labour. The subjugation of labour at this period is founded simply upon the direct and unmediated power of private property. Thus the craftsman is denied his skill by virtue of the legally enforceable absolute right of the capitalist to use and abuse, and exclude others, at his will, from the means of production. Separation from the means of production in the form of private property backed by coercion is the key not only to the generation of the class of wage labour, but also to the control of wage labour within the manufacturing division of labour itself. Hence the double significance and centrality of the Blackstonian conception of property especially in eighteenth-century English formulations of the rule of law, in which security of private property is the dominant end.[5]

The division of labour and simple co-operation within the workshop on the other hand present a different problem. The division of labour in manufacture served primarily to bring together spatially and temporally individual skilled craftsmen, and the problem of capital in the organization of production lay precisely in bringing and keeping that labour together. To this end the power of property as control is, typically, complemented by coercive legislation and common law which tied the worker in time and place to capital, for example the later use of the Statute of Labourers 1349, the Statute of Artificers 1563 and of course the Poor Laws. In a sense then it can be said that organization in the labour process of manufacture is guaranteed from outside the workshop while control is guaranteed from within it. At this period both control and organization obtain through direct force.

But if the division of labour within the workshop sees increasingly difficult problems of organization and control from the point of view of capital, the rapidly expanding social division of labour (in the form of expanding markets, the growth of the towns, communications etc.) sees the initial generation of the conception of liberty in commerce, of which Adam Smith and the eighteenth century political economists were the theorists. Freedom and equality in the commodity market, and the free alienation of real property, the sweeping away of the entail, of localized customary law and of outmoded legal fiction in the interest of certainty and predictability in exchange relations formed the demands of the day (cf. Smith 1776 and Bentham 1977 *passim*). In this respect it is true that the sphere of circulation and bourgeois legality has its own separate existence in the other worldliness of the market. But even as late as Bentham it was recognized that such liberty was premissed upon the security of private property – as indeed it was – and that as such liberty must always play second fiddle (cf. Halevy 1972, pp.37-54). Strictly within these limits then the separation of bourgeois legality from the organization and control of relations of production holds good. With the advent of the machine, however, there comes a qualitative shift in the nature and problem of control, to which this 'general rule' is no longer applicable (for an alternative reading see Chapter 6 in this volume).

The period of manufacture saw and, indeed, necessitated the production of a class of wage labour economically and legally subordinated to capital. The complex and contradictory transition to factory production as the dominant form of the labour process radically restructured the social basis of the class of labour breaking the hierarchical and cultural differentiations which existed within that class during manufacture by deskilling and rendering labour homogeneous.[6] Of course this process met with intense resistance. Resistance to the machine at the turn of the century marks crucially this break, and yet by 1836, Andrew Ure was writing that 'Arkwright created order' (cited by Marx 1970, p.347). The qualitative difference in control which was occurring is visible in three broad dimensions. First, as I have already mentioned, it is visible in the abstraction and deskilling of labour and the creation of an urban proletariat; secondly in the redefinition and extension of the notion of commercial liberty, and thirdly in the machine itself which now dictates as an apparent technical necessity the intensity and detail division of labour.

The despotism of the factory rests upon the use of the machine as the embodiment of a distinct set of social relations. Many of the mechanical devices and inventions of the eighteenth century had been inapplicable in the complex of culture, tradition and hierarchy which typified the class of labour of the manufacturing period. But the extension of factory production 'once fully developed breaks down all resistance', quite brutally creating mass labour, displacing the skilled and irreplaceable labour-power of the craftsman and replacing it with the living average and replaceable labour-power of the urban proletariat. In such conditions, for capital, the problem of the control and organization of the labour process gradually assumes new shape. With the employment of women and children undifferentiated both in terms of skill and strength from the male worker, labour-power is reduced in practice to the common denominator: average or abstract labour. In consequence the need to restrict the mobility of labour and separate the craftsman from the tools of his trade gives way to its opposite. The abundance of average labour-power available on the market shifts the location of control to the market place itself. This movement – although obviously this is a simplification – receives formal legal recognition in the Truck Act 1831. Therefore, whereas the truck system during the period of manufacture may be seen as a means of tying down labour, the Truck Act 1831 marks the formal reconstitution of the control of the factory owner in terms of simple dismissal and the threat of unemployment. Again by the 1820s, and certainly by the time of the Master and Servant Act 1830, the system of annual hirings established under the Statute of Artificers was being dismantled, setting up in more recognizable form the 'free' contract for the sale of labour-power. In legislation such as this we can see how commercial liberty is gradually extended to include the free alienability of that very special commodity, labour-power. In short we can say that in principle the 'authority' of the capitalist inside the workshop gives way to the dull compulsion of economic need outside the factory doors. The weapon of control in this instance is then symbolized in the 'lock-out' rather than the 'bastille' of the manufacturing period. 'Direct force outside economic conditions is of course still used', Marx tells us, 'but only exceptionally'. For the capitalist, moreover, direct force is inflammatory. Spearheading this movement, Joseph Townsend wrote in 1786:

> Hunger will tame the fiercest animals, it will teach decency and civility, obedience and subjection to the most perverse. In general it is only hunger which spur and goad (the poor) on to labour; yet our laws have said they shall never hunger. The laws, it must be confessed, have likewise said, they shall be compelled to work. But then legal constraint is attended with much trouble, violence, and noise: creates ill-will, and can never be productive of good and acceptable service: whereas hunger is not only peaceable, silent, unremitting pressure, but, as the most natural motive to industry and labour, it calls forth the most violent exertions. [quoted in Scull 1977, p.28]

Thus the creation of abstract labour and homogeneity of labour by the introduction of machinery releases capital from the fetters of craftsmanship and from the need to co-ordinate labour by direct force. Replaceable (abstract) labour-power takes the place of the irreplaceable (particular) labour-power in the labour process. But this in turn presupposes the availability and therefore the mobility of labour. The liberty of the individual to sell his labour-power in the contract of employment is set alongside the security of property as the maxim of the rule of law.[7] Both become necessary conditions of capitalist appropriation. The commodity market and the exchange of abstract labour becomes the focus of legality. As Pashukanis so correctly noted, the legal person – the abstract subject of rights and duties – becomes the focal point of legality, and the principle of the rule of law becomes the facilitation of commodity exchange between the formally free and equal (cf. Pashukanis 1978 *passim*, and Kinsey 1978). On the market capital and labour meet as equal before the law. But again the transition is never simple and straightforward. The legal relation of master and servant, the legal position of the independent contractor, of lump labour etc., are all instances of the complex and uneven development of historical reality only behind which can this trend be identified. But, as a characterization, I would argue that with the mediation of control and organization through the social relation of man to machine, the law is increasingly, although never finally, released from direct regulation of the labour process and becomes at this stage principally concerned with the organization of the exchange of commodities – including now labour-power – providing the ever more complex juridical framework of commodity exchange.

But in talking of economic need and the market as the locus of control we must not lose sight of the problem of organization and co-ordination of labour within the factory – of what Marx refers to as the 'factory code'. While the market and the power of dismissal are perhaps sufficient to control and break the resistance of the worker, the introduction of machinery places the organization of the labour process squarely in the hands of the capitalist:

> The factory codes, in which capital formulates, like a private legislator, and at his own good will, his autocracy over his work people unaccompanied by that division of responsibility in other matters so approved of by the bourgeoisie, and unaccompanied by the still more approved representative system; *this code is but the capitalist caricature of that social regulation of the labour process which becomes requisite in co-operation on a great scale, and in the employment of common, of instruments of labour and especially of machinery.* [Marx 1970, p.400; emphasis added]

It is important to emphasize that Marx relates the 'factory codes' to the organization rather than to the control of the labour process, for here a common confusion frequently arises. This 'disciplinary' power of the factory owner as private legislator is not, in form, the power to control labour but the power to organize and co-ordinate production. Once this formal distinction is recognized we can see that in the transition from manufacture to factory production there is a complete, formal reversal of the location of control and organization in the labour process. Whereas the organization of social labour in manufacture had to be guaranteed from outside the workshop through legislation and the common law, in factory production co-operation is established within the factory in the form of the factory code. On the other hand, whereas in manufacture the control of labour takes the form of direct and face to face property relations, in factory production control is rooted externally to the labour process in the indirect relations of the labour market. As such, any relation which obtains between the sphere of circulation (legality) and the sphere of production in manufacture is inverted in the despotism of the factory. In relation to Renner we see that private property, although a necessary condition of capitalist production is a sufficient condition neither for the organization nor the control of the labour process. As Marx wrote in the passage cited on page 9 that

> It is not enough that the conditions of labour are concentrated in a mass at one pole of society while at the other are grouped masses of men who have nothing to sell but their labour power.

The despotism of legality

> From the perspectives of the capitalist entrepreneur the essential characteristic of the production process for which he is responsible is that it must operate itself. The controlling power of the capitalist hinges on this postulate of the self-acting or 'automatic' character of the labour process of production. [Sohn-Rethel 1978, pp.118-19]

The rising organic composition of capital in the advanced production process places the emphasis on productivity not only upon increasing and improving technology but also, and crucially, upon the maximization of its efficient use (see Chapter 5 for a detailed discussion of this argument). The introduction of homeostatic and simple feedback mechanisms on the machine, such as the aptly named 'governor' on the steam-engine, had ensured a constant and regular centralized source of energy within the labour process and a technical determination of the division and intensity of labour. The problem that now faced capital in its constant search for increased productivity and the production of relative surplus-value, was to reproduce in *living* labour that same mechanism of self-control, thus to constitute the labour process as an enclosed and self-regulating system. In so far as this is attainable capital reaches towards the most highly developed form of despotism. Crucial to this form is the realization of the *voluntary* contract of employment.

In his analysis of labour process, Braverman (1974, p.52) has specified three necessary conditions of capitalist production which must become generalized throughout society:

> First workers are separated from the means with which production is carried on. Second workers are freed of legal constraint such as serfdom or slavery, that prevent them from disposing of their own labour-power. Third the purpose of the employment of the worker becomes the expansion of a unit of capital belonging to the employer who is thus functioning as a capitalist. The labour process therefore begins with a contract or agreement governing the conditions of sale of labour-power by the worker and its purchase by the employer.

It is unclear perhaps whether Braverman is pointing to essential conditions for capitalist production or simply to moments in its development. If the latter is so, then I would agree with his presentation except and in so far as the final statement is concerned, which at least needs much greater elaboration than Braverman recognizes. For, I would argue, the contract of employment is the most highly developed medium of despotic relations, in that it presupposes 'voluntary' and willed obligations obtaining reciprocally between capital and labour as formal equals. As we have seen, the grounds of this juridical relation are first established in the early period of factory production in the extension of commercial liberty to include the commodity of labour-power. It is however only in conditions of advanced capitalist production that the voluntary contract for the sale of labour-power becomes the generalized form of control and organization of the labour process;

at this moment despotism assumes legal form, and the possibility of the self-regulating labour process takes ideal shape.

Under the conditions of early factory production Marx had described the paradox wherein the worker is under compulsion to sell his labour voluntarily. Subsequently, the attempt is made to remove that appearance of compulsion. In the words of F.W.Taylor, speaking of his own notorious study of manual labour: 'the task before us narrowed itself down to getting Schmidt to handle 47 tons of pig-iron per day and making him glad to do it' (cited in Braverman 1974, p.104). We have already seen with the introduction of the machine and the deskilling of labour direct legislative interference was rejected not only as unnecessary but as an obstruction to the production of a reliable or peaceable supply of labour on the free market. But in the capital-intensive labour process the 'reliability' of labour takes on a very different connotation. The typical complaint becomes the unreliability of the work-force within the factory, the lack of 'pride' in the job and so on. The reproduction of the reliable and responsible worker takes priority where the dominant end is the efficient use of the machine. The primary locus of control thus shifts back, from the market to the factory, where the increasingly detailed time and motion studies of 'modern' management techniques are utilized to ensure both control and organization of labour. The reliable worker or 'trained gorilla' becomes once again irreplaceable, not now in terms of his skill but in terms of his tractability or docility. Scientific 'man' management becomes increasingly concerned with the individual psychology of the worker as much as with the splitsecond timing of routinized tasks and the Pavlovian reflex becomes the dominant paradigm of the routine itself. Thus Taylor had set about constructing a voluntary and as far as possible reflexive commitment on the part of labour to the labour process, particularly through the use of incentives and reward. In so far as Taylorism succeeds in this project the self-activating, self-regulating labour process would seem to be realized. But the problem of this science of man management as with its academic counterpart – the physiological and behaviourist psychology of Huxley and Maudsley – lies in the problem of subjectivity.[8]

The production of a human automaton is by no means an impossibility – witness the product of long term prison routines. The problem arises however in that a machine cannot operate itself, no matter how sophisticated. (Whether or not that is so, by definition the possibility is disallowed within the capitalist mode of production.) Hence the problem of subjectivity to which I point, is not the problem of so-called 'alienation' from work, of disenchantment or *arbeitsunlust*, but a problem familiar to the fetishized social relations of generalized commodity exchange. Thus Marx wrote of commodity circulation that: 'Commodities cannot go to market and make exchange of their own account.' Commodity exchange requires that the 'guardians' of commodities

> . . . place themselves in relation with each other as persons whose will resides in those objects and must behave in such a way that each does not appropriate the commodity of the other, and part with his own except by means of an act done by mutual consent. They must therefore recognize in each other the rights of

private proprietors. This juridical relation . . . expresses itself in a contract . . . . [1970, p.88]

Thus it is that commodity exchange requires an ascribed relationship of wills; that exchange obtains between formal and abstract legal subjects. The argument of this passage, especially as it has been developed by Pashukanis, is important in so far as it provides us with the point of entry to the problem of subjectivity in the labour process.

Pashukanis developed these comments of Marx to show how in relations of generalized commodity exchange the fetishized negation of subjectivity in labour (in the form of exchange values in which labour as abstract or average labour becomes the common unit of measurement) must be complemented by the ascription of formal legal subjectivity or personality. In the market the individual exists as a legal subject only, and exercises his 'will' as the bearer of abstract rights and duties which constitute him as the formal equal of all others who appear in this 'Garden of Eden'. This legal fetishism, argues Pashukanis, of which the hallmarks are consent, reciprocity and the abstraction and generality of rules, is a necessary counterpart of the fetishism of commodities. Thus embodied in the concept of commercial liberty, expanded in the initial stages of modern industry to incorporate the sale of labour power but as yet not realized in the labour process itself, is the notion of voluntarism and consent (see Kinsey 1978 for the argument in greater detail). The problem faced by capital in the labour process was precisely analogous: how to ascribe subjectivity to the object of scientific management. Labour must be personified, and as such becomes the personification of objectified social relations.

In relation to the facilitation and organization of commodity exchange Marx pointed out that the ascription of will or subjectivity need not necessarily occur within the framework of a developed legal system. A 'business' morality, shared conceptions of reasonable commercial practice – still very much present within the English common law – may be sufficient. The same is true of the labour process. Subjectivity can be ascribed in a number of different ways. For example, Taylor found that by rigorous selection of the 'right man for the job' and that by detailed moment by moment instruction and supervision the labour process could be controlled and organized quite efficiently, its major drawback being its cost-effectiveness. What is important, however, is to note that in the detailed job description and instruction cards so painstakingly implemented by Taylor's foremen, supervision provided the medium of both control (in the formal ascription of subjectivity which is denied in substance by the minute control of movement), and of organization of labour (in the detail division of labour). Both control and organization are focused at the point of production and for the first time coincide in the same instrumentality. It is in this coincidence of organization and control that discipline, properly so called, obtains. Thus conceived discipline is clearly to be distinguished from the exercise of arbitrary power and/or coercion. Furthermore, we now see that whereas the organization and control of labour in earlier moments of the development of the labour process were distinct, they have now come together in the idea of 'management'. Braverman (1974, p.617) correctly notes, 'The specifically capitalist mode of management did not become generalized until relatively recent times; that is within the last hundred years'. Integrally related to the development of management techniques of discipline is the development of the modern contract of employment as the dominant mode of ascribing subjection to labour. Thus in 1896 we see, for example, the formal embodiment in law of the power to discipline *within the factory* in the Truck Act. This legislation effectively legitimated the new form of disciplinary practices which had developed during the middle to late nineteenth century by making its basis the contractual acceptance by labour of the disciplinary power of capital. Indeed it is notable that throughout the 1890s an immense emphasis is placed upon 'voluntarism' in labour relations, as for example the Conciliation Act 1896, as increasingly the market is of less importance as the focus of control.

There is, therefore, a significant difference between the power of discipline now exercised by capital and the unfettered power to enforce co-operation under the earlier 'factory codes'. It is a difference I am sure which some will dispute but it is of the essence. We have seen that in writing of the factory codes Marx had pointed to the autocracy of the capitalist, and the absence of 'the division of responsibility . . . so approved of by the bourgeoisie . . . unaccompanied by the still more approved representative system'. It is precisely that representative system which is now embodied in 'contractual' discipline of modern management. Thus we find the following comment upon disciplinary power in a recent work on the law of employment:

> During the performance of an employment contract the employer may find it necessary, through his appropriate manager, foreman or committee charged with this responsibility, to exercise some form of disciplinary power over the employee, which may take a number of different forms. But any notion that such power can be used without strict lawful authority can be discounted. We must however draw a distinction between manual workers and other employees. [Selwyn 1976, p.98]

The modern contract of employment thus differs substantially from its earlier 'embryonic' form. It must detail specifically or by implication the terms of employment and the mode of punishment for deviation from those terms. For example, in one case (*Davies* v. *R. Johnson and Nephew Ltd.* 1934) it was held – not surprisingly – that there is an implied term in the contract of employment that the employer is entitled to ensure improved performance of work and that work is done in a proper manner by engaging time and motion experts.

The voluntary contract of employment formally embodies the reciprocal definition of the terms and conditions of work and the extent and range of the employer's power of discipline. One immediate consequence of this is that disputes as to the control and organization of the labour process are displaced from the factory floor to the tribunal or the court (cf. Chapter 9 below). John Lea has referred to this as the 'democratic' form of discipline (Chapter 5 below).

We can now return more directly to the problem of the ascription of subjectivity in the contract. Too often law is thought of solely in terms of disputes, as a mode of conflict resolution etc. Much more importantly however law serves to define the very contours of everyday life.

Walter Bagehot – no fool when it came to the problem of order and control – knew this well; here the conservative liberal of the nineteenth century gives perhaps the clearest indication of fetishism of legal subjectivity and the nature of legal ideology – not as a spider's web of conspiracy but as a concrete practice of routinized social relations:

> [for anti-political man] morality . . . was to be found in the wild spasms of 'wild justice', half punishment, half outrage – but anyhow, being unfixed by steady law, it was intermittent, vague, and hard for us to imagine. Everybody who has studied mathematics knows how many shadowy difficulties he seemed to have before he understood the problem, how impossible it was when once the demonstration had flashed upon, ever to comprehend these indistinct difficulties again, or to call up the mental confusion that admitted them. So in these days when we cannot by any effort drive out of our minds the notion of law, we cannot imagine the mind of one who had never known it, and who would not by any effort have conceived it. [1956, p.16]

It is precisely this taken-for-granted, routinized expression of everyday relations which informs the analysis of the fetishism of legal subjectivity as the basis to the voluntary contract of employment. In capitalist society generalized commodity exchange not only presupposes, but reproduces and confirms the ideology of legality in the subjectivity of the legal person as commodity owner. That subjectivity – the organizational form of commodity exchange – is the concrete medium through which the social division of labour is practised and expressed within capitalism. In so far as legal subjectivity – initially articulated for the purposes of simple commodity circulation – comes to express the social relation obtaining between capital and labour in the labour process in terms of formal equality, reciprocity and consent, the fetishism of the commodity form of labour-power is reproduced in the labour process itself. The value relation or commodity form of social relations becomes the generalized modality of organization and control within the labour process as it is in generalized commodity exchange. Thus, the spheres of circulation and production are reproduced each in the other. So it is that in the developed capitalist production process the rights as well as the particular and detailed duties – the subjectivity of the worker – are ascribed in the contract, and lived in the voluntary subordination of labour to capital. This revolution in control is embodied in the practice of law. Gramsci wrote that

> The revolution that the bourgeois class has brought to the conception of law and hence to the function of the state consists especially in the will to conform. [1973, p.230]

This then is the despotism of legality; the content of the contract may be disputed but the form is never questioned. It is seen to be beyond negotiation. In the labour process the despotism of legality forms the necessary counterpart to the fetishized inversion whereby the machine appears to take on a life of its own and in which production becomes truly automatic. The dream of the capitalist becomes a lived, if transient, reality.

In these spacious halls the benignant power of steam summons around him his myriad of willing menials. [A. Ure, cited in Marx 1970, p.396]

Conclusion

In the course of this essay I have suggested that the control and organization of the labour process reaches its highest expression in the despotism of legality. In earlier stages of its development we have seen that control and organization of production were mediated through separate and distinct instrumentalities, sometimes obtaining at the point of production itself and sometimes beyond the immediate relations of the labour process. In developed capitalist production on the other hand I have argued that both control and organization of production necessarily coincide at the point of production but that discipline – as it is constructed through the form of law – is established in the form of the contract of employment. Relations of production are construed not as direct relations obtaining between the class of capital and the class of labour, but as indirect relations obtaining between equals. It is only in this way that law stretches down throughout the social relations of capitalism and becomes the dominant expression of capitalist order.

In the earlier stages of the development of the capitalist labour process the use of legislation, and the common law as coercive vehicles of class power is undeniable, but the form of law – the expression of social relations on legal relations – was not a necessary constituent element of the production process itself. Increasingly, however, it would seem that that is the case. E.P. Thompson wrote of eighteenth-century farming that

if we look closely into (the) agrarian context the distinction between law on the one hand . . . and the actualities of productive forces and relations on the other becomes more and more untenable. For law was often a definition of actual agrarian practice as it had been pursued 'time out of mind'. How can we distinguish between the activity of farming or of quarrying and the rights to this strip of land or that quarry? The farmer or forester in his daily occupation was moving within visible or invisible structures of law. [1975, p.261]

The point is well made but notable changes occurred especially in the nineteenth century. The content and composition of those 'visible and invisible structures of law' was qualitatively rewritten. The property rights of the eighteenth century have given way to the 'right to work'. No longer are the common rights of the farmer or forester denied: the rights of women, of the poor, of the illiterate, of the unemployed, of the delinquent, of man are universally asserted at law. Few if any aspects of social life fall beyond the reach of the legal definition, of the hegemony of legality. The legal subject has become truly universal. Status is ascribed in rights, social being becomes legal being.

The problem of socialization of production thus becomes much more than the mere reallocation of property and property rights as suggested by Renner. The whole edifice of rights and duties must be reworked and re-examined. This remains a task for the future, but a signal note of warning should be sounded. Too often radical analysis has slipped back to the eighteenth century and to the insidious anarchism of Godwin, satisfied with the rejection of legality lock, stock and barrel. Half an acre and a cow is simply not sufficient. No socialist society will be 'free' from organization any more than it will be free from the need to produce. But then, no more than the capitalist labour process is free from contradiction, is the form of bourgeois law free from its internal contradiction and the possibility of its transformation.

4 Bentham's fear of hobgoblins: law, political economy and social discipline

John Annette

In the dark of night Jeremy Bentham was afraid of hobgoblins. He wrote that

> In no man's judgement can a stronger persuasion of the non-existence of those sources of terror have place than in mine; yet no sooner do I lay myself down to sleep in a dark room, and my eyes keep open, these instruments of terror obtrude themselves . . . . My fear of ghosts had been implanted in my mind from earliest infancy by the noxious weed, domestic servants . . . . [*Works*, vol. 9, pp.83-4 and vol. 10, p.64] [1]

While attending the lectures of Sir William Blackstone at Oxford in 1763, which would later be published in 1765 as the *Commentaries on the Laws of England*, Bentham once again experienced the fear of hobgoblins (ibid., p.45). This time they were in the form of fallacious fictions contained in the English common law. It would be Bentham's task to exorcise these hobgoblins and establish a new materialist 'science and art of morals and legislation'. It was in the role of Legislator that Bentham saw his life's work. He wrote,

> Have I a genius for anything? . . . What of all the earthly pursuits is the most important? Legislation was the answer Helvetius gave. Have I a genius for legislation? . . . I gave myself the answer fearfully and tremblingly – yes. [*Works* vol. 9, p.271]

As a Legislator Bentham saw himself not only as a law reformer but as one who would transform the existing legal and moral basis of society.[2] He would be the Newton of morals and legislation.

Law, for Bentham, was the means to establish and maintain a rationally ordered society and was therefore the key element in his social and political thought. Bentham, however, was not a utopian social engineer. His view of law as a means for rationally ordering social change was the product of his critique of the existing legal system and of his understanding of the nature of the economic and social changes taking place in late eighteenth century England. Douglas Hay in his excellent essay, 'Property, authority, and the criminal law' (in Hay *et al.*, 1975, p.39) states that Bentham could not understand the 'personal terms' of justice in the practice of the English law in the eighteenth century in contrast to the sense of justice in terms of 'rational bureaucratic decisions made in the common interest'. I would argue that Bentham was aware of how this system of order and deference worked and that his theory was not based solely on the normative principle of utility but upon a subordinate set of principles which would provide a new system of social discipline (cf. Holdsworth 1952, vol. 13, p.46). Recent commentators on Bentham's vision of social discipline have failed to appreciate the historical significance of his materialist analysis of the changes in the form of the law required for the ordering of the social relations of production necessary for the development of industrial capitalism (Foucault 1977; Melossi 1976a, 1976c; and Scull 1977). The rule of law would not only provide 'directly' for the maintenance of 'liberty', 'equality', and 'property' within the sphere of the circulation of commodities but it would also provide 'indirectly' the social discipline necessary for the sphere of the production of commodities.[3] The sphere of circulation, Marx writes:

> within whose boundaries the sale and purchase of labour-power goes on, is in fact a very Eden of the innate rights of man. It is the exclusive realm of Freedom, Equality, Property, and Bentham, because both buyer and seller of a commodity, let us say labour-power, are determined only by their own free-will. They contract as free persons, who are equal before the law. Their contract is the final result in which their joint will finds a common legal expression. Equality, because each enters into relation with the other, as with a simple owner of commodities, and they exchange equivalent for equivalent. Property, because each disposes only what is his own. And Bentham, because each looks only to his own advantage. [Marx 1976, p.280]

Bentham followed Marx in the company of the capitalist and the worker from the 'noisy sphere' of circulation 'into the hidden abode of production, on whose threshold there hangs the notice 'No admittance except on business' (ibid., p. 279).

Bentham's materialist analysis of the form of law is significant because it recognized the inadequacy of the practice of the common law to maintain social discipline and because it suggested ways in which law could be used 'indirectly' to establish the new social discipline of the labour process in response to the changing composition of the labouring class in the eighteenth century. It is important to note that for Bentham the rule of law was not just a set of rational commands establishing a system of social control. The rule of law should not be seen in terms of the exercise of direct social control. It represents a legal definition of changing social relations whereby the law can be the mediation of class struggle (cf. Linebaugh and Thompson 1972; Linebaugh, 1976). Law was not viewed simply as an instrument of hegemony but as a rational mediation of existing class relations. It would provide artificially an identification of interests by the realization of the principle of utility through the establishment of a system of 'direct' and 'indirect' legislation. To illustrate the historical significance of Bentham's materialist jurisprudence I will examine its relation to classical political economy and then its application to the reform of the poor laws and the problem of poverty.

Many of the *philosophes* and radicals of the Enlightenment were practical reformers who sought in the establishment of a materialist psychology based on the association of ideas a basis on which to form a social science at once theoretical and capable of being transformed into an art (Baker 1975; Halevy 1972). In 1768

Bentham, having read Helvetius and Beccaria, began to construct his 'Elements of a critical jurisprudence' based upon the principle of utility which was derived from his materialist psychology. Essential to this materialist psychology was a complex linguistic theory (Annette 1978). In 1776 Bentham, now a young lawyer at Lincoln's Inn, published a work entitled 'A fragment on government', which was a scathing critique of Blackstone's interpretation of the common law (Bentham 1977; Holdsworth 1952, vol. 13; and Posner 1976). In the *Commentaries on the Laws of England* Blackstone declared it self-evident that

> There is nothing which so generally strikes the imagination, and engages the affections of mankind, as the right of property; or the sole and despotic dominion which one man claims and exercises over the external things of the world, in total exclusion of the right of any other individual in the universe. [Blackstone, 1973-5; Hay *et al.*, 1975]

Blackstone's view of the natural right basis of civil government was largely influenced by John Locke. It was Locke, the Whip apologist, who stated that 'Government has no end but the preservation of property' (Locke 1970, p.347; Dickinson 1977). Bentham regarded the notion of 'natural right' as a fallacious and even dangerous fiction. All 'rights' according to Bentham were social conventions designed to protect private interests. The political language of natural right theory was dangerous because it could lead to either despotism or anarchy. Important legal fictions like 'power', 'right', 'trust' and 'property' needed to be clearly defined. Bentham wrote,

> Power and right and the whole tribe of fictitious entities of this stamp are all of them, in the sense which belongs to them in a book on jurisprudence, the results of some manifestation or other of the legislator's will with respect to such an act. Now every manifestation is either a prohibition, a command, or their respective negations . . . . Power, whether over a man's own person, or over other persons, or over things, is constituted in the first instance by permission; but in so far as the law takes an active part in corroborating it, it is created by prohibition and command. [1970, p.206, n.2]

Like Hobbes, Bentham was concerned to analyse scientifically the structure of power existing in the real world. Power, for Bentham, was not a thing but a relationship between persons or things. It was essentially a relationship of control. Power over persons or things can produce pleasure or pain for human persons. The legislator would create an artificial structure of power relations which would maximize pleasure and minimize pain for the whole of society.

Bentham in 1776 identified with the critique of the common law influenced by the writing of Adam Smith, Lord Kames, and the judicial decisions of Lord Mansfield (Holdsworth 1952, vols. 12 and 13; Stein 1970). Although there were important developments in commercial law, the reform of the property law seemed impossible. In the late eighteenth century there was a tremendous increase in legislation of capital statutes mostly concerned with the protection of the 'natural right' of property (Radzinowicz 1948-68, vol.1; and Hay *et al.*, 1975). Despite the influence of Beccaria and the increasing influence of the ideas of law reform among lawyers Parliament resisted all attempts at reform. Bentham believed that the members of Parliament were ignorant of the art of legislation. Knowledge of this art would have prevented the growing uncertainty which even Blackstone tried to prevent as the result of this increase in unscientifically established law.

By 1780 Bentham completed the initial formulation of his 'art and science of morals and legislation' which is contained in his 'Introduction to the principles of morals and legislation' (Mack 1962, pt. 2). The science of morals and legislation is a discourse that is architectonic in that it structures the relationship between other forms of discourse. The art of morals and legislation is also architectonic in that it provides the legal framework of society within which power relationships are established and maintained. There are also some other important works like 'Of laws in general', 'Essays on the influence of time and place in matters of legislation' and 'Essay on indirect legislation', which Bentham completed around 1780. In the 'Essay on the influence of time and place in matters of legislation' Bentham dealt with the problem of legal relativism and social change. He recognized that the establishment of a totally reformed rational system of law would not produce a utopian society. He wrote,

> Perfect happiness belongs to the imaginary region of philosophy and must be classified with the universal elixir and the philosophers' stone . . . . Painful labour, daily subjection, a condition nearly allied to indigence will always be the lot of numbers. Among the higher as well as the lower classes, there will always be desires which cannot be satisfied . . . reciprocal security can only be established by the forcible renunciation by each one. If we suppose, therefore, the most reasonable laws, constraint will be their basis. [*Works*, vol. 1, pp. 169-94]

The 'Essay on indirect legislation' is perhaps one of the most important and also most neglected of his legal essays (Ogden 1932). It is in this essay that Bentham acknowledges the importance of custom and tradition in the establishment of the art of legislation. He wrote,

> Indirect means, then, are those which, without having the character of punishments, act upon a man physically or morally, to dispose him to obey the laws, to shield him from the temptations, to govern him by his inclinations and his knowledge. [BC MSS no. 99, p.110]

Indirect legislation or social therapeutics aimed, therefore, to condition human behaviour as manifested in contemporary society. This process of 'conditioning' would be through social legislation and the creation of social institutions like prisons, poor houses, schools, etc. Bentham recognized that the reform of the civil and penal laws of his society would also need to be supplemented by the reform of the constitutional laws. It would not be until later in his life, however, that as an advocate of 'democratic' administrative reform Bentham would come to write his tracts on Parliamentary reform and his 'constitutional Code'. It is in these early writings on jurisprudence and law reform that Bentham laid the framework for the establishment of a new system of legislation which would produce new forms of social discipline. This social discipline would be produced not simply through the imposition of direct control or punishment but through indirect or social legislation. By 1780 Bentham's vision of a 'science and art of morals and legislation' was now clear to him and he was confident of the benefits it would confer upon society.

It was in the 1780s that Bentham, now under the patronage of Lord Shelburne, began to examine more systematically the nature of the changes that were taking place in English society. Lord Shelburne, man of letters, wealthy landowner, Whig politician, had been impressed by the progressive ideas of Bentham in his 'A fragment of government'. At Bowood, his estate, he introduced Bentham to a wider circle of intellectual and political influences and encouraged him to continue his work on the reform of the law and to consider more extensively contemporary social and political problems. It was at this time that Bentham read Adam Smith's *Wealth of Nations* (1776) and became interested in the study of political economy. According to T.W. Hutchinson, Bentham is not an important political economist in terms of his contribution to the 'scientific knowledge' of economics. Hutchinson (1956) writes:

As an 'economist' as today defined, Bentham made no attempt to develop an economic calculus or a theory of relative values and prices. His economic theorising is . . . rather practical, 'macro-economic', concerned with aggregate monetary problems, and if not statistical, at any rate concerned to exploit such crude statistics as were available while being ready for and calling for more. [see also Stark 1952-4]

The importance of his writings on political economy are, I would argue, in their relationship to his essays on the 'science and art of morals and legislation'. Bentham for example, saw his 'Essays on indirect legislation' as having a clear relationship to his 'science of political economy'. His first economic work, 'The defence of usury', was written in 1787 in the form of letters from Russia where he was assisting his brother Samuel to set up a factory system for the enlightened despot Catherine the Great. In this work he criticized Adam Smith for inconsistency by making the usury laws an exception to his *laissez-faire* principle. He had accepted Smith's principles and was now going to push them to their logical conclusion.

This work has given rise to an interpretation of Jeremy Bentham as a strict *laissez-faire* theorist. There has been, however, considerable recent literature on 'Benthamism' and the 'nineteenth-century revolution in government' which rejects this interpretation (Hume 1967; Fry 1979). A consideration of the meaning of the *laissez-faire* principle to the classical economists is relevant. A.W. Coates (1971) writes:

contrary to the view expressed by innumerable commentators, they [the classical economists] did not advocate laissez-faire, if that expression is taken to mean an essentially negative conception of the economic and social role of government . . . . Not only did the classical political economists admit many exceptions to the general rule of government non-intervention they also recognized that the law was supplemented by a variety of non-legal social controls.

The classical conception of *Ordnungspolitik*, referring to policy formation concerned with the maintenance of a legal and social framework for economic activity, left the actual economic process within this framework largely under its own dynamic. *Prozesspolitik* meanwhile referred to the more clearly economic objectives like levels of employment and economic growth.

The classical conception was established basically in the political economy of Adam Smith. It is important, however, to examine not only his *Wealth of Nations* but also his *Theory of Moral Sentiments* and his *Lectures on Jurisprudence* to fully appreciate the concept of justice and the legislative framework Adam Smith regarded as important for economic development (Smith 1976 and 1978; Winch 1978). Following Adam Smith only Jeremy Bentham and J.S. Mill among the classical economists would attempt to fully examine the relationships between legislation, political economy, and social and economic policy formation (Robbins 1952; Samuels 1966). For Adam Smith the dynamics of economic development would help establish a 'natural' identity of interests in society. Bentham in his writings recognized that 'interests' could only be harmonized by legislative activity and especially by indirect legislation. In economic matters, however, he argued that the legislator should only intervene in special circumstances. In his 'Manual of political economy', written in 1793-5, he stated that there were various 'agenda' and 'non-agenda' activities of government with regard to the economy. He wrote:

> A general rule governing the agenda of government . . . is that . . . nothing ought to be done or attempted by government for the purpose of causing an augmentation to take place in the national mass of wealth, with a view to encrease of the means of neither subsistence or enjoyment, without some special reason. Be quiet on those occasions to be the motto or watchword of government. [Stark 1952-4, vol.3 p.333]

Compared to Adam Smith and most of the other classical political economists his list of governmental activities that were agenda was much more extensive. The important point, however, is not the question of the extent of government intervention directly in the economy but the significance of the legislative framework necessary for the development of the economy. The legislator would provide this legislative framework through the art of direct and indirect legislation based on the materialist science of morals and legislation.

In his 'Principles of the civil code' Bentham argued that although the principle of utility was fundamental it was also an ideal or goal to be realized. He stated that there were four subordinate principles or goals of legislation which would provide the means for the realization of the principle of utility. These were security, subsistence, abundance and equality. Security was for Bentham the primary immediate goal of legislation. He wrote,

> We have now arrived at the principal object of the laws; the care of security. This inestimable good is the distinctive mark of civilization; it is entirely the work of the laws. Without law there is no security; consequently no abundance nor even subsistence. And the only equality which can exist in such a condition is the equal-

ity of misery . . . . Among the objects of the law, security is the only one which embraces the future; subsistence, abundance, equality, may be regarded for a moment only; but security implies extension in point of time with respect to all the benefits to which it is applied. Security is therefore the principal object. [*Works*, vol. 1, p.302]

It is for the maintenance of 'security' that property is instituted by law according to Bentham. Also 'liberty', which is simply 'negative liberty' or freedom from the coercion of the law, is the product of security. Bentham wrote, 'When most of us speak of liberty what we mean is security – and security is the work of law, coercing those who would interfere with or injure those whom it means to favour.' It is clear that for Bentham without security the other ends of legislation – subsistence, abundance and equality – cannot be realized. The primary goal of the legislative framework of society necessary for capitalist development is the provision of security. The question of the extent of direct governmental intervention in economic activity is therefore related to the provision of security. Bentham accepted that the legislator need not exercise direct power over the economic interests which were exercising economic power for the provision of subsistence and abundance. It was only when that exercise of economic power threatened the security of the society in terms of its aggregate subsistence and abundance that Bentham favoured direct government interference in the economy. The provision of security is the primary goal of legislative activity. This would be brought about through the art of direct and indirect legislation.

The debates in the 1790s about the reform of the Poor Laws and the problem of poverty provide a good example of how Bentham combined his art of legislation with his rather frightening skill as a social engineer. They illustrate how Bentham would provide for the realization of security, subsistence, and abundance within a society under the impact of Industrial Revolution (Poynter 1969; Rose 1971; Scull 1977). In the 1790s the pauper problem became critical and Bentham suggested a complete reform of the old Poor Laws. In order to plan the reform of the Poor Laws he turned to the government for statistical information about paupers and found there was none. He printed a blank Pauper Population Table in Arthur Young's *Annals of agriculture* in 1797 and appealed to parish relief officers to fill it in and return it to him. Only a few, like Patrick Colquhoun, actually did so. In 1797 Sir Frederick Morton Eden published his 'State of the poor'. As a disciple of Adam Smith he argued that the Poor Laws were against economic liberty and that they provided unnecessary competition to free employment. In 1798 the Rev. Thomas Malthus, in the first edition of his *Essay on the principle of population, etc.*, argued that the natural rate of increase in population was much greater than the highest conceivable rate of increase in subsistence. It was Malthus's further argument that the Poor Law in a way actually created poverty. Earlier in 1786 the Rev. Joseph Townsend had argued in his *Dissertation on the Poor Laws* that poverty was necessary for social discipline. He wrote,

There must be a degree of pressure, and that which is attended with the least violence will be the best. When hunger is either felt or feared, the desire of obtaining bread will quietly dispose the mind to undergo the greatest hardships and will sweeten the severest labours. [Townsend 1786, pp.39-40]

The significance of the debate over the Poor Laws following the introduction of the Speenhamland System in 1795, Samuel Whitbread's Reform Bill of 1795, and Pitt's Reform Bill in 1796 goes beyond the level of moral ideology. It was in the debates concerning poverty that the classical economists first began to consider the implications of the ever-increasing subjection of labour to the needs of capital.[4] There was an increased awareness of the relationship between unemployment and the accumulation of capital. For Bentham this debate also involved the question of how the art of legislation could provide for the process of capital accumulation. He recognized that it could provide means also to maintain the subjection of labour to capital in the labour process. Bentham wrote,

The law which offers to poverty an assistance independent of industry is, so to speak, a law against industry itself, or at least against frugality. The motive to labour and economy is the pressure of the present and the fear of the future: Want: The law which takes away this pressure and this fear must be an encouragement to idleness and dissipation. This is the reproach which is reasonably brought against the greater number of establishments created for the poor . . . . [*Works*, vol.1, p.314]

In his unpublished 'Essay on the subject of the Poor Law' of 1796 Bentham established the definition, object, and theory of Poor Law legislation. In this essay he made an important distinction between poverty and indigence. He wrote,

Poverty is the state of everyone who in order to obtain subsistence is forced to have recourse to labour. Indigence is the state of him who being destitute of property . . . is at the same time either unable to labour or unable even for labour to procure the supply of which he happens thus to be in want. [BC MSS no. 153*a*, p.21]

Labour was therefore the only natural source of subsistence. It was necessary for the market to provide subsistence for the labour market.

In 1786, in a fragment entitled 'Poor's cry', Bentham argued that the government could do nothing for employment except for removing unnecessary burdens upon the labour force. In another essay in 1796 Bentham argued that the decline of wages was an indication of the decrease of capital in proportion to labour. This seemed to anticipate the Malthusian argument although Bentham did not arrive at the position of Malthus which called for the abolition of the Poor Law (Poynter 1969, p.125). Although Bentham was familiar with Joseph Townsend, who also called for the abolition of the Poor Law, he believed that the problem of indigence should be relieved by the law. Bentham's main writings on the Poor Law were written between 1795 and 1798. His major work, 'Pauper management 'improved', appeared in Arthur Young's *Annals of agriculture* in 1797. His other writings which remain in manuscript are massive in number. These include an essay on the 'Independent labourer', 'Three essays on the Poor Laws', and a large work entitled 'Pauper systems compared' (*Works*, vols. 8, 13; BC MSS nos. 151-4). The only printed work by Bentham on the subject of the Poor Law is 'Observations on the Poor Law Bill introduced by the Rt. Hon. William Pitt' which was written in 1797 but not printed until 1838, six years after his death, by Sir Edwin Chadwick (Bentham, *Works*, vol. 8).

What characterized the confused state of the Poor Law debate at the time was not only a lack of statistical information about its operation and effects but also the lack of a general theory about its operation. Bentham, as I have previously mentioned, actually did attempt to gather what statistical data he could find. In his 'Essay on the subject of the Poor Law' he attempted to formulate the principles of a theory of the Poor Law. The Poor Law is an important example of how Bentham applied his 'Essay on indirect legislation' to the problem of establishing and maintaining social discipline. His distinction between 'poverty' and 'indigence' led him to the position that poverty was essential to the creation of wealth. He wrote that, 'As labour is the source of wealth so is poverty of labour. Banish poverty, you banish wealth.' (BC MSS no.153*a*, p.25). In his criticism of Pitt's Reform Bill he argued that the condition of the non-labouring recipient of poor relief must be less eligible than that of the industrious poor otherwise the very incentive to work hard would be removed.

The proposals which Bentham put forward for pauper management are actually quite staggering in terms of their scope and detail (Himmelfarb 1970a). It was an application of the 'Panopticon plan', which had been published in 1791 as a model prison, to the problems of pauper management. The central control of the Poor Law administration was to be vested in a joint stock company with a board of directors called the National Charity Company. The board was to build about 150 'Industry Houses' all over the country and each house would contain about 2000 persons. These Industry Houses would be built on the Panopticon principle of central inspection. That is, they would be circular buildings in which the governed could be inspected from the centre as structured by an architectural plan (ibid., Foucault 1977; Evans 1971). No relief would be granted except upon the terms of the Industry House which would be that of entering into productive industry. Mendicants and vagrants were to be apprehended and brought into the work house and given employment. Children or non-adult paupers were to be received as apprentices. The insane, dumb, deaf, or blind were to be segregated. The same plan of management was to be observed in all of the Industry Houses. The use of the inspection principle and the principles of the factory system would not only provide for the management of paupers but also through the 'time and work disciplines' of capitalist production transform the paupers into productive labour.

What is interesting about the pauper management proposals are that they combine Bentham's 'technology of power', as observed by Foucault, with Bentham's concern for the maintenance of the labour market. As Bentham began to extend the original purpose of the Industry Houses from the treatment of the temporarily indigent to the control of the permanently indigent, his pauper management system became the model of a micro-social system which would exist within and in some sense compete with society. Influenced by his brother Samuel, he was fascinated with the possibility of using unskilled labour in manufacturing with completely standardized parts. The application of the 'piece-work' system is a most novel feature of the application of factory discipline to the Industry Houses. The sketches contained in the text were done by Samuel Bentham (Bentham, BC MSS no.154*a*, p.31). Bentham saw child labour as an essential part of his organization of the labour force. The Industry Houses would provide training, medical treatment, and moral discipline. The use of education to instil social discipline is an important feature of his plan (Johnson 1970; West 1975).

The Industry Houses became for Bentham a laboratory for social discipline far more extravagant than his original 'Panopticon plan'. He wrote,

> The institutions of the proposed company would afford the first opportunity ever presented to mankind of enriching the treasure of useful knowledge by contributions furnished on a national scale and on a regular all-embracing plan and would thus form an epoch . . . . [BC MSS nos. 151-4]

Some of the other experiments carried on within the Industry Houses would be Registry Offices, Loan Offices, Frugality Banks, Charitable Remittance Offices, Frugality Inns, Dispensaries, Lying-in Hospitals, Mid-wifery Lecture Schools, Veterinary Lecture Schools, Military Exercise Schools, Marine Schools, etc. This was no utopian vision for Bentham but part of his overall plan to provide security and subsistence through indirect legislation. Humanitarians would find it useful in its provisions for charity while lawmakers and political economists would find its utility in its provision of security, subsistence, and even abundance. Bentham wrote, 'A secure provision for the indigent is to the philanthropist what a pineapple is to the epicure.' Unfortunately for Bentham by 1811 his proposals for the Panopticon plan and for the Industry Houses were rejected in the committees of Parliament. Bentham, although severely disappointed did not give up his vision of a rational, legally ordered society as he spent his later years on devising various proposals to reform the structure of government.

The emergence of a market in labour provided the necessity of distinguishing poverty and indigence. It was considered necessary to transform the indigent who was not capable of labour into the pauper who was still capable of labour. A basic prerequisite of capital is not only the existence of a mass of 'free' wage labourers but also social discipline over that labour. Pauperism, like certain forms of criminal activity, seemed to threaten that control over the labour market. Georg Rusche and Otto Kirchheimer (1968), for example, have demonstrated that the prison system in the late eighteenth century was an attempt to maintain the labour market by preventing crime as an alternative to wage labour (see also Melossi 1968). This thesis, I would argue, can also be applied to the debate about the Poor Laws. The problem was for capital to control the reproduction of the working class.[5] This control over labour would be brought about not only through new 'technologies of power' but also through legally maintained social relations of production.

In order to fully understand Bentham's writings on political economy or proposals like the 'Panopticon plan' or the 'Pauper management plan' it is necessary to see them as part of his materialist science and art of morals and legislation. According to Bentham only through such a science could the changes taking place in the existing structure of power relations be analysed and only through such an art could a rational structure of power relations be maintained. Bentham argued that legislation could directly or indirectly provide not only for the realization of the principle of utility but also for the subordinate ends of legislation, namely security, subsistence, abundance and equality. Bentham's reform of the Poor Law by the principles of indirect legislation would help to maintain the ever increasing subjection of labour to capital. It would maintain labour as a commodity of exchange within the sphere of circulation and within the sphere of production it would introduce the discipline of the labour process, which by establishing co-operation and the division of labour would turn man into a machine (cf. Marx 1976, p.799).

Bentham was aware of the 'antagonistic character' of capitalist accumulation. He believed that through scientific legislation the maintenance of the social relations of production necessary for capitalist development would be provided. While being an advocate of democratic rights Bentham would use his materialist science of morals and legislation to establish a system of legislation which would create the 'carceral archipelago' (Foucault 1977, pp.293-308) of the Panopticon Prison and the Industry Houses. There would be no hobgoblins allowed in this machine of legally maintained social relations. Bentham could finally sleep peacefully.

5 Discipline and capitalist development

John Lea

This essay is an attempt to develop certain themes and hypotheses relevant to a general understanding of the dynamics of the subordination of labour to capital and their changing nature with the maturation of capitalist societies. The first part consists of some critical remarks on approaches to the study of this process derived from, among others, the recent work of Michel Foucault. This is followed by the elaboration of an hypothesis regarding the changing nature of subordination in modern capitalist societies. The discussion in this essay is limited and restricts itself to a consideration of those structures of control to be found in and around the process of economic production.

The analogy of the two spheres

In *Discipline and Punish* Foucault (1977, p.222) remarks:

> Historically, the process by which the bourgeoisie became in the course of the eighteenth century the political dominant class was masked by the establishment of an explicit, coded and formally egalitarian juridical framework, made possible by the organization of a parliamentary, representative regime. But the development and generalization of disciplinary mechanisms constituted the other dark side of these processes . . . . And although in a formal way, the representative regime makes it possible . . . for the will of all to form the fundamental authority of sovereignty, the disciplines provide, at the base, a guarantee of the submission of forces and bodies. The real corporal disciplines constituted the foundation of the formal juridical liberties.

The distinction between the political liberty and social slavery of capitalism is not a new or unfamiliar theme. It is to be found throughout Marx's writings. One of the clearest formulations from his earlier writings comes from the *Poverty of Philosophy* (1976a, p.126):

> It can even be laid down as a general rule that the less authority presides over the division of labour inside society, the more the division of labour develops inside the workshop and the more it is subjected there to the authority of a single person. Thus authority in the workshop and authority in society, in relation to the division of labour, are in inverse *ratio* to each other.

More recently the theme has formed the starting point for Dario Melossi (1976) in his own study of social control in capitalist societies:[1]

From the crisis of the feudal system of production down to the epoch of laisser-faire a process developed in which the more relaxed became the relations of direct dependence in society as a whole, the more there became organized and perfected the particular structures of authority of bourgeois society, structures based on the fundamental contradiction . . . between political liberty and social slavery. Such slavery manifests itself in the conditions which permit the extraction of surplus value, which guarantee, that is, the process of exploitation. *The totality of these conditions finds its real basis in the factory situation* but, contemporaneously, is reproduced in a whole series of other institutions which . . . have by various instruments and methods, the functions of forming and controlling the factory proletariat and guaranteeing the adaptability of labour power to be used and handled as one commodity among many. [emphasis added]

Thus social control under capitalism, or at least under classical nineteenth century capitalism, is paradoxical in nature. It is rooted, according to the view outlined above, in the existence of the factory and its key ancillary institutions: the prison, the school, the workhouse, poorhouse etc., which enforce an authoritarian moulding and disciplining of the individual and which constitute the 'dark side' of the immediately visible relations of political and legal equality and the general contractual nature of social relations in capitalist societies.

I wish to challenge two aspects or implications of this view. Firstly, that the mechanisms of control resided solely or predominantly in *institutions* without in any way denying their crucial role. Secondly, that the 'discipline' of the institutions, specifically of the factory, was and is simply identical with the subordination of labour to capital.

Let us begin with the mature Marx. In the first volume of *Capital* Marx clearly makes the distinction between the 'two spheres' in a way similar to Melossi and Foucault and to his own earlier formulation in the *Poverty of Philosophy*. He speaks of the

sphere of circulation or commodity exchange within whose boundaries the sale and purchase of labour power goes on [and which] is in fact a very Eden of the innate rights of man. It is the exclusive realm of Freedom, Equality, Property, and Bentham . . . .

But

when we leave this sphere of simple circulation or the exchange of commodities . . . a certain change takes place, or so it seems, in the physiognomy of our *dramatis personae*. He who was previously the money owner now strides out in front as a capitalist; the possessor of labour power follows as his worker. The one smirks self importantly and is intent upon business; the other is timid and holds back, like someone who has brought his own hide to market and now has nothing else to expect but – a tanning. [1976, p.280]

However, it should be noted that the purpose for which Marx makes this distinction between the sphere of circulation – the market and the realm of legal and political equality, and the sphere of production – within the factory, is not to show that it is the factory that is the site of control and discipline over labour *by contrast* to the Eden of the innate rights of man. Marx's purpose here is altogether different. He is concerned simply to examine how the production of surplus value takes place on the basis of the exchange of equivalents – labour-power for wages – in the sphere of circulation. In no way is he setting out to show that the worker, in the sphere of circulation as the seller of labour-power, actually exists as a free being independent of capital even though he may appear to do so. Later, Marx makes this explicit:

> From the standpoint of society, then, the working class, *even when it stands outside the direct labour process*, is just as much an appendage of capital as the lifeless instruments of labour are . . . . The Roman slave was held in chains, the wage labourer is bound to his owner by invisible threads . . . . The appearance of independence is maintained by a constant change in the person of the individual employer and by the legal fiction of a contract. [ibid., p.719; emphasis added]

In other words the equality of the sphere of circulation is a necessary appearance but nevertheless an appearance. It is in fact the realm of 'invisible threads' of control. Thus Melossi, for example, is incorrect to suggest that, as far as the conditions which guarantee the exploitation of labour and the production of surplus-value are concerned, 'The totality of these conditions finds its real basis in the factory situation.' It finds at least some of them outside the factory situation in the sphere of circulation, in the realm of invisible threads appearing as the innate rights of man. It remains to specify what those invisible threads consist of.

The market as an instrument of social control

The first and foremost 'invisible thread' is of course the very separation of the worker from the means of production and his dependence upon the price received for the sale of his labour-power for his individual consumption which 'provides on the one hand the means for the workers' maintenance and reproduction; on the other hand by the constant annihilation of the means of subsistence . . . provides for their continued reappearance on the labour market' (Marx 1976, p.719). But once a participant in the labour market, the worker faces the competition of other workers which maintains the price of his labour-power at a level corresponding to its value, to the level necessary for the capitalist to be able to accumulate a surplus-value as a result of its purchase. The competition between workers under classical capitalism took the form of the ever present industrial reserve army of unemployed which:

> during periods of stagnation and average prosperity weighs down the active army of workers, (and which) during periods of over production and feverish activity . . . puts a curb on their pretensions. The relative surplus population is therefore the background against which the law of supply and demand for labour does its

work. It confines the field of action of this law to the limits absolutely convenient to capital's drive to exploit and dominate the workers. [Marx 1976, p.792]

Thus during the early phases of capitalist development the advance of factory production and the deskilling of crafts served not only to undermine worker autonomy and facilitate the development of the capitalist labour process and the regime of factory authority and discipline, but also to widen the sphere of competition between workers through the homogenization of labour thereby to make more effective the operation of the reserve army of labour.

Panopticism, discipline and the market

According to Foucault (1977, p.215):

Discipline may be identified neither with an institution nor with an apparatus; it is a type of power, a modality for its exercise, comprising a whole set of instruments, techniques, procedures, levels of application, targets; it is a 'physics' or an 'anatomy' of power, a technology.

In Jeremy Bentham's plan of the Panopticon – the model prison – Foucault identifies the perfected architectural embodiment of discipline. The architecture that achieves this is the perfection of *surveillance* embodied in the relationship between the central observation tower and the peripheric ring. The inmate never knows whether or not he is being watched. For this reason it is as if he is being *constantly* watched. He becomes the bearer of his own surveillance.

The perfection of power should render its actual exercise unnecessary: that this architectural apparatus should be a machine for creating and sustaining a power relation independent of the person who exercises it, in short that the inmates should be caught up in a power situation of which they themselves are the bearers. [ibid., p.201]

Panopticon can be considered as a particular case, the architectural case, of a type of power; power carried by those against whom it is directed. The underlying mechanism of such a system of power is Bentham's philosophical psychology, the utilitarianism of the *hedonic calculus*. In Bentham's Panopticon his philosophy is made manifest. In his utilitarianism he formulated as a general law of human behaviour precisely the behaviour dictated by the architecture of Panopticon. Granted that the Panopticon is 'a machine for dissociating the see/being seen dyad: in the peripheric ring one is totally seen without ever seeing' (Foucault 1977, p. 202), then one submits, precisely as the hedonic calculus dictates.

But there are other structures besides that of the architecture of Bentham's model prison which embody power in this way. One such is that of the competitive market which operates as a sort of *decentralized panopticon*. The fear of being watched at any moment finds its equivalent in the homogeneity of the commodity, in the knowledge, on the part of the bearer of the commodity, that his commodity is identical with and thus potentially replaceable by any other. The total surveillance of the central tower finds its equivalent in the perfect knowledge of the market on the part of the purchaser of the commodity. If Panopticon constituted the *ideal type* of architectural control over the physical body of the labourer through surveillance then 'perfect competition' constituted the *ideal type* of control over the distribution and price of labour-power. Like Panopticon the market constitutes a power situation independent of the presence of the exerciser of that power: capital.

Indeed, in its ideal-typical form the competitive market approximates more closely even than Panopticon Foucault's conception of power as a relation carried by its bearers. The bearing of the power relation by the inmates of Panopticon is contingent on the presence of a specific architectural structure. The structure which guarantees the working of the market as a system of power is entirely located in the characteristics of the 'inmates': their homogeneity (or rather the homogeneity of the commodities that they bring to the market), their knowledge, and their fragmentation from one another, and finally the fact that each bears a sufficiently small proportion of the total supply or demand as to be unable to affect the working of the market through individual action. The market as a realm of freedom standing in contrast to the discipline of the institutions is thus an appearance:

> In reality the worker belongs to capital before he has sold himself to the capitalist. His economic bondage is at once mediated through, and concealed by, the periodic renewal of the act by which he sells himself, his change of masters, and the oscillations in the market price of his labour. [Marx 1976, pp.723-4]

In *Discipline and Punish* Foucault specifies (part 3, ch. 1) what he considers to be the various modes or ways in which discipline is articulated within institutions. In the chart opposite I have attempted to show how some of the modes of institutional discipline have their parallels in the functioning of the market.

It is important to stress that the actual operation of the labour market even in the heyday of classical capitalism prior to the 'imperfections' introduced by mass-organized trade unionism fell short of the ideal world portrayed by the economists of the 'hidden hand'. The geographical mobility of workers was physically limited and the breakup of communal ties between workers could never be perfected. Indeed, one of the very conditions which in early nineteenth century capitalism assisted, as I shall argue below, the development of a degree of panoptic surveillance on the part of the factory owner, namely the company town, or one industry town, tended to work against the perfection of the market mechanism as a technology of control. Rather, such developments tended to assist in the establishment of the whole working class community of the area as a base for solidarity against the local employer. Nevertheless strong tendencies worked in favour of the market. The large rural periphery and the mass of urban unemployed sustained the reverse army of labour while parochialism and regional/ethnic divisions within the working class enabled employers to arrest the development of class solidarity

Mode	Institution	Market
The art of distributions	the enclosure and breaking down of collective dispositions on the part of individuals and their allocation to 'functional sites' in accordance with a precise hierarchy	the individualization of labour power as a commodity fragmentation and competition among workers
The control of activity	the wedding of the body and its gestures to the requirements of the object to be acted upon in accordance with temporal and functional codings of the body and its actions	the composition of particular labour forces in relation to tasks through the hiring of specific amounts and types of labour
The organization of geneses	carefully graded stages for the acquisition of skills	the separation of labour-power from other, variable attributes of the individual worker (religion, race, etc.)
The composition of forces	the distribution of bodies to maximum effect in accordance with the technology employed regulated by a precise system of signals and commands	the rational distribution of labour in the economy in accordance with the structure of supply and demand

and maintain competition among workers.

Finally, Foucault's conception of discipline presents a paradox. Discipline is a type of power; a 'physics' of power. Yet a perusal of the modes of its existence in the chart above will reveal the elements of co-ordination necessary in *any* complex organization requiring collective activities. For Foucault such collective activity in modern society appears inexorably fused with surveillance and authority as embodied in the architecture of Panopticon, the paradigm case of disciplinary power. In the discussion above it has been argued that the market provides an analagous mechanism for the distribution and collective co-ordination of individuals. Like the Panopticon it is a system of power: it works against, and without reference to, the conscious decisions of the individuals who are its bearers.

Yet it is vital to distinguish discipline (as the co-ordination of collective activities) from the means (external power embodied either in the architecture of Panopticon or in the structure of relationships between individuals in the market) whereby it may be achieved. This is a distinction that Foucault does not dwell upon and yet, as we shall see, one that becomes of increasing importance with the maturation of capitalist societies.

The Panopticon and the factory

Having specified the sphere of circulation as an addition to rather than as a contrast to the power of the institutions of classic capitalism it remains to investigate how far institutional power specifically in the factory in fact corresponded to the type of power embodied in Bentham's Panopticon and elaborated by Foucault in *Discipline and Punish*. To the extent that there was such a correspondence enabling the factory of classic capitalism to be portrayed as a structure of total power analogous to the prison (which is the main object of Bentham's and Foucault's deliberations), then there is a temptation to seek an understanding of the transition to newer forms of social control in modern capitalism mainly in terms of changes in the labour process and factory organization. If, however, the factory was unable to approach panoptic forms of organization and required the market as its constant accomplice in the sphere of control then it may be more fruitful to understand changes in modern capitalism in terms of changing relationships between the factory and the market in addition to the internal development of each.

Under what conditions, then, could the factory of classic capitalism approach the Panopticon in its mode of operation? There are two distinct aspects to the question. Firstly that of how far discipline, in the sense of the co-ordination of activities in the labour process, was inexorably fused with a technology of power; of the subordination of labour to capital. The answer to this question is a simple question of historical fact, well-documented by Marx in the first volume of *Capital*. The application of science to the process of production and the development of a collective disciplined labour process arose not spontaneously from the knowledge of the workers but from their subordination to capital such that:

> The entire development of the productive forces of *socialised labour* (in contrast to the more or less isolated labour of individuals) and together with it the *use of science* (the *general* product of social development), in the *immediate process of production* takes the form of the *productive power of capital*. It does not appear as the productive power of labour, or even of that part of it that is identical with capital. And least of all does it appear as the productive power either of the individual worker or of the workers joined together in the process of production. [Marx 1976, p.1024]

Given that the transition to factory production and the development of collective socialized labour was fused with the subordination of labour to capital, the second aspect of the question now presents itself: how far did the structure of that subordination correspond to that of Panopticon? In other words how far in the factory could the codification and distribution of labour of the workers take the form of 'a power situation of which they themselves are the bearers'? Taking the Panopticon as the analogy the question resolves itself into one of the opportunities for the factory owner to erect a system of surveillance on the Panopticon model.

In the early phases of the development of factory production capital accumulation through the production of *absolute* surplus-value predominated. By absolute surplus-value Marx denoted surplus-value extracted via the driving down of wages and the maximization of both the length of the working day and the intensity of labour. The maximization of the working day meant that many if not the majority of workers were in the factory for the best part of their waking hours. In addition the spatial organization of early capitalism: the predominance of the company town and the tendency for the local employer of labour to be also the owner of the local process of distribution and consumption, and finally the tendency for most family members to be simultaneously employed; all these factors tend to maximize the power of surveillance of the employer over his work force.

But despite this there remain two crucial differences between the factory and the type of institution that could closely approach the mode of Panopticon. Firstly, the capitalist, as the purchaser and consumer of labour-power, is basically only concerned with the labourer during the time that the latter is in the factory. It is during that period alone that the capitalist is productively consuming the commodity he has purchased. Of course, he may well appreciate the necessity of maintaining a police force for the general supervision of his work force, or of paying taxes to the state to do the same thing, but such expenses are fundamentally a deduction from accumulated surplus-value. The expense of a system of *total* surveillance penetrating deeply into the home, cultural and other activities of the worker under conditions in which the arrangements of the latter do not take the architectural form of the prison or barracks[2] is not one that the capitalist is normally prepared to bear, especially knowing that the market and the ever present industrial reserve army are added forces of discipline standing by his side. Unlike the inmate of the Panopticon the factory worker, however stringent the regime during the time he or she is in the factory, cannot easily be deprived of the area of private space outside the surveillance of capital from which to recompose a measure of cultural and political autonomy.

If this is correct then it introduces a crucial modification into the argument concerning the nature of panoptic power. To achieve the *automatism* of the Panopticon it is not sufficient that the architecture correspond to Bentham's blueprint. Of equal importance is the fact that the inhabitant of Panopticon is an *inmate* as opposed to a visitor, that is, that the Panopticon is his/her total world. Or conversely any time spent outside a given Panopticon be spent in similar Panopticons such that the social world consist of a linked series of panoptic institutions. Outside this Orwellian nightmare (of which more below) *partial* habitation of even the most rigorous Panopticon is unlikely to prevent the emergence of a measure of resistance.

But, and this is the second difference, there are crucial internal differences between factory and Panopticon quite apart from the question of the differential amounts of time spent in each by the respective inhabitants. In the prison[3] such labour as takes place save in the exceptional circumstances of the industrial use of prison labour[4] is subordinated to the task of embodying habits of discipline in the minds of the inmates. Its distribution spatially and temporally need not be allowed to interfere with the maintenance of a regime of total surveillance. The factory on the other hand is above all devoted to the production of goods to be exchanged as commodities on the market. The factory owner stands in competition to other capitalists, he has to get his goods to market. The worker knows this and even in the most rigorous system of factory discipline has a certain autonomy from which he can launch an attack on his master knowing well the inconveniences for example of 'accidental' breakages, etc. of machinery to the capitalist anxious to meet his delivery date.

In conclusion then, power in the factory could not and did not achieve the ideal world of Bentham's Panopticon during the period of early capitalism. Nevertheless it approached it more closely than that of modern monopoly capitalism. However, more importantly, it is a mistake to consider that, as far as nineteenth-century capitalism is concerned, the power of capital lay in the institutions – above all the factory – as a *counter* to the formal juridical freedoms of the sphere of circulation. The sphere of circulation, the market, is the realm of Marx's 'invisible threads' which bind the worker to capital every bit as much as the authority of the capitalist in his factory, and by methods which, as I have suggested, meet Foucault's criteria of disciplinary power certainly no less, and possible more closely than those of the factory.

The crisis of social control

On the basis of the above discussion it is possible to advance a hypothesis as to the nature of the increasing problems faced by what we might term the 'classical' system of capitalist social control towards the close of the last century. The transition to the modern system of capital accumulation through the production of relative surplus-value served to increase the autonomous space available to the worker, to further distance the factory and factory life from anything approaching Panopticon. It involved the reduction of the working day as part of the process of raising labour productivity, the increased size of the factory and the decline of the company town and the ownership of the local means of consumption by the individual employer of labour. By the last third of the century this process is joined by a revolution in technique within the labour process itself. A rising organic composition of capital leads eventually to the predominance of fixed costs which do not vary in relation to fluctuations in output. This leads to an emphasis on reduction of the turnover time of fixed capital leading to a reduction in unit costs: speed of operations in the utilization of plant becomes of the essence. The revolution in techniques for speeding up the work process is indissociable from the name of F.W. Taylor and 'scientific management'. What the latter involved was as far as possible the removal of the application and control of human labour from the hands of the workers and placing it at the disposal of a centralized and effective enterprise management thus ensuring that plant would be used in the most effective way possible. The attempt to eliminate worker autonomy in the production process involved the breaking down of the physical actions of the worker into precise coded, measured, and timed gestures which are then presented to the worker as norms to be adhered to. Alfred Sohn-Rethel (1978, p.156) has summed up the significance of this with precision:

the wedding together rather than the confrontation of labour and machinery [and] the conversion of the worker from a machine operator into part of the machinery.

Scientific management in the general sense, it would thus appear, is the perfection of the discipline of the body as a structure of power spoken of by Foucault. However Sohn-Rethel draws other conclusions from the conversion of the worker into part of the machinery. Disciplined work can now be:

either . . . the subordination of labour to the machinery or it can take the shape of the subordination of the machinery to labour. It must be one of the two; it cannot remain indifferent to this alternative. [ibid., p.162]

In other words, the consequences of the wedding together of labour and machinery are paradoxical. Only when the worker stood in contrast to and, in terms of method of operation, confrontation with the automatism of the machine was the disciplining of his body fused with, and contingent upon, his subordination to the authority of capital. With the fusion of worker and machine, discipline is built into the design and pacing of the machinery. The worker's actions are set out in advance as part of the structure and process of the machine, quite irrespective of the authority of capital. Indeed, as Gramsci remarked (1973, pp.809-10), the new automatism of the labour process frees the worker mentally from subordination to the authority of capital:

Once the process of adaption [to the new methods of production] has been completed, what really happens is that the brain of the worker, far from being mummified, reached a state of complete freedom. The only thing that is completely mechanised is the physical gesture; the memory of the trade reduced to simple gestures repeated at an intense rhythm, 'nestles' in the muscular and nervous centres and leaves the brain free and unencumbered for other operations. One can walk without having to think about all the movements needed to move, in perfect sychronisation, all the parts of the body, in the specific way that is necessary for walking . . . . One walks automatically and at the same time thinks about whatever one chooses. American industrialists have understood all too well this dialectic inherent in the new industrial methods . . . not only does the worker think, but the fact that he gets no immediate satisfaction from his work . . . can lead him into a train of thought that is far from conformist.

In these passages from Gramsci and Sohn-Rethel we find the basis of a firm critique of the conception of the disciplined articulation of the actions of the human body as inevitably inseparable from a structure of power: the automatism of a discipline built into the machinery leaves the worker freer to reflect on the conditions of his labour under capitalism (Gramsci) while a collective co-ordination of labour dispensing entirely with the authority of capital, based instead on the objective synchronization of integrated flow production, presents itself as a historical possibility (Sohn-Rethel).

For the fact that this historical possibility remains unrealized capital has to thank processes increasingly located outside the factory and the labour process:

> the assumption being that the workers, while working as a combined force with their hands, in their minds remain divided in conformity with their pay packets. [Sohn-Rethel 1978, p.162]

Here Sohn-Rethel perceptively hints at the new structure of social control which has grown up to replace and reinforce the weakening structures of early capitalist discipline. The increased severance of working discipline from capitalist authority forces capital, within the factory, to take for granted as far as the labour process is concerned, the 'decision to participate' on the part of the workers and to rely upon factors external to the factory. Ultimately, of course, the decision to participate is generally guaranteed by the separation of the worker from the means of production. In this respect of course capitalism has not changed. But the other vital 'invisible thread' binding the worker to capital, the market, which subordinated the worker to the labour process as a process of capital valorization, and that above all else, by virtue of the fragmentation and competition within the working class for employment and which dominated the worker with his knowledge of his own replaceability by another also weakened during the latter decades of the last century at the same time as the technical changes in the labour process were emerging. The process of capital expansion itself acted to break down regional particularisms, communications were made easier between groups of workers and the level of competition in the labour market was further reduced by the decline in the 'latent' portion of the reserve army still in agricultural areas. The crisis in the mechanisms of capitalist social control took the manifest form of the rapid growth through the latter decades of the last century of trade union organization among the mass of the previously unorganized unskilled and semi-skilled workers and of a general increase in the intensity of the class struggle.

Monetization and the new structure of social control

The solution for capital lay in the acceptance of a new relationship between the 'two spheres' of the market and the factory. This involved the acceptance of the mass trade unionism of the industrial working class and the relinquishing, in the main, of attempts to smash union organization through the direct use of the industrial reserve army. But, instead, the trade union organization itself becomes a crucial vehicle of social control: a vehicle for the deflection of the class struggle from the labour process into the market. Capital maintains and deepens its control of the labour process and the factory through concessions on wages, including the 'social wage'. The material precondition for this strategy is the rising organic composition of capital and the rising productivity of labour (as opposed to the lengthening of the working day) as the main method of increasing the mass of surplus value. Wage increases can parallel productivity increases; the results of the latter can be shared between labour and capital on the condition that wage increases take up less than the full effect of increases in productivity.

Under the new system of control the terrain upon which compliance is generated shifts outside the factory – the door is finally closed upon Panopticon – *and* outside the market (as the fragmentation and competition among workers) into a new relationship between the two, into a trade-off of gains in the market, in the price of labour, in return for compliance in the labour process. Around this relationship, which we can term the 'monetization' of the class struggle, is gradually erected a new structure of political and social control. Monetization is the basis of the consolidation of reformism as the mass ideology of the labour movement. Such ideology may have originated as an expression of the market situation of the older labour aristocracy, but monetization strengthens it and extends it as the dominating ideology for the working class as a whole. Reformism is thus a modern ideology, the ideology of the working class under *modern* capitalism. As the basis for a stabilization of the class struggle at the industrial level it acts to transfer that struggle 'peacefully' to other arenas, notable among which is the state where the class struggle takes the predominant form of a political struggle for increases in the social wage. Monetization thus underpins the political incorporation of the working class into the state structure and the establishment of the 'hegemony' of the latter. It is not apparent neutrality of the state and its structures that provides the basis for its 'hegemony' and the forcing of the working class into the channels of reformist politics. It is monetization and the establishment of a reformist politics that enables the state to take on the appearance of a neutral terrain which then acts to reinforce the situation that made possible its emergence.

The replacement of the older structures of control, or rather their relative stepping back to make way for the new structures of monetization, forces upon capital the task of campaigning for its authority within the sphere of monetization. 'Let us educate our new masters' is the slogan of capital as it develops through the expansion of the media and the mass education that is a presupposition of the media a campaign to win the working class to 'responsible' behaviour when it comes to establishing the terms of the contract of monetization. At the same time the perfection of the techniques of mass surveillance of the working population gathers pace with the increasing scale of social life in the city outside the sphere of production and the discipline of the market. While the penetration and surveillance of the working class has been a continuous activity of the capitalist state, its expansion and the use of increasingly sophisticated techniques of data-gathering incorporating the welfare institutions into this role is a response to the decline of the discipline of factory and market and their replacement by the inherently fragile structures of monetization. In this context Foucault's remarks (1977, pp. 276-7) on the *real* importance of the prison, which never succeeds in its ostensible role, are of interest:

> the prison, apparently 'failing' does not miss its target; on the contrary, it reaches it, in so far as it gives rise to one particular form of illegality in the midst of others, which it is able to isolate, to place in full light and to organize as a relatively enclosed, but penetrable milieu . . . . This form is, strictly speaking, delinquency.

exactly what we are doing with our students

The penetration, classification, and surveillance by the agencies of capital of a working class which has passed, in its culture and organization well beyond the confines of the factory and the small industrial town into the modern capitalist city, becomes the task of almost the entire social apparatus of the state which, meantime, continually fails in its ostensible tasks of eliminating poverty and crime.

State and Panopticon

But such structures of surveillance must be distinguished from any hypothesis of the transference of the methodology of Panopticon from distinct institutions such as the factory or the prison, to civil society in general. The methodology of Panopticon is, as we have seen, a system of power of a special type; one in which the inmate is 'totally seen without ever seeing' and fears the consequences of being seen, and therefore submits automatically irrespective of the actual presence of surveillance in any particular situation. The growth of the apparatus of state surveillance within the context of monetization and liberal democracy is governed by dynamics of a different order.

Firstly, one is not totally seen without ever seeing. In Orwell's *Nineteen Eighty Four*, the precise actualization of a social Panopticon, the entire world of private space is deprivatized and subject to total surveillance. No one knows whether at a particular moment his actions are being watched, but in Orwell's nightmare, like Bentham's, he has no way of knowing either way and, fearing the consequences, submits. The type of surveillance characteristic of the modern democratic capitalist state is not a technology or a 'physics' of power in this sense. Its mode of operation contrasts with that of panopticism: it assumes, correctly, that the majority of the population is unaware either way of the presence of surveillance and either believe in its complete absence or, if aware of its presence, have little understanding of the actual or potential use to which information thus gathered can be put. Surveillance is an information-gathering exercise aimed at dealing with specific individuals or small groups deemed a potential threat to social stability. It is the construction of the rudiments of an apparatus to stand in readiness should the unstable parameters of monetization break down, it is, irrespective of what its practitioners may wish, not aimed at inducing a fear of surveillance as part of a general 'technology' for the maintenance of those relationships. For the apparatus of surveillance of the modern state to be considered as an automatic technology of power it would be necessary to radically redefine the state as identical with the fabric of social existence as such in which discipline, knowledge and co-ordination become defined in themselves as sources and forms of power. This direction is precisely that taken by some of Foucault's adherents. Thus Pasquale Pasquino (1978, p.52) finds it necessary that:

> one rids oneself of the idea of the State as an apparatus or instance separate from the social body, the focus of all political struggle, which must be either democratised or destroyed, once its veritable nature has been revealed, or which must be appropriated in order to take power: if one rids oneself of this old idea . . . .

This would resituate the analysis of relations of power wholly within the interior of the social body. The state would then be like a topographical survey, or rather the name given to such a survey.

Thus the physics of power is at last, with this conception, freed of any location in distinct institutions or *particular* structures of social relations. In a way this formulation parallels that of Althusser in his essay on the 'Ideological state apparatuses' (1971), in which 'churches, parties, trade unions, families, schools, newspapers cultural ventures etc. etc.' become part of the state apparatus. There is of course a radical difference in the starting points of Althusser and Pasquino. While the former wishes to subsume civil society into the state as part of a continuous series of coercive institutions, the latter wishes to decompose the state and its institutions into the very fabric of civil society. Nevertheless the end result is similar, the effect being to render difficult if not impossible any account of the changes in the structure of social control in capitalist societies especially in terms of the role of the state.

The danger of this type of analysis is that it clouds our ability to identify with precision the potential and actual instabilities of modern capitalism which disrupt the delicate balances of monetization and render it necessary for capital to periodically seek radical modifications in the state form. It is above all under the fascist regimes that capital abandons the structures of monetization and calls for the establishment of a social Panopticon in a barbarous attempt to recapture the automatism of power once located in the combination of factory and market. The evolution of discipline from an identity of the labour process with the mental and physical subordination of the worker to the authority of capital towards a rupture in which collective labour stands juxtaposed to the demands of capital valorization is the foundation of the modern authoritarian state.

6 Institutions of social control and capitalist organization of work*

Dario Melossi

I wish to emphasize that what follows is not in any sense a completed piece of work but, rather, the elaboration of some directions for further research in the study of social institutions and themes concerning social control in general. These hypotheses originated during research into the origins of penal institutions in the period of the formation of the capitalist mode of production (Melossi and Pavarini forthcoming).

Classical capitalism and social control

I shall define the institutions that I am going to consider as *ancillary* institutions. The real nature and function of these institutions in classical – that is, nineteenth century – capitalism is revealed through an understanding of the nature of *authority* and *discipline.* Marx wrote:

> The sphere of circulation or rather the exchange of commodities within the limits of which moves the purchase and sale of labour-power, is in reality a veritable Eden of the innate rights of man. There reigns only Liberty, Equality, Property and Bentham. [1976, p.280]

Thus the sale of labour-power respects the general principle of the exchange of equivalents. However at the end of the process the capitalist ends up with a value greater than he had at the beginning. It must therefore be in the particular nature of the commodity that he has bought that the secret of surplus-value resides. This consists in the fact that the consumption of the use value of labour-power itself produces value. But that only occurs under particular conditions. The capitalist in fact buys only the individual labour-power of single labourers, not their combined force. In so far as he finds the latter already given as the method of use of the labour-power he has bought then: 'the co-operation of wage labourers is entirely brought about by the capital that employs them' (ibid., pp. 449-50). By means of his authority the capitalist puts to use the labour-power he has bought, that is, organizes the labour process. It is this specific form of use, this despotism, which alone allows the extraction of surplus-value. The authority to organize and regulate the factory in accordance with an ordered plan is a question of life and death for the survival of the capitalist mode of production.

* Translated by John Lea.

As Marx notes in the *Poverty of Philosophy* (1976a, p.126) there is clearly an inverse relation between the development of authority in the factory and in society whereby, in the long period of gestation of the capitalist mode of production, authority withdraws from the wider social universe to concentrate and direct itself in certain well defined spaces, notably, in the factory. From the crisis of the feudal system down to the epoch of *laissez-faire* the more relaxed became the relations of direct dependence in society as a whole, the more became organized and perfected the particular structures of authority of bourgeois society, structures based on the fundamental contradiction between political liberty and social slavery. Such slavery manifests itself in the conditions which permit the extraction of surplus-value which guarantee the process of exploitation. The totality of these conditions finds its real basis in the factory situation but contemporaneously is reproduced in a whole series of other institutions which are born or receive new life and significance with the advent of bourgeois society. These institutions have, by various instruments and methods, the function of forming and controlling the factory proletariat, of guaranteeing the adaptability of labour-power to be used and handled as one commodity among many.

By what mechanisms and through what institutions are such results achieved? Jeremy Bentham – in this case the social architect Bentham rather than the 'juridical' Bentham who 'reigns' in the sphere of circulation – envisaged in his great eighteenth-century project for a Panopticon (1838-43, vol. 4, pp.37-173) the embodiment of a new principle of construction. The principle was to be applicable to any type of establishment in which people were to be placed under discipline, including penitentiaries, workhouses, poor houses, factories, lazariums, hospitals, and schools. With particular diligence Bentham dealt with the application of the Panopticon to his project for a new model prison. In this establishment the aims of custody, of isolation and solitude, of forced labour and of instruction, are pursued simultaneously. A study of this institution in particular reveals clearly how that instrument becomes one of control and instruction of labour-power, as the site of the production of the proletariat.

The functional connection between the prison and the factory is made in the concept of *discipline*. This is the fundamental lesson that the prison expounds to its inmates and at the same time is the way in which the authority of capital presents itself to the workers. The capitalist organization of work and discipline thus arise together, as interrelated concepts separable only in so far as one is considering separately the two aspects of capital: the organization of constant capital: machinery, and variable capital, labour-power. But from the historical study of the prison another result emerges; namely, the related origins of all the various institutions which to the mind of the bourgeois utilitarian Bentham, appeared as united in function and in structure. These institutions have progressively differentiated themselves, in the transition from the mediaeval to the classical capitalist eras, from what Foucault calls '*grand internment*'. But their theoretical and practical roots are the same even though their functions become more specific and articulated.

The research of Foucault in *Discipline and Punish* (1977) starts out from precisely this point of view. The emergence of the institutions of incarceration is described by Foucault together with other institutions – the school, the army, the hospital, the factory – or rather, Foucault presents us with the emergence of a certain idea, a certain way of conceptualizing social organization which is of some importance in defining diverse structures, diverse architectonic, ideological and verbal spaces. The central nucleus around which these different forms organize themselves is *discipline*. But Foucault does not rest here. He shows us precisely what discipline means. He shows us how the rules, the practical written ones, of the army, of the instructional institutions, of the prison and hospital, of the *ateliers*, come, during the seventeenth and eighteenth centuries, to take on the aim of a constitutive and architectonic idea of the body. The body is reconstructed and redefined in accordance with precise rules which are minutely described by Foucault according to certain general principles which he terms the *political economy of the body*.

Let us follow the categories which Foucault draws out in the process of dissecting these institutions: the art of distributions, the control of activities, the organization of geneses, the composition of forces, and then; hierarchical observation, normalizing judgement, the examination. These are the elements of discipline (ibid., pp. 135ff.)[1] But at the same time they are the elements of the capitalist organization of labour and the pattern they follow is that of the production of variable capital, of the worker. Their object is the production of the individual as a machine, as part of the complex capitalist machine. The great merit of Foucault's work lies in the fact that it allows us to see how the production of the individual as a machine – that is as labour-power – is not something that has to do only with his mental state but also something which transforms his body, remodelling it as part of a complex organization. The human individual becomes redefined during this period as *worker* (Melossi 1975). It is through the use of certain techniques that the body can be habituated to determinate movements, to repetition and regularity, in such a way as to enable it to function obediently as the appendage of a machine, or rather, as a machine. The role of institutions outside the factory is thus clarified as the production and reproduction of variable capital. The political economy of the body reveals itself as simply political economy *tout court*.

Another notable result of the work of Foucault is to put the concept of ideology back on its feet. The ideological base which constitutes the general cultural atmosphere of capitalism parallels the understanding of technique and can be seen as nothing other than the mode of conceptualization of labour-power. In this way, ideology no longer occupies the 'sphere of circulation', of the free reign of the juridical and political institutions, it is on the contrary located in the areas of servitude: the factory, the prison and the school. Ideology, in the last analysis, is nothing more than the appearance with which a specific technique of the reproduction of labour-power presents itself to the consciousness of the labourer. Any conception of ideology as a sort of 'holy spirit' rising up from the economic sphere is thus swept away. It lies so much more in the regular rhythmic movements normatively prescribed, with which the pupil has to sit at the desk and take the pen in his hand, than in all the philosophy of Hegel.

Ideology, before being spoken of or read about, can be measured and touched. In this way Foucault, the idealist, presents a materialist theory of ideology, a theory far more informative about structure and super-structure than the architectonic metaphor (Althusser 1971) a theory which perhaps goes as far as to allow only a single and all-embracing structural space to subsist within the category of the reproduction of labour-power. Such a foundation as Foucault's makes it difficult to sustain the distinction between the *repressive* and the *ideological* apparatus of the state in the way presented by Althusser. For a whole series of state institutions at least, both these concepts would be unified within that of the construction and teaching of a certain basic nucleus of behaviour. Another important consequence is that of distinguishing within the vast corpus of ideology, the real nucleus of an epoch and (in accordance with Marxism rather than Foucault) of a mode of production,[2] of a constitutive ideology of the complexity of the capitalist organization of work and in particular, labour-power.

From the outset of capitalism therefore, there exist areas of control by capital outside the factory. The sphere of production extends itself far outside the factory gates. And it is from the outset the state which operates this extension of capital in the form of an interventionist strategy, a strategy entirely characteristic of the period of origin of these institutions – mercantilism. It was the merchants presiding over the municipality of Amsterdam who created, at the end of the sixteenth century, the first house of work and correction, the first modern prison in Europe organized along factory lines and endowed with particular economic privileges (Melossi and Pavarini 1977). Similar processes were at work with the hospitals, the military institutions, the schools and the modern penitentiaries. It is worthwhile also to dwell on one last institution of crucial importance hitherto undiscussed – the family.

Predominantly private institutions, Althusser reminds us (1971), following Gramsci, can function perfectly as ideological state apparatuses. In the transition from the religious structure of medieval society to the secular and impersonal structure of bourgeois society (even if the latter remains apparently dominated by religion), authority and the complex social universe withdraws – on the level of appearance – to the factory and to other segregated institutions. The authority structure, and thus the possibility of an orderly exploitation of labour-power and an efficient accumulation of capital, would become extremely fragile if it were not possible to sustain the old *belief* in authority by means of an instrument which could develop the same potentiality for the organization of consensus as the rural religious world of the middle ages.

The weapon forged for this purpose is that of education in the patriarchal nuclear family. It is achieved through the over-valuation of the role of the father who becomes the secular priest of the new social structure. Marx observed:

Luther certainly conquered servitude based on *devotion* but only by replacing it with servitude based on *conviction*. He destroyed faith in authority but only by restoring the authority of faith. He transformed priests into laymen but only by transforming the laymen into priests. He freed mankind from external religiosity but only by making religiosity the inner man. He freed the body from its chains only by putting the heart in chains . . . it was no longer a question of the layman with the priest *outside himself* but rather of his struggle with his own *inner priest*, with his priestly nature. [1975, pp. 251-2]

It is the new 'reformed' urban bourgeois family which takes on the most important part of the function of providing the enduring ideological basis of consensus through the channelling of the instincts in accordance with social needs. It is this which is precisely the nucleus of Freud's entire research. It must be emphasized that the connection between the capitalist organization of work and the reproduction of labour-power does not follow ideological communally enforced channels but *passes through* the body and head of the individual, at the stage of primary socialization of the infant. The result is the physical constitution of a personality ready to be immersed in the work process, and, which is the same thing, to learn the necessary work skills. The foundations of this instruction of the body, which becomes reinforced and perfected during the phase of secondary socialization, are located already within family education. The family and other institutions which are created or restructured during the birth of the capitalist mode of production are thus with good reason to be defined as *ancillary* to the factory. This is the first general hypothesis of this article which is presented for further research and elaboration.

The crisis of neo-capitalist social control

All this, as I have said, is from the standpoint of the competitive capitalism which securely dominated the last century. In the period stretching from the last decades of that century over the entire first half of the present, we witness, throughout the capitalist world, a gathering momentum of profound modifications to the underlying economic scenario. The present discussion is focused around two developments.

The rapid increase in the predominance of fixed capital inside the factory allows an increasing integration of capitalist authority with machinery in the organization of work. The guarantor of the extraction of surplus-value is decreasingly the capitalist, or his overseer, and is increasingly located in the very technical 'rationality' of production itself. The first systematic computation of the scientific organization of work is elaborated, in the United States, by the ex-worker, Frederick W. Taylor. It is Gramsci who draws out the strong connection between 'Taylorism', 'Fordism' and the whole sphere of custom, culture and, above all, the 'sexual question':

The history of industrialism has always been a continuing struggle (which today takes on an even more marked and vigorous form) against the element of 'animality' in man. It has been an uninterrupted, often painful and bloody process of subjugating natural (i.e. animal and primitive) instincts to new, more complex and rigid norms and habits of order, exactitude and precision. [1973, p.298]

And it is Gramsci who links the battle on this terrain with the entire question of hegemony:

Life in industry demands a general apprenticeship, a process of psycho-physical adaption to specific conditions of work, nutrition, housing, customs, etc. This is not something 'natural' or innate, but has to be acquired and the urban characteristics thus acquired are passed on by heredity or rather are absorbed into the development of childhood and adolescence. As a result the low birthrate in the cities imposes the need for continual massive expenditure on the training of a continual flow of new arrivals in the city and brings with it a continual change in the socio-political composition of the city, thus continually changing the terrain on which the problem of hegemony is to be posed. [ibid., p.296]

Thus, increasingly, from the beginning of the period in which Gramsci wrote these notes, in addition to the ancillary institutions the *city* begins to be considered a new terrain of conflict.

The second development is that the progressive centralization of capital, carried forward by the accumulation process, transcends competitive capitalism and creates a new structure of monopoly – or of oligopolistic equilibrium – in which the sphere of circulation is increasingly integrated into and subordinated to that of production. The separation between the 'two spheres' outlined in the first volume of *Capital* is progressively fading away. In the process of the capitalist socialization of work, capital, working through the state, extends its real base from the factory out to the whole of society. Panzieri (1976) expresses this clearly:

The factory *fades away* as a specific moment. The same type of process which dominates the factory, characteristic of the moment of production, tends to impose itself *throughout society* and therefore the characteristic features of the factory – the particular structures of the subordination of living labour power to capital – tend to pervade all levels of society reappearing in specific forms.

The sphere of circulation, of consumption, becomes subsumed under the direct domination of capital; decisions on prices, the organization of the market and at the same time the organization of consensus are becoming unified. Not only are the traditional instruments of social control strengthening themselves, that is those 'areas of the sphere of production' outside the factory, in existence since the origin of capitalism, but also new instruments are evolving. The underlying principle is no longer that of enclosing the individual but of following him to where he is normally enclosed: outside the factory in the localities. The structure of propaganda and the mass media, a new and more effective system of policing and social surveillance, are the carriers of neo-capitalist social control. The crisis of the segretive institutions is countered by the reconstruction of the city as factory and the displacement of the focus of surveillance from the factory to the city.

These developments are not without their impact on the system of secondary social control, the ancillary institutions. This is the second main hypothesis that I want to put forward. It is above all the prison system which feels the effects of the new developments. Rusche and Kirchheimer (1964) show how, from the end of the last century up to the 1940s, the prison population fell considerably in Great Britain, France and Germany. In Italy the period clearly begins in the 1880s and extends to the present, with the exception of the fascist period. The decline of the incarcerated population is accompanied by the adoption of increasingly extensive penal measures for open control like probation, widely practised in the United States. Already during the last century the prison system had entered a profound malaise rooted in its own internal contradictions. Any prison system oscillates between the alternatives of, on the one hand, transformation into a productive institution modelled on the factory and, on the other, of becoming a pure instrument of terror. The former results in loss of ability to terrorize, the latter renders the prison useless for any task of resocialization of the inmates but allows it to function, as Foucault observes, to preserve a social zone labelled as delinquent and as the carrier of a whole series of services (not least that of scapegoat) for the dominant class (1977, pt.4, ch.2)[3] For the entire present century, therefore, the prospects for reform have lain in the direction of a progressive diminishing of penalties involving incarceration, together with increasing repression for certain categories of crime, a typical 'scissor-like' process. The *predominating* tendency however is for social control to move from the secondary to the primary level and, within the former, to displace control away from detention towards police measures of various forms of social surveillance.[4]

This entire process, hastily described above, cannot be understood except as an expression of class conflict, as the result of continuing incessant effort on the part of the contenders, capital and labour, to bring themselves up to the level achieved by the mode of production and the social relations inherent in it. In particular, the entire process of the socialization of capitalist control which began in the 1920s was a response to the task of defending the level of exploitation and profit placed in jeopardy by the workers' struggles and in particular by the profound crisis which followed the First World War (Cacciari 1972; Bologna 1972). The subordination of the working class to the process of capitalist development is not given at the outset but is the result of strategies that capital is constrained to carry out to safeguard the extraction of surplus-value. Such processes are rooted in the class struggle and hence do not present themselves simply as a linear development.

Typical here is the prison. On the one hand we witness the underlying process described above and on the other hand the steady loss of the re-educative connotations of the prison (of resocialization). The latter implies that the institution turns increasingly towards the use of terroristic and authoritarian measures, as a result of which it performs particularly well in crisis situations requiring a turn towards authoritarianism. This was the case during the fascist period and seems to have been the case in other countries in more recent years.

Likewise the case of the family. In several cases during the present century it has been the focal point of attempts to 'regroup' consensus around an authoritarian and reactionary ideology. An analagous example, even if opposite in form, is the entire administrative apparatus of the modern welfare state in which conquests of the working class are turned to the real advantage of capitalism. All these questions were posed with particular clarity during the late 1960s.

It is with the present crisis, beginning in the late 1960s, that the profound connection between social control and the capitalist organization of work emerges into the consciousness of the masses and is reflected in practical politics. Today it is possible to pose the problem clearly because of the new dimensions taken on by the struggle itself. The present stage of working-class combativity has become generalized throughout the entire Western economy and at the same time has been accompanied by the development of movements which have shaken to the foundations the most important ancillary institutions of our society. It is obviously necessary to keep in mind the determinate specificity of each particular institution, as well as the effect of national particularities.[5] It is nevertheless surprising how, beyond the differences, however profound, the movement against psychiatric practices, the revolt in the prisons, the unprecedented mass movement in the schools and universities, the process of democratization in the army, and the profound crisis of family institutions, have rocked the social equilibrium of advanced capitalism. These movements have combined with one of the most intense manifestations of the international working-class struggle. Under such conditions the discussion which has arisen in a conscious and manifest way around the institutions has itself provided material for the actual struggle around the question of power in the factory. It is not by accident that the explosion of the anti-institutional and anti-authoritarian movement has coincided with the development of the class struggle and has captured and generalized not only the force and generic impact of the working class but also the level and the specific contents of this historic movement and its capacity to shatter the social universe.

Certainly this process has assumed new and profound dimensions in the Italian situation due, in my view, to the particularities of socio-political development. Two aspects (present also in other countries) are superimposed: the struggle against the capitalist organization of work at the social level (in the ancillary institutions) has on the one hand brought to light the inadequacy of these institutions for securing the development of the mode of production, and on the other hand this struggle has aimed at throwing such institutions into internal chaos at the highest level. Certainly in Italy, more than elsewhere, the extreme dysfunctionality of specific institutions like the school for the task of capitalist rationalization is evident everywhere. That does not, however, detract from the fact that at the end of the 1960s the movement against the organization of work in the factory came up against the entire social universe of disciplinary and formative institutions based upon the factory. The very possibility of an analysis of these institutions arises only upon the basis of their entry into crisis in the face of practical struggle. In this sense there is no more profound a reflection upon the events of 1968 than the text of Foucault. To use Foucault's own language, one begins to *dismantle*, to disjoint, to take to pieces, that complex machine which was created by the bourgeoisie with its ascendancy to power.

Perhaps the institution which is most readily connected with the general development of the workers' and students' movements is the prison. Here the main dynamic of struggle is for the assimilation of the internal regime of the prison, especially as regards labour, to the standards of 'free' existence and on the other hand to open up the institution itself to the outside world. It is unnecessary to recall the impressiveness with which these struggles emerged in the school, the fundamental apparatus of the entire process of the reproduction of labour-power. It was no accident that they emerged here as Althusser (1971) has noted. But most relevant on the level of theory are the implications of the workers' campaign for the '150 hours'.[6] The concept of the school which is posed by this struggle and which we can now grasp theoretically is its breakdown as a separate segregated institution and its integration into the organization of work but *starting from the needs of the working class*. Study becomes an instrument of the class struggle.

This process, however, is not yet generally understood on a class basis. In the immediate situation there seems to be a contradiction whose origins are to be found in the lack of social development corresponding to the level of capitalist work organization and the struggle around it: the integration of various institutions with the factory in this complex of 'factory-society' (Panzieri 1976) also signifies the possibility of a new and higher order of social control, a reinforcement and an extension of the command of capital. An examination of certain reform processes at work, during the 1960s, in various European countries reveals tendencies which were at the centre of the struggles of 1968. While these tendencies became the subject of radicalization, the state on the other hand attempted to counteract the movement and re-exhume the old apparatus of control.

To sum up what is necessarily an extremely diffuse discussion. On the one hand the integration of the various social institutions under the command of capital and the consequent increasing unity of the factory and the other social institutions results from the exigencies of the process of capitalist rationalization. On the other hand, however, this process of unification of all the institutions involved in the reproduction of labour-power and its use, has produced a more immediate and explosive communicability of struggles against the capitalist organization of work in all spheres of society. This has served precisely to uncover the ancillary character of various institutions. In this situation it is extremely likely that the defence of conservative positions and the old repressive apparatus of control by capital will endure only in so far as this is necessary for the control of the crisis and while new solutions to the problem of control are in the process of development.

These new systems of control will not be worked out 'at the conference table'. Given that the entire system of social control is modelled on the relations of production, then it will only be through the restabilization of the power of capital in the factory (which implies a new morphology of the relations of production) that new types of social control can become a reality. And so a fundamental theme for research at the moment must be the attempt to identify the extent to which there is being constructed a new correspondence between the social and the productive spheres, a correspondence of the clarity symbolized under classic capitalism by the Benthamite model of the Panopticon.

Here is not the place to present even a preliminary sketch of such a hypothesis. It is sufficient just to observe that in the leading capitalist country, the United

States, the *territorialization* of social control has progressively advanced on a massive scale.[7] It must be emphasized on the other hand that such directions as these which may be followed by our research presuppose clearly the standpoint of a class which is in a position to link together the present militancy of workers and popular masses under a strategy on the terrain of social control. The real movement is, once again, as we have attempted to show for past phases of the struggle, dialectical. In other words it is necessary to distinguish clearly, within the new terrain of conflict, between the objectives of the valorization of capital and the restoration of its command in the form of new techniques of social control on the one hand, and on the other, the structures which correspond to the needs of the popular masses. These cannot but be closely connected to the level of struggle in the factory.

At this point the discussion of social control becomes the discussion of the state, given that the hegemonic apparatus of the state is the most fundamental vehicle of social control. The struggle for hegemony, therefore, is not a question of more struggle *within* the institutions or *in* the localities, generically understood, but the construction, in the same way as did the bourgeoisie, of real vehicles of hegemony, of a real apparatus and structure. The hypothesis of a democratic social control (that is, one practised by the masses) fuses the fight for an anti-capitalist use of the state which does not simply run parallel to, but is currently strictly co-ordinated with the struggle against the capitalist organization of work. And thus it seems, also on the terrain of social control, that the only direction of significant progress for the working class and the popular masses is that which has as its objective the *reform of the state*.

7 'Decarceration' and the fiscal crisis

Roger Matthews

It has by now become quite clear that it is impossible to discuss current developments in particular institutions of social control, or the dynamics of social control practices more generally, except in the context of a broader analysis of the changes taking place in advanced capitalism. What has made this clear is that the current capitalist crisis has had a definite impact on the state, not only in terms of pressures to reduce state spending but, further, to reorganize the very ways in which social control is exercised.

One aspect of this in the recent period has been the changing relationship between traditional institutions of control, notably the prison, and emerging forms outside the 'total institution' such as the so-called 'community care' programmes. The immediacy of this process of transformation has put into question the adequacy of the existing framework of subjectivist deviancy theory. In particular the emphasis in such theory on exposing the fundamentally despotic character of *all* control institutions is hardly viable in the light of the considerable political significance of such changes. Further, the tendency of the old deviancy theory to contrast the despotism within the total institution with the relative freedom outside is undermined by the apparent turns in state policy and ideology. Yet it is important to try to penetrate behind the ideological terms in which such changes in state policy are formulated to grasp their real substance.

The aim of this paper is to examine such questions through a critical review of the theses advanced by Andrew Scull in his book *Decarceration: Community Treatment and the Deviant – A Radical View.* The strength of Scull's approach is his explicitly political starting point. The problematic of the book begins from a questioning of what Scull sees as the 'growing harmony of interests within conventional politics, including hard line conservatives who have lent support for decarceration and the increased use of "community-care" '.

To the extent that criminologists and practitioners have been aware of this development, Scull argues, they have been predominantly concerned with the most *effective* methods of implementing the policy, rather than to question and in turn to analyse why such a policy should emerge at all.[1] To this end Scull begins from a rejection of familiar subjectivist and pragmatic approaches, and advocates instead a historical and structural analysis which, he argues, is the only methodological approach which can adequately account for the process of decarceration. However, I shall argue that although Scull is critical of 'official' versions of the significance of decarceration, the weakness in his own theoretical approach leads him to an analysis which in practice does not radically break with appearances: first, in accepting too readily the notion that 'community care' is a substitute rather than a *complement* of incarceration, and second in failing to analyse the roots of the *actual* changes in control that have been taking place.

Theoretical issues

The decarceration thesis

Scull's thesis is deceptively simple. Its starting point is a double-edged critique of humanistic accounts on one hand, and contemporary 'liberal' accounts on the other.

Following Rusche and Kirchheimer (1968)[2] he argues that changes in control practices are not motivated primarily by humanistic concerns and the assumption that community care is necessarily more 'humane' than incarceration is built on questionable assumptions.

> Most people's conception of the 'humane' does not embrace placing senile men and women in the hands of rapacious nursing home operators or turning loose the perpetrators of violent crimes, under conditions which guarantee that they will receive little or no supervision. [Scull 1977, p.1]

Secondly, he rejects the two contemporary liberal accounts which explain the growth of community treatment as the result either of the development of psychoactive drugs or as a result of social scientific critique of the 'total institution'.

The first of these two accounts argues that the recent growth of decarceration is due to the revolution in the use of psychoactive drugs, which has allowed larger numbers of people to be managed within a non-institutional setting. Although recognizing the general significance of this development Scull argues that its claims as an adequate explanation of decarceration are exaggerated since many of those decarcerated, particularly the young, are not on the whole subject to drug treatment.

The second 'liberal' account often presented is that the growth of decarceration results from the critique of 'total institutions' forwarded by social scientists, particularly during the 1960s. They are credited with managing to persuade policy-makers to seek 'community-based' alternatives. Critiques of total institutions, however, are as old as institutions themselves, and arguments that these institutions only exacerbate the problems which they set out to solve have a long and distinctive pedigree. What is interesting about recent critiques is that they, unlike their predecessors, should fall on such willing ears.

In contrast to these 'humanistic' and 'liberal' accounts, Scull argues that decarceration only became possible in the second half of the twentieth century with the development of a welfare infrastructure which made 'segregative modes of control far more costly, in relative terms, and far more difficult to justify'. This tendency was compounded by the simultaneous development of a 'fiscal crisis of the state' in the post-war period which forced policy-makers to adopt less costly forms of control than institutionalization.

In sum, therefore, Scull argues that it is economic considerations which have forced the increased substitution of community-based control for traditional forms of incarceration. Community control and incarceration are seen to be two mutually interdependent phenomena; moreover, 'it is precisely the expansion of the one which made both possible and desirable the contraction of the other.' [ibid., p. 135].

Defining decarceration

In the introduction to the book Scull defines decarceration as simply a word which is 'shorthand for a State-sponsored policy for closing down asylums, prisons and reformatories' [ibid., p.1]. However, in his attempt to demonstrate that decarceration is taking place on a large scale, and also to relate decarceration to the growth of community care, the term comes to take on a wider meaning and embraces a complex set of practices which includes not only the removal of people from institutions, but also the processes by which they are diverted away from such institutions.

In Scull's usage the term 'decarceration' comes to involve four distinct processes. Firstly, the most dramatic form, which involves the physical expulsion of inmates as a result of the closure of institutions. Examples of this process are limited to the famous 'Massachussetts experiment' and a small number of mental institutions, but has not been operated to date in prisons. Secondly, the potential level of incarceration has been reduced, Scull suggests, through fiscal measures which have frozen or withdrawn funds designated for this area. Examples of particular cutbacks can be found, no doubt, throughout the history of incarceration, but what is significant about the post-war period is the dramatic increase both in Britain and America in the amount of funds which have been made available to this category of public expenditure (see Gough 1975; Platt and Takagi 1977), and the continued expansion in the building of segregative institutions.

Thirdly, Scull identifies a process which 'involves re-classifying whole categories of offences and offenders'. There has, in the post-war period, been a tendency to 'decriminalize' certain categories of offences (see Greenwood and Young 1979); however, the general movement in this period has clearly been towards greater state intervention with the consequent creation of new, and expansion of existing, categories.[3] The final form in which decarceration is effected, Scull argues, involves the increased use of discretion by the police and the courts in an attempt to divert people away from the possibility of incarceration. This discretionary process is for obvious reasons extremely difficult to quantify, but there is some evidence that the control agencies have not been unresponsive to pressures of overcrowding in institutions or the piling up of cases before the courts. However, what is significant is that since the 1930s, and particularly in the post-war period, the overall conviction rates have dramatically increased as well as the number of people incarcerated (see Radzinowicz and King 1977).

The rationalization of the use of incarceration and attempts to reduce the incarcerated population are by no means a distinctive characteristic of the post-war period. Rusche and Kirchheimer (1964, p.146), for example, have shown that the number of people imprisoned in Britain during the period from 1880 to 1931 fell steadily from 32,990 to 13,838 – a tendency which was repeated, with a few minor fluctuations, all over Europe during this period.

Also, as Hawkins (1975, p.281) has emphasized:

> The search for alternatives to imprisonment has, of course, been going on for more than the last thirty years. The Probation Officers Act 1907, The Childrens Act and The Prevention of Crime Act (both 1908), The Mental Deficiency Act 1913, and The Criminal Justice Act, all attempted to remove certain kinds of offenders from prison.

Prior to this period, in the eighteenth and nineteenth centuries, decarceration in one form or another was in operation, although offenders were not placed in other forms of state control but left in their communities. It must be remembered that in Europe, at least, this process was mediated by the use of transportation, which acted as ameliorate the generic problems of overcrowding and security which has threatened incarceration since its inception.[4] Decarceration, as Scull comes to define it, is nothing more or less than the negative moment of incarceration: the process by which offenders are selected or diverted from segregative forms of control. It is therefore not reducible to the growth of a welfare infrastructure or the 'fiscal crisis of the state', although these factors may have some effect on its specific form in any particular historical period. Moreover, decarceration and community care are not two mutually interdependent phenomena, but rather two distinct processes which, again, may become related under specific social and historical conditions.

Further, the generality with which the term 'decarceration' is often employed fails to adequately conceptualize the relation between segregative and non-segregative forms of control. For example, placing people in 'twenty-four-hour detention hostels' in the 'community' instead of traditional institutions is not adequately reflected in the term 'decarceration'. More importantly, a large percentage of apparently 'decarcerated' individuals are not placed outside of the general network of control and surveillance, but are diverted into more flexible programmes only to reappear in traditional institutions at a later date.

It becomes increasingly clear that the changes in the nature of incarceration in the post-war period in particular, and more generally since the eighteenth century, are substantially different than those described by Scull. However, this in itself does not entirely undermine his thesis, which does not refer to the number of people incarcerated at any one time (the prison population has almost doubled during the period from 1951 to 1971) or the percentage of the total population (which has increased in roughly the same proportion over the same period), but to the *percentage* of people incarcerated who have been convicted of indictable offences (HMSO 1971). Thus the decarceration argument is built upon the very dubious presupposition that all those convicted of indictable offences should naturally or automatically be incarcerated.

For Scull, then, 'decarceration' means the difference between the number of indictable offences and the number of people incarcerated. Curiously, within this equation the growth of the crime rate is taken as relatively unproblematic. There is no analysis of the content of this figure or any discussion of why it should have risen so rapidly. Every apprentice criminologist learns not to take official statistics on crime as 'given'. The nature, object, definition and reaction to crime is not static; the social and political preoccupation with crime varies from one period to the next.

> The obvious but frequently neglected point is that crime is differently defined (in both official and lay ideologies) at different periods, and this reflects not only the changing attitudes amongst different sectors of the population, as well as real historical changes in the social organization of criminal activity but also a shifting application of the category itself, by the governing classes to different groups and activities in the course of – and sometimes for the purpose of providing the ground for – the exercise of legal restraint and political control. [Hall *et al.*, 1978, p.189]

Any approach which purports to be 'historical' must consider not only changes in control practices but examine its relation to changing forms of social and 'criminal' activity. The concentration on the control side of this relation will tend to make such processes appear arbitrary. The growth of crime, even during the post-war period, has been anything but linear or unilateral.[5] Within Scull's presentation we have, in effect, an unknown on each side of the equation: thus making any attempt at substantive analysis extremely difficult and seriously detracting from the plausibility of the thesis.

A remaining part of Scull's thesis which requires closer examination is the effect on control strategies of the so-called 'fiscal crisis of the state' in recent years.

Crisis: what crisis?

There is little disagreement amongst the general population that the recent period has been one of crisis. There are, however, serious differences in the way in which this 'crisis' has been conceived.

For Scull the crisis is located in the state apparatus and is 'engendered by capitalism's need to socialize more and more the costs of production', which has resulted in a situation in which state spending exceeds available revenue. This, for Scull, explains why the state is forced to search for cheaper methods of control.

The initial problem with this account is its crude *economism* which fails to explain why the state should want to cut back on this area as opposed to any other (defence, industrial grants, etc.). The recent period has seen massive cutbacks in state expenditure; however, they have not been universal or automatic.

The analysis of the crisis is taken predominantly from the work of Gough (1975) and O'Connor (1973), from which he quotes freely and uncritically, which is surprising since the work of the former is an *explicit critique* of the latter. In his attempt to marry the two accounts he does injustice to both.[6]

Within Scull's analysis the state is depicted as a quasi-autonomous mechanism which acts rationally to compensate for the anarchy of the capitalist market system. The state is seen as 'functional' in relation to capital, and he fails to see, as Gough certainly does, that the contradictions of capitalist accumulation are not 'solved' by the state apparatus but are increasingly reproduced within the state. The basis of the crisis as Holloway and Picciotto (1978) have argued lies in the 'capital relation' and the failure to analyse it on this broader context leads, they argue, to the twin limitations of economism and politicism. Only by locating the crisis in this broader context of a 'crisis of capital accumulation' is it possible to understand why, in periods of crisis, capital is redirected away from the unproductive sectors (the state) into productive sectors (industry) in order to regenerate accumulation. The parameters of this reorganization of capital are set, not solely by the 'depth' of the crisis, but by the level of class struggle.

The restructuring of the capital relation also involves a restructuring of the relation between the state and civil society which involves a major offensive against the working class (and sections of capital) producing a potential disruption, precisely at a time when capital is being redirected into the more productive sectors. Thus, what is evident, in opposition to Scull's (functionalist) conclusion, is that law and order tends to become a major political issue precisely at this conjuncture. The result being that rather than funds being directed away from this area, there are pressures for these to increase. As Gough (1975, p.75) has pointed out:

> Expenditure on the police and the judiciary is the only item in this category to have consistently increased since the war, at least in Britain. This is a response to both the growing need for regulating functions given the complexity of modern urban life (e.g. traffic control) and to the growing class and other antagonisms in these societies particularly since the mid 1960s. It is significant that in the U.K. that expenditure on the police and prisons is planned to increase faster than average over the next five years.

The percentage of the GNP allocated to the police and prisons has risen dramatically from 0.8 per cent to 1.4 per cent from 1961 to 1973 (ibid., p.62).

Scull points out in passing that this 'process' which he is trying to identify has proceeded further in the US than it has in Britain and yet the 'crisis' in Britain has been 'deeper' and more sustained than in the US, and suggests that an explanation of this process is, to say the least, incomplete.[7]

A second major problem arises with Scull's 'fiscal crisis' theory, and involves the assertion that community care is increasingly replacing incarceration because it is cheaper. This does not take into account that the costs of institutions are fixed and stable whether the institutions are full or not (and of course they are 'over-full') and that the use of community care must therefore involve an *additional* cost. It would be precisely in the area of community care and not institutions that any effects of the fiscal crisis would be expected to be most effective.

Also, as Greenberg (1975) has noted, the arguments that 'community treatment' is necessarily cheaper are dubious.[8] Many forms of community treatment in fact would be, if implemented properly, more costly than incarceration. Neither has community treatment been found to be more effective in reducing the rate of recidivism.[9]

In sum, Scull's analysis of the crisis falls into the limitations of an economism, and a functionalism, and misconceives the basis and nature of the crisis. As with all functionalist accounts it omits or misplaces the role of class struggle and the contradictions engendered in the state apparatus itself; it is therefore unable to identify the *limits* of state intervention.[10]

What is clearly missing from Scull's account is any substantive analysis of the changes within the capitalist mode of production over the last century. By concentrating entirely on the level of the state (political) the changing control practices appear to be determined either by the 'desires' of the state agencies (politicism), or the 'needs of capital' (functionalism). The crisis of capitalist accumulation since the end of the 1960s has had an important influence on control practices (as well, of course, as in most other areas, for example, education) through a reorganization and re-evaluation of the 'law and order' industry. There have been massive cuts in public spending, but they have been differentially distributed and subject to a complex set of pressures of a political and ideological, as well as an economic, nature.

Who is decarcerated?

In the post-war period there have been a number of significant developments in policies of incarceration, policing methods, amount of funds available which would bear detailed investigation.[11] A general overview of the period indicates that there has been a changing official response to *certain categories* of offenders, an increased preoccupation with crime which has produced three interrelated developments which are not adequately reflected in the abstract category 'decarceration'.

Expansion The policy of expansion of control has been a general post-war phenomenon and has been particularly evident among the category of juvenile offenders. The growth of intermediate treatment, diversionary programmes, suspended sentences, 'improved' detection and surveillance techniques, and the like, has meant that more, particularly young, people are coming into contact with the formal control apparatus of the state and being contained within it. This has forced a reclassification and a rationalization of control practices.[12]

Acceleration The widening of the control net has exacerbated the existing problems, particularly overcrowding and security, which has prompted a policy of 'accelerated discharge', by which more and more offenders go through the control system faster and faster. This has been most evident in the case of mental patients where, although the number of residents has 'fallen over the past two decades, this fall has been accompanied by a steep *rise* in the overall admission rates' (Scull 1977, p.67). In England and Wales the admissions to mental hospitals rose from 78,586 in 1955 to 170,527 in 1970 (ibid., p.67).

Bifurcation While the control net is expanding and the turnover rate is increasing for certain categories of offenders, there are other categories whose period of incarceration is lengthening. The implication of this bifurcated process through the 'removal' of marginal or less dangerous offenders from long-stay institutions is that the 'seriousness' of those who remain incarcerated is relatively increased. As Cohen has argued (1977, p.220), this has important implications for the future of prisons:

> What this all means is that we have entered into a new era of penal policy, one in which the problem will become not short-termers, the pathetic men who go in and out of our over-crowded prisons but the existence of an increasing number of long-term 'dangerous' men, who pose entirely new difficulties of control, security and discipline. And the paradox is that because of the liberals' success this group will be defined in ever-more negative and destructive terms. They will be the hard-core at the bottom of the barrel, the recalcitrants, the incorrigibles, those for whom one can do nothing more than shut them away in dispersal prisons or security wings. Prisons for this group of offenders are destined to become human warehouses; places where people are stored until society can think of something else to do with them.

At the same time as diversionary programmes are being outlined and implemented for certain categories of offenders (youth, first offenders, etc) control units are being constructed in the heart of the prison system. While some categories are being 'decriminalized'[13] (sexual offences, drugs) 'life' sentences are increasing in length and capital punishment re-emerges on the political agenda.

On the level of theoretical exposition, Scull's account dissolves in economic reductionism. This crude determinism is confounded by the evidence that during the post-war period there has been a significantly increased level of investment into the law and order industry, despite the general level of cutbacks from unproductive sectors. This development only becomes intelligible by locating the state within the contradictory framework of the capital relation.

The abstract notion of decarceration, the negative moment of incarceration, is neither dependent on the development of 'community-treatment' or synonymous with the term de-institutionalization. Its history is uneven and contradictory. The term itself is devoid of any substantive content and any reference to changing definitions and reactions to crime; remaining vague and of limited heuristic value. An examination of some of the major developments in the post-war period indicates that changing control strategies are more adequately grasped through the interrelated processes of expansion, acceleration and bifurcation. Although Scull's thesis has some tenability in relation to mental institutions, it seems largely inappropriate when extended to prisons and borstals.

Methodological considerations

Scull raises a number of issues which he is unable to adequately theorize and falls into a series of half-truths and inconsistencies. However, he also raises serious questions about method which required consideration.

However, he does not offer a detailed outline of his method but expresses it negatively by way of a somewhat gratuitous attack on what he defines as 'liberal' criminology in the form of 'labelling' or 'societal reaction' approach, which largely employs a subjectivist and descriptive methodology. In opposition Scull offers the inverse – a subjectless structural analysis which is historically informed – which rather than transcend the one-sidedness of these 'liberal' approaches, inverts them and presents an oppositional but equally one-sided account. We are ushered into the eternally circular debates of sociology between micro/macro, individual/society. subjectivist/objectivist dichotomies. Instead, it might have been more fruitful if he had examined in some detail those historical studies which *have* emerged from this tradition by Platt (1969), Erikson (1966)[14] and others and shown how his approach differed from *theirs*. There is limited mileage in attacking positions for not being historical or structural when they, often explicitly, do not aim to be either.

But, for Scull, the advantages of his approach lie not in 'abstract polemics', but in 'a practical demonstration of its analytic utility'. The limitations of the 'analytic utility' of his approach have been discussed above, however it would be premature to reject his method on these grounds alone.

To be fair, it is to Scull's credit that he opposes the ahistorical and astructural tendencies which have become prevalent in criminology, which tend to naturalize or eternalize existing social relations rather than treating them as necessarily dynamic and transient. Also Scull's chapter on the process of incarceration is one of the most comprehensive to be found, and moves beyond explanations, such as that presented by Rothman,[15] which sees incarceration as the result of either the growing 'complexity and diversity' of 'industrial' society, or the results of the efforts of a number of well-meaning individuals. Scull, instead, locates the process within the changing mode of production and the changing forces and relations of production in an attempt to outline the conditions which made incarceration both 'possible and desirable'.

Unfortunately, however, history comes to an abrupt halt at this point. Those who might have expected a detailed history of incarceration related to the dynamics of the capitalist mode of production, would be bitterly disappointed. The narrative breaks off somewhere in the eighteenth century and we are thrust headlong into the second half of the twentieth century. Except for a brief analysis of the growth of the state apparatus through 'capital's need to increasingly socialize the costs of production', capitalism appears as a static entity locked in its 'early' form. It appears as a static structure – a structure without history.

From this point history is severed and the remainder of the book moves to the present period in an attempt to demonstrate the decarceration thesis, on the assumption that decarceration and community treatment are post-war phenomena. This erroneous assumption/conclusion derives from his failure to follow his object logically and historically. Instead, having assumed that the growth of decarceration is based on the expansion of 'commodity control' all that remains is to 'prove', or 'demonstrate', this relation. In fact the two phenomena do *appear* to be mutually interdependent. What we need to explain, through an analysis of their specific histories, is why they should arrive at this apparent relation in the era of monopoly capitalism. Simultaneously we need to explain the relation between the removal of a number of individuals from segregative forms of control which appears to be an emptying of institutions and the *underlying* processes by which these empty places come to be immediately filled by new inmates.

It is noticeable throughout the book that a wide range of terminology and concepts are borrowed from Marxism (dialectic, crisis, etc.) plus a number of direct and indirect references to Marx. This is representative of the growing Marxist influence in the social sciences.[16] However, the manner in which Marxism is co-opted is far from satisfactory. For

> sociology invariably tears elements of Marx's thought out of context, which embraces both a theoretical grasp of capitalism and the practice of the Workers revolution to overthrow it. Instead Marx's ideas are converted into abstractions independent of capitalism and of Marxism which can be married to equally 'independent' abstractions. [Shaw 1975, p.48]

Marx's work is often used by these sociologists as a useful weapon against competing theories and epistemologies invariably without following through its radical implications, with the result that the very real and important differences between Marxism and sociology are obscured. It is, therefore, worth considering briefly some of the immediate differences between the method employed by Marx and that employed by Scull and other sociologists.

Unlike Scull, Marx does not start with a *definition*: an abstraction which presupposes that the object is 'known', but from the concrete material and social relations of (capitalist) society. Neither does he accept as 'given' the very phenomena which he sets out to explain: this practice, particularly evident in positivist sociology, Marx refers to as 'giving the science before the science'. As Engels states (1962, p.462), commenting on Marx's method:

> The general results of the investigation of the world are obtained at the *end* of the investigation, hence are not principles, points of departure, but *results*, conclusions. To construct the latter in one's head is ideology. [emphasis added]

Only after years of detailed study was Marx able to abstract the 'laws of capitalist motion' and isolate the genesis of the contradictions of capitalist accumulation embedded in the commodity form. Scull, as we have seen, does not follow the logical and historical development of his object in detail and rather than attempt to understand the process of decarceration/incarceration, moves immediately to attempt *direct* empirical confirmation of his assumption/conclusion. Marx (1968, p.106) precisely pointed out the dangers of this approach in relation to Ricardo's analysis of value:

He at once allows himself to be influenced by considerations of all kinds of concrete conditions . . . one must reproach him for regarding the phenomenal form as immediate and *direct proof* or exposition of these general laws.[17]

Scull's preoccupation with the economic might be seen by some as an attempt to emulate the method of Marx, for it is usually in this reductionist manner that Marx is presented by his critics. However, nothing could be more antithetical to Marx, and on numerous occasions he remonstrated against those who adopted such procedures (Marx and Engels 1976, pp. 2-5 [thesis on Feuerbach]). It is, however, in social science (which is continuously, although not always explicitly, engaged in a debate with Marx)[18] which is structured around ideological divisions of economics, sociology and psychology which are treated as discrete entities and lead subsequently into the reductions of economism, sociologism and psychologism. Lukács (1971, p.27) has emphasized:

It is not the primacy of economic motives in historical explanation that constitutes the decisive difference between Marxism and bourgeois thought, but the point of view of the totality.

For Marx, transforming Hegel's dialectical method, the aim is to transcend the limitations of one-sided approaches.

Scull's method, on the other hand, although characterized by the assertion that economic and material forces play a preponderant role, disassociates the control practices of advanced capitalist society from the internal contradictions of the system itself. This leads him into a functionalist explanation which sees all developments as resulting from the 'needs' of capital. This undialectical approach, ignorance of class struggle, and political and ideological forces, leads him into a 'one dimensional criminology'.

Although we might agree with Scull (and Rusche and Kirchheimer, and Foucault) that 'humanitarianism' is not the primary force behind changing control practices, it does not follow that the ideology of humanitarianism is not significant in explaining such developments. Platt's study of *The child savers* has demonstrated the practical and material effects of the adoption of a humanitarian philosophy by sectors of the middle class. Ideologies such as humanitarianism do not descend from heaven – they have a real material basis, and practical consequences. Humanitarianism in the nineteenth century played an important part in strengthening the bourgeoisie's claim to represent the public good and as a progressive movement in history.

Historical materialism is concerned to identify the material conditions for the production of ideology and assess its relation to other social and political forces. In the *German Ideology* Marx identifies the aims of a materialist conception of history:

This conception of history depends on our ability to expound the real process of

> production, starting out from the material production of life itself, and to comprehend the form of intercourse connected with this and created by the mode of production (i.e. civil society in its various stages) as the basis of all history; and to show it in its action as State, to explain all the different theoretical products and forms of consciousness, religion, philosophy, ethics etc. etc. and trace their origin and growth from that basis; by which means of course the whole thing can be depicted in its totality (and, therefore, too, the reciprocal action of these various sides of one another). [Marx and Engels 1976, p.272]

Scull's approach, which loses track of 'the real process of production', fails to grasp the complex interrelations which are involved in the history of incarceration. Scull's method has little in common with Marx except the use, or rather the misuse, of certain Marxist categories.

Political problems

Radical criminology?

Scull's attempt to provide a radical analysis is deeply flawed by his functionalist metaphysics which fail to analyse capitalism as a dynamic contradictory whole, and thus gives an inflated importance to the state devaluing all attempts at mobilization within the social formation. The implications of such an analysis are, at the root, inherently conservative.

Scull's failure to provide any concrete analysis of 'crime' in capitalist society detracts enormously from his account of decarceration. This abstentionism, Ainlay (1975/76, p.222) has argued, has become inculcated into the general approach of radical (or critical) criminology and stems from the fear

> that to squarely face the question of crime would only be to provide (albeit unintentionally) administratively useful information – has finally led them to solve the problem by virtually abolishing the question of crime as such, shifting the primary focus of their efforts instead to such palliative pursuits as the critique of Liberalism.

Such abstentionism severely forecloses the possibility of radical practice. In Scull, however, not only is there no analysis of crime but also no substantive analysis of the developments of incarceration. Thus there is no point of comparison between institutional and non-institutional forms of control. Scull's invectives against community control thus disappear in a whirlpool of moral indignation.

Scull's self-characterization as standing alone outside the 'growing harmony of interests' across the political spectrum supporting decarceration is seriously mistaken. He is, in fact, in 'good' company. An influential group of radical conservative criminologists are also arguing against community control and for the stricter application of prison sentences. Scull's moral invectives could be usefully accommodated within the body of this 'New Realist' theory.[19]

However, his possible contribution to this conservative tradition is limited by his lack of consistency. At times he does not seem to be sure whether community control is a 'good' or a 'bad' thing.

> After all, many of those subjected to processing by the official agencies of social control have all along been scarcely distinguishable from their neighbours who were left alone, and presumably they can be expelled from institutions without appreciable additional risk. But for many other ex-inmates and potential inmates the alternative to the institution has been to be herded into newly emerging 'deviant ghettos', sewers of human misery and what is conventionally defined as social pathology within which (largely hidden from outside inspection or even notice) society's refuse may be repressively tolerated. [Scull 1977, p.193]

Within Scull's ambivalent conclusion there is no discussion of the political implications of his analysis, but what is more serious is that there is no political practice which is *discernible*. The analysis falls back into the 'appreciative' or 'non-interventionist' framework which reproduces the 'liberal' positions which he so readily attacks. Scull's account of decarceration does not, in the end, differ significantly from these other accounts he presents, and 'economic motives' can unproblematically be married to existing 'humanitarian' and 'liberal' accounts as another *factor* in the explanation. His explanation would therefore be, if the process of decarceration were happening as he assumes, merely an attempt to fill the gaps left by these idealist accounts.

Alternatives to prison

The major issue which Scull raises, but fails to confront squarely, is the debate about 'alternatives to prison'. This debate has normally focused around discussions of the cost-effectiveness of newer forms of control over traditional forms (see Greenberg 1975). Others have argued that the day of the prison is over and is to be replaced by more 'suitable' methods of control. The advocates of this latter position constitute what is loosely defined as the 'decarceration movement'. Their arguments refer in the main to juveniles; categories of violent criminals, psychopaths, child molesters and the like, are invariably excluded from the arguments of these penal reformers.

Against these general arguments it has been stated above that the combined processes of expansion, acceleration and bifurcation better characterize the main trends in control practices, all of which tend to *reinforce* the position of prisons in society.

The control net itself is widening and more and more people are going through faster and faster. The institutions of state control are becoming more diverse with finer gradations from the least to the most severe, producing what Foucault has eloquently described as a 'carceral archipelago'.

The growth of so-called alternatives to prison, it must be emphasized, cannot be seen as autonomous – the very possibility of these 'alternatives' is dependent upon the prison as a *final* resort; their growth does not endanger the existence of prisons and other institutions but reinforces their existence.

The relationship between prisons and more recent alternatives/extensions are better seen as analogous to the relation between gold and money. Once the basic currency is accepted it allows the development of more flexible and convenient methods of exchange. However, the value of paper currency is always dependent upon the viability of gold itself, and at the end of the day must always be realizable.

The arguments for alternatives do not in any fundamental way threaten the existence of prisons. Rather they reinforce the legitimacy of punishment and state control apparatus by accepting the 'need' for some form of punishment, and by implicitly sanctioning the need for prisons to accommodate the 'hard' cases. The general agreement between many criminologists, penal reformers and prison staff that a large majority of those incarcerated should never be there in the first place, does not necessarily require the application of more 'appropriate' strategies of treatment or correction, but raises fundamental questions, often overlooked in this context, about a legal process which produces and selects so many 'unnecessary' and marginal offenders for punishment.[20] The discussion of alternatives presupposes a critical examination of crime and the legal process itself, and the production of 'problems of control'; also an examination of the changing importance of the prison within the control structure of capitalism and its movement from a primary institution of control in early capitalism to an institution of last resort in monopoly capitalism; and the changing relation between prisons and other ancillary institutions (the media, education, etc.)

Finally, the changing role of prisons needs to be related to community strategies of control together with an analysis of the political implications of this process.

Contradictions and community control

'Community' has become one of the dominant ideological notions to develop in the post-war period. Precisely at the time that notions of community care, community treatment and community control were becoming most popular, sociologists in Britain and America were mourning the death of the community (see, for example, Young and Wilmott 1962).

It is also paradoxical that the beginning of community control at the turn of the twentieth century registered a break with the community; whereas previously offenders not sentenced were able to remain in their locale, the growth of probation and the like distinguished and separated people from their community. It becomes important to distinguish those people who are left in their community and those who come under state forms of regulation and surveillance.

But why should the state seek more flexible, non-segregative forms of control? To answer this question it is necessary briefly to examine the changing nature of productive and social relations under capitalism during this period which made such developments 'possible and desirable'.

The problems of control in the era of what has been termed 'liberal capitalism' became less and less the direct control of the worker in his productive relationship; he had become adapted to the time and work discipline required by the capitalist mode of production. Established trade union organizations had acted as buffers between the owners and the non-owners of the means of production. The focus of attention turned to the problems of reproduction; of providing a healthy, educated and disciplined work force, and particularly to the 'social problems' emanating from urban areas. This concern was reflected in the work of Park and Burgess (1927) and other members of the Chicago school. Problems were seen as being located in certain geographical areas; and in turn it was in these areas that control was primarily directed. Also the growth of structural unemployment, through the increased use of technology, was located primarily in the areas which Park and Burgess had isolated, and affected primarily youth, minorities and immigrant workers. The increasing severity of cyclical crises during the first half of the twentieth century, culminating in the 'depression' of the 1930s, provided an incentive to expand welfare provisions through a policy which attempted to prevent the increase in class struggle by *anticipating* it. Important changes occurred during this period which have been identified as:

> a general tendency towards the organization of consensus through the simultaneous use of the means of mass communication and high wages and consumption. These are the fundamental bases of the new state of affairs. The school, the mass army, the family become, therefore, more important than the prison and other adult correctional institutions of the last century, such as the poorhouse. The school, itself, with its increasing extension towards the first years of the present epoch is more important than the family. At the same time one finds a tendency towards the progressive unification of the various apparatuses of social control at the level of the city as a total institution towards a city-system of complete social control. [Melossi 1976]

During this period, then, there was a decline in the importance of the prison in relation to other ancillary institutions of control – a decline which began when it ceased to be a profit making institution. Simultaneously we find a move towards *territorial* control more directly associated with the reproduction of capital.

One result of this intervention has been an 'embarrassment of riches' – an overproduction in the number of people coming within the control net, which finds its material expression in the 'bottleneck' in the legal system. The police are being encouraged to develop more sophisticated detection and surveillance methods, while the courts are trying desperately to divert offenders away from already overcrowded prisons. The police feel that much of their effort is 'wasted' and understandably feel antagonistic and suspicious towards these other control agencies.

'Community', or more specifically, the areas of reproduction, distribution, and consumption have become new terrains on which struggles are being fought – terrains where the working class has been least organized and least militant. However, the experience of the recent decade has been that the nature of the struggle has been broadened to embrace these areas. As Cockburn (1977, p.163) notes:

We have to recognize that alongside struggles at the point of production, in the mines and in the factories there is a struggle at the point of reproduction, in the schools, on housing estates, in the street, in the home.

The development of community or territorial control has not *solved* but extended the problems, and generated new contradictions and new terrains of struggle. In practice, community corrections have not proved to be necessarily more cost-effective, humanitarian or effective in reducing the rate of recidivism (see Greenberg 1975; Empey 1973). All the problems of punishment and reform, once laid at the door of the prison, are being displaced and reproduced within community corrections.

The introduction of parole, probation, indeterminate sentences, diversion programmes and the whole array of recent control strategies have served, invariably, to either increase lengths of incarceration, loss of liberty, or surveillance on one hand, and to introduce many, particularly the young, into the control net for 'offences' that prior to the setting up of such programmes would have gone unnoticed or seem to be inconsequential. Such control organizations carry with them their own inertia, through the professionalization, specialization and the need to continually 'produce' deviant populations on whom their livelihood depends.

The expansion of social work and correctional agencies has absorbed a stratum of the middle class who, themselves, have been displaced from direct production into the service sectors and who not only look and dress like their clients, but have a significant overlap of real interests and experiences. This has the potential, which to some extent has been realized, of such community strategies having consequences which were not initially anticipated. The recent past in Britain has seen the emergence of a number of broad-based movements inside and outside these organizations, amongst claimants, prisoners, mental patients, and the formation of radical groups of social workers, lawyers and probation officers (see Fitzgerald *et al*., 1977).

The increasing emphasis on community corrections allows new strategies of intervention which were difficult within the closed fortress of the prison. But:

To the extent that criminal activity represents a rational response to the absence of opportunities realistically available community corrections may be largely irrelevant because it is in a position to generate few new opportunities. [Greenberg 1975, p.5]

For those who picture a return to the 'community' as a return to a golden age of collective living, the reality is unfortunately entirely different. The history of capitalism has been the history of the systematic destruction of the community. Those not incarcerated, or semi-incarcerated (hostels, halfway houses, etc.), are returned invariably, not to the community but to ghettos in the inner city. One must ask, as Greenberg suggests, 'why if the "community" is so therapeutic, the offender got into trouble there in the first place?' (ibid., p.4).

Summary

The terms 'decarceration' and 'community care' have been absorbed within a short period of time, often uncritically, into the conceptual repertoire of criminologists. However, such terms can easily become ideological veils which obscure more than they illuminate. Inasmuch as this process of 'decarceration' is occurring it only reflects the phenomenal form of changing control practices in the post-war period. Although a large number of offenders are now dealt with in more flexible non-segregative forms of control it must be emphasized that many of these people would not in previous periods have been embraced by the control network at all, and that many are processed as a result of minor offences and in a significant number of cases have never even committed an offence. Meanwhile traditional segregative forms of control are reinforced and secured.

Scull's thesis that it was the growth of community care which made decarceration possible is anachronistic. For Scull, in all periods, those offenders not incarcerated are in one form or another decarcerated. Up to the end of the nineteenth century the majority of these offenders did in fact return to their communities but it was paradoxically with the emergence of community control that the ex-offender became differentiated from the community and became a special object of surveillance or intervention. Incarceration was the response to the imperatives of labour, work discipline and social upheaval in nascent capitalism. State-sponsored community or territorial control at the end of the nineteenth century were a response to the problems of reproduction particularly associated with urban areas. The locus of control thus expanded from production to reproduction: from the factory to the home.

In the post-war period the two forms of control have become less distinct; each has expanded out to meet the other; to adopt each other's practices, and reinforce each other's existence; resulting in a finer gradation of punishments from the most trivial to the most severe.

The recent crisis of capitalist accumulation involved severe cuts in public expenditure but not in the area of law and order. It did, however, result in a rationalization and a reorganization of the 'law and order industry' as part of a changing relation between the state and civil society. Certain categories of offences have received a less formal reaction while other categories have been introduced, together with changing strategies and styles of control.

As opposed to the methodology adopted by Scull, such changes are neither reducible to the 'economic' or the 'needs' of capital. Rather they are imbricated within the dynamic, contradictory totality of the capitalist mode of production. Each new strategy of control is enmeshed in conflict and struggle (see Thompson 1975). Class struggle is not episodic, but a continual and permanent antagonism between the producers of surplus and the owners and controllers of the means of production extracting the surplus.[21]

Scull's methodological inadequacies, theoretical confusions and political impotence are inextricably related. The merit of his work is that it relates some important issues; its weakness lies in his failure to provide the means even to begin to resolve them.

Through the evaluation of Scull's work it has been necessary to suggest some alternative hypotheses and different lines of enquiry. Much, however, remains tentative and awaits further concrete and detailed investigation. Any such analysis which aims to transcend the limitations of economism, politicism or functionalism must necessarily relate the changing strategies of control to the dynamic and contradictory productive and social relations of capitalist society together with the changing nature and object of 'criminal' activity in any particular historical period.

8 Policing the working-class city

Phil Cohen

The changing role of the police force has increasingly become a central theme in the current debate on the left – over the road to socialism in advanced capitalist societies. Those who argue for the parliamentary road are almost invariably committed to a civil libertarian position – that the powers and practices of policing can and must be made accountable to democratic institutions of control, as part of a broader struggle to transform the state. Consequently the attempt is made to radicalize and extend the functions of the traditional 'Liberal Watchdog', and to give a structural edge to the 'rotten apples' thesis concerning police behaviour.

On the other side are those who maintain they are holding to the revolutionary road, and who argue that state power must be seized or smashed, through the autonomous organization of proletarian struggle. For the ultra left, the police force is the brutal repressive arm of the ruling class, which must be confronted and shown up for what it is at every opportunity. This could be called the 'all coppers are fascist pigs' thesis, and generally goes with the view that Britain is on the way to becoming a police state.

The current campaigns against legal repression (against the 'sus' laws, against the extension of powers of detention and arrest) cannot help but highlight the issue of bourgeois democracy, and the relation of state to civil society, even if the gulf between street activist and academic Marxist seems to grow even wider. But are the terms of the theoretical debate adequate to the task of formulating principles of political practice?

At present the argument seems to be bogged down in a series of antinomies:

Either the freedoms and structures of accountability which characterize bourgeois democracy contain within them the conditions of their socialist transformation, *or* they are pure sham, designed to mystify the masses, and must be exploded

Either the state can be transformed so it reflects, or is subordinated to, the institutions of civil society *or* civil society is the basis on and from which the apparatus of the state is to be eroded, and ultimately destroyed.

Like all debates that go round in circles, the arguments continually pass each other going in opposite directions. But that would at least indicate that there is some 'common ground'. And there is.

Civil libertarians and ultra-leftists agree that there is a fundamental contradiction in the mechanisms of bourgeois democracy, between the formal and substantive aspects of law enforcement; between, for example, the neutral and impartial administration of justice, enshrined in juridical ideology, and the material practices which ensure there is 'one law for the poor, another for the rich'.

Where they diverge, of course, is on what to do about it. For the ultra-left it is a question of stripping away the appearance of neutrality, to reveal the hidden essence of class justice; for the civil libertarian, of suppressing the residual elements of class practice, so that the formal principles become substantive guarantees.

Marxists like to pride themselves on having gone beyond such either/or positions, and the Manichaean division of the struggle into goodies and baddies. Yet they are not able to account for the fact that this superior dialectical view is nowhere reflected in their political practice, other than by appealing to the usual get out clauses about the 'relative autonomy of theory'. Yet what if the problem turned out to be theoretical after all? What if it lay in the terms which Marxists themselves have contributed to the debate?

Several recent studies have suggested that the problems lie less in the terms themselves than the way they are used to generate false dichotomies. Balbus (1973) argues that the police force must be considered in its structural specificity as a site of contradictory practices, between those which are required to guarantee public order, those which safeguard the legitimacy of the state as a neutral arbiter of justice, and those which are required for the organizational maintenance of the force itself, as a bureaucratic apparatus. These contradictions are reproduced in a whole series of split perceptions about the functions of the police, which is reflected also at the level of public debate.

Edelman (1979) has argued that juridical ideology is not something confined to the law courts; it is a representation of a material transformation which class relations undergo in the sphere of commodity circulation and exchange, and as such penetrates the basic conditions of subjectivity in capitalist society. The law gives class subjects legal being; it determines the most intimate relations between parents and children, as well as the most public aspects of everyday life.

What both studies point to is the need for additional concepts to denote the range of institutions and practices, which are not wholly 'in' the state or civil society but are interpenetrated by them, and which serve to both condense and displace their contradiction on the terrain of class conflict.[1]

The terms 'bourgeois' and 'proletarian public realm', popularized by the Frankfurt school, seem to me to be useful here, once they are divested of their idealist problematic (see in particular Negt and Kluge 1973 and 1975). For they can be used to make sense of a space of articulation between *specific habitats of class practice*, and *specific conditions of legal subjectivity*, a space which is far from metaphysical and, as I hope to show, has a very material history. For it is here and nowhere else that the policing of the working-class city takes place.

Cuffs and capes

The modern police force emerged out of the crisis of urban administration in the Victorian city. It was the first branch of the British state to develop an ideological as well as a purely repressive function. As such, the official task of policing was both to protect the institutions of private property, and to enforce statutory norms of public order primarily designed to ensure the free circulation of commodities, including the commodity of labour power.

In London especially, the metropolitan force was both the strong arm and the advance guard of municipal reform.[2] As a population formed by pre-industrial and rural conditions crowded in and colonized the archaic urban infrastructure, it became less a question of enforcing their segregation from the upper classes than of policing their usage of social space and time so that it did not obstruct the traffic of industry and commerce. The potential sources of obstruction included not only strikes, political mobilizations and organized crime, but also the development of street cultures and their irregular economies, upon which whole working-class communities came to depend as a means of local livelihood and identity against the anarchy of impersonal market forces. In such areas as these, the question 'Who rules around here?' was no mere metaphor of a class struggle waged essentially elsewhere: it was itself that struggle. For here the new instruments of bourgeois law and the traditional instruments of popular order became quickly locked in a brutal, if everyday, confrontation. Inevitably the slum neighbourhoods adjoining the inner industrial perimeter, with their volatile, visible and organized social systems, mounted the most violent and sustained opposition to these new urban reformers in blue. Islington was no exception.[3]

Henry Mayhew noted in the 1850s that the costermonger community was in the vanguard of resistance. To 'have' a policeman was the bravest act a coster could perform, and those who were sent down were regarded as local martyrs and heroes. When they came out of prison, subscriptions were organized. Coster boys adopted 'guerrilla' tactics based on superior knowledge of the local terrain, waiting hidden down an alleyway until the policeman came past, lobbing their stone or brick, and then just as quickly disappearing. Mayhew suggests that the costers' hatred of the police was due to a residual Chartist influence amongst them, but his own evidence suggests that the main motive was economic rather than political. As one coster told him.

> They drive us about, we must move on, we can't stand here and we can't pitch there; they are trying to drive us out of business. [Mayhew 1851, p.22]

Resistance was not confined to the coster colony around Chapel Street market and the Pentonville Road. From the 1880s onwards, as Islington became increasingly proletarianized in the south and the middle class retreated northwards behind the barriers of property and income, it was those traditional occupational groups concentrated geographically and socially between the two, still tied to the irregular street economy, its seasonal patterns of casual labour and drift migration, who became the special targets of policing. For nearly half a century Popham Street and Packington Street off Essex Road, and Gifford and Bemerton Streets off the Caledonian Road, saw numerous affrays between constabulary and local populace. The local press records 146 such incidents in these areas between 1880 and 1920 – inevitably only those leading to arrest, and hence presumably only a fraction of the real number of cases.

A report in the *Islington Gazette* of January 1881 gives some sense of these occasions. A certain Mr Savoury, a horse-keeper in his mid twenties who lived in Gifford Street, was charged with assault and wounding a policeman. On the Sunday night, after the pubs had closed, there had been a fight in Gifford Street and a crowd of a hundred or so had gathered round to watch and cheer on their man. The police arrived to break it up and proceeded to arrest one of the contestants. This infuriated the crowd who set on the policemen, gave them a thorough beating, and rescued the prisoner. Mr Savoury had apparently played a leading role in the counter-attack, and when a policeman drew his staff to arrest him, he grabbed it and 'knocked him about so severely that he's been under the surgeon's hand ever since'. In court the next day, a large crowd from Gifford Street turned up to support their hero, only to see him sent down for six months' hard labour, the stiffest penalty the magistrate could inflict for such an offence at this period.

It is interesting to note that in evidence the police claimed that they had intervened to 'quell a riot', whereas in fact, by breaking up the popular recreation of a Sunday night spar, their actions had actually provoked one.

The ancient tradition of collective self-defence still existed in this areas two generations later, as shown by a report (*Islington Gazette*, June 1924) from the 1920s. A policeman arrested a local woman in the Caledonian Road, when a large hostile crowd – but this time *mainly of youths* – gathered round to rescue her. Stones, cans, bottles began to fly, and one nimble 16-year-old errand boy wriggled his way through the crowd and tripped up the policeman. However, the police had become increasingly efficient at dealing with these situations: reinforcements were summoned, and several more arrests were made.

Even arrest might not be the end of the story. One Islington resident (Mr Malone: oral testimony) recalled how in his youth, before the First World War, the police would strap a particularly obstreperous offender on to an open stretcher and wheel him back, still followed by the crowd, to the station. Once there, the crowd would wait outside and, if they heard a noise, claim the police were beating up the man, even on occasion retaliating by stoning the windows. He also remembered how during this period, in the tenements where he lived, the arrival of the police on what was regarded as the residents' own territory would be greeted by a hail of flower pots, and this was not an infrequent occurrence of his childhood!

What outraged these communities was not just the law's attack on what they regarded as legitimate means of livelihood or secondary income – these were in any case being increasingly eroded by wider and purely economic forces – but the criminalization of traditional street pastimes which were solely recreational. From the 1870s onwards, it was young people who were particularly singled out on this front. Mayhew (1851) noted that street gambling, in the form of pitch and toss, held a special fascination for the costers, Kings Cross being a popular venue:

It is difficult to find in the whole of this numerous class a youngster who is not a desperate gambler . . . every attempt by the police to check this ruinous system has been unavailing and rather given a gloss of daring and courage to the sport.

In the 1850s, men as well as boys had been addicts of pitch and toss, but by the 1920s adults had taken to other forms of betting, notably of course horse-racing, while pitch and toss had retained its popularity as an integral part of general street youth culture, now reinforced by the imposed leisure of unemployment. Secondly, while pugilism was being taken off the streets and refined in the boxing club, the rise of the professional football club had given a powerful impetus to its amateur emulation in the back alley.

During the 1920s, Islington police seem to have made a special drive against these two sports, and it is therefore not surprising to find that they account for over half the reported arrests of juveniles during this period. Given the scale of these activities and the local police's limited manpower, there was no attempt at mass roundups. Instead the police attempted a more selective strategy of arrest. They concentrated harassment in those streets associated by reputation or tradition with *adult* crime. The geographical distribution of arrests for street football (which has no possible criminal connotations) closely follows that of youngsters for playing pitch and toss, which *may* conceivably have been used as a cover for working as bookies' runners. Policing tactics thus consisted of general physical intimidation coupled with systematically arbitrary arrests.

Another Islington resident, Mr Spendriff, remembers:

If we'd been playing football or something in the street, there used to be a policeman – we used to call him Flash Harry – and he used to throw his cape at you as you'd run away. He'd throw it right between your legs. Yes. He'd just cuff you round the ears and let you go. [oral testimony]

Cuffs and capes seem to have been the favourite methods of discipline, as they could be applied apparently randomly against isolated kids. Officers who specialized in such attacks were of course especially feared and hated. Here is a vivid account of one such incident in Chapel Street in the late 1930s:

There was this copper, he was a real bully; all the kids were scared of him. In those days the Law was mostly brawn, big fellas, and they'd clout you as soon as take a look. Well there was this one, he was called King Kong – you know, after that monster in the film. Well, one day, it was around Christmas time and I'd been helping my uncle out on the barrow and he'd given me a few bob for myself; so I was quite chuffed, thinking what I was going to spend it on, and just walking along thinking my own thoughts, and then WHAM! it was like I'd walked into a lamppost or something. And it was this copper, King Kong. He must have been standing in a doorway 'cos I didn't see him. And then he just came out and got hold of me and smacked me in the teeth. You know I was so shocked I couldn't do nothing, say anything. I just sort of looked at him and he smiled and said 'Well son, if you want to know what that was for, I'll tell you: disturbing the peace. And you'd better scarper off home before you get another one for whistling about like you own the place'. And you know what it was – I'd been whistling in the street, and it was agin the law he reckoned. Anything like that, the littlest thing, you'd get the Law down on you. But they rarely took you to the station – just belted you! Of course in them days you sort of expected it, same as the teachers gave you, or the old man if you didn't behave. So it was all the same sort of thing. [Mr Spencer, oral testimony]

The sense of shock registered is not then at the actual violence metered out. That is accepted as a normal feature of relations between adult authority and youth. What does hurt is the sudden and arbitrary nature of its occurrence.

Nevertheless, in the decade after the First World War, the whole pattern of relations between the police and the working class in North London had begun slowly, but subtly, to change from outright physical confrontation to an unwritten system of tacit negotiation. The antagonism was not resolved, but it was pursued by means other than street beatings and set-tos. The reasons for the change are complex: they are partly to do with changes in the conditions and composition of the local working class, partly with the position of youth within the generational division of labour, and partly the result of the changing function of the police force in the developing structure of the capitalist state. Let us look at each in turn.

The years after 1919 saw the disintegration of many of the material supports of traditional street culture. The casual labour market generated by the irregular economy declined; while the associated criminal subculture split off and became the preserve of an increasingly professional fraternity, whose scale of operations and organization embraced not just Islington but also Kentish and Camden Town. Secondly, access to job opportunities was no longer so dependent on highly localized social networks of information and patronage. Apart from odd jobs, the street corner labour exchange was actually less efficient than the official version under conditions of widespread, and not just local, unemployment. Thirdly, the local Irish presence had tended to become both geographically more dispersed and culturally more entrenched, largely through its involvement in trade unionism and local labour politics. The traditional techniques of hardness and brawling expertise, while still called on, tended to play a supporting rather than a leading role. Concentrations of the old 'dangerous class' had been broken up through sustained harassment or rebuilding. Campbell Road was demolished to make way for a factory. Slum tenements began to give way to municipal housing. Clissold and Finsbury Parks, Highbury Fields, various youth clubs, uniformed organizations, all claimed a share of youthful energies from the overpoliced streets. Finally, the expanding lower middle class consolidated *their* presence in residential neighbourhoods previously monopolized by the carriage trade, and added to the weight of civic consciousness in numerous local institutions patronized by manual workers and their families. Furthermore, the sheer physical fact that large numbers of the men and boys, who had previously dominated the traditional street culture, were away from it during the war years, meant that women and children were left in charge and, in a sense, domesticated some of its functions.

All these changes, small in themselves, uneven in their development, nevertheless combined to alter the contexts of policing and the practices of social control at street level. In the process, the local working class had become more sedimented, less autonomous, their public behaviour to an extent domesticated by an urban environment which was beginning to bear the first marks of properly capitalist planning. But this does not mean that it had become sedentary, dependent, or privatized.

In part, the patterns of street and neighbourhood usage remained remarkably consistent, given the changes in economic infrastructure. It was the moral ideologies associated with that use which were modified, harnessed to specific working-class notions of *public propriety*.

The notion was one of the great distinguishing characteristics of the labour aristocracy; and by the 1870s it was firmly established as an active principle amongst the large colonies of skilled print and railway workers in Islington. Nor was it just a notion, for these groups spun a whole cocoon of institutions around themselves to make substantive, and to preserve, the connection between superior occupational and moral status. What this in practice meant was a more or less ritual avoidance of contact with street cultures, a preference for more rational recreation over its popular diversions. It meant drawing a socially, and often geographically, visible line between the two habitats of working-class subjectivity – here the workshop, there the street – serving as a principle of territorial affinities and enmities. But if the skilled worker drew a line under his own feet, it was not always so neat or so visible for his children. Nevertheless, up until the First World War there were two quite clear-cut apprenticeships into working-class masculinity and manual labour.Those for whom apprenticeship was a material institution were kept firmly under the patriarchal thumb of the master craftsman in the workshop and, because of their prolonged financial dependence, kept under the parental thumb as well. From this basis, the parent culture had little difficulty in extending its strategy of social closure to embrace the free time of its youth. Those new institutions of public property, the woodcraft organizations and the boys' clubs, were dominated by the children of skilled workers – and of course in many cases it was only they who could afford the cost of membership.

There is no greater contrast than with the way coster boys and girls were informally apprenticed to their street trade. The aristocracy of the irregular economy ensured that their children started learning the trade almost as soon as they could walk. By the time they were 12 or 13, girls as well as boys had familiarized themselves with all the essential tricks of the trade, as well as having learned how to negotiate the local underlife and still stay out of trouble with the law. Just as importantly, they were often able to save enough from what they learned on the family barrow and through odd jobs to hire a pitch of their own, and set up in competition with their parents. Even more scandalous in the eyes of juvenile reformers, almost as soon as they reached puberty coster boys and girls could afford to leave home, rent lodgings and live as husband and wife. With money in their pockets, their own bosses, free from irksome family constraints (which did not, however, mean that they were not part of a close network of kin and could not rely on it for support when times were hard), no wonder coster youth were often the envy of their peers, the local youth style leaders, and their style was dead set against public propriety and all it stood for!

In between these two extremes stood the mass of unskilled and semi-skilled manual workers and their families. It was this stratum which now began to move away from the moral economies of street culture, and find in the institutions of public propriety a means, not just of respectability, but of material advancement.[4] For them, involvement in trade unionism and local labour politics has been the great pathway to these twin goals. Labourism is the working-class politics of public propriety and conscience, and it is no coincidence that its spokesmen have always been in the vanguard of those advocating the strictest legal repression of 'hooliganism', 'juvenile crimes', and working-class youth cultures in general. In Islington, the rise of the New Unionism and, after the war, of the Unemployed Workers Movement not only organized the hitherto unorganized, but helped give them a stake in the new urban order that was taking shape. Unemployed men still gathered at the unofficial labour exchange on the High Pavement of Essex Road, but to talk politics or racing results rather than to jeer at passing toffs or spit at the police, as was their regular habit in the 1890s. Their courting children no longer scandalized the older citizenry by obscene catcalls or by jostling them off the pavement, as they were recorded as doing up until 1914. By the 1920s, the monkey parade had retired to the greater privacy – if not decency – of Highbury Fields.

A railway porter summed up the span of change neatly enough, comparing his own childhood before the First World War with that of his son before the second:

> When Johnny was growing up in the flats, people had started using flower pots to grow flowers in. When I was a lad there, they kept them empty to throw at the Law. [Mr Elder, oral testimony]

But perhaps the most sensitive indicator of change comes from comparing the accounts given by mainstream-strata young workers about their encounters with the law before and after the war. In the descriptions on the pre-1914 period, the policeman remains a shadowy almost anonymous figure. A van driver recalls one such childhood encounter:

> They were generally all stereotyped. Big black moustaches – you couldn't tell one from the other. All we knew was they was all down on us the same. We never got a chance to recognize them; we were too busy running away. [Mr Freeman, oral testimony]

But in the accounts of the 1920s and 1930s the portraits are filled in. Personal idiosyncrasies are mercilessly characterized, not least in nicknames. Wee Willy Winkie. Droopy Dan. Flash Harry. King Kong. Terms, certainly not of endearment, but of some familiarity. These are no longer shadows, but larger than life figures in the scenarios of youthful experience. This growing personification is one index of the gradual ideological penetration of 'The Law' into the basic conditions of working-class life during the period.

Another is the way certain aspects of routine policing became perceived as part of public ceremonial, a legitimate drama punctuating working-class life, as in this account *circa* 1920 by a warehouseman, then in his late teens:

> Well, the police, you could tell the time by them. The posse we used to call them. At ten o'clock at night you'd see them marching down the road, relieving the various beats . . . . Course, Saturday nights, if you wanted to enjoy yourself, you'd go down with your mates to see the drunks being brought in to the station. [Mr Jackson, oral testimony]

So instead of an angry crowd representing a whole neighbourhood, solid with one of their own in the nick – a not infrequent occurrence in the earlier period – here, a quarter of a century on, we have a group of footloose youngsters enjoying the spectacle of arrest as a free Saturday night entertainment.

It is impossible to be absolutely certain how typical these different responses were, or how accurate the accounts. But since they are all drawn from the mainstream elements, rather than from the extremes of rough or respectable, it seems likely that they do register substantive qualitative changes in popular attitudes to policing over this period. Given that police and court records were not available, it is difficult to construct any precise quantitative index of change. However, by comparing local press reports of 'disturbances' from 1880 to 1935, a distinct pattern begins to emerge:

1 After the First World War the number of reported incidents of public disorder per year drops considerably. On the other hand, there were episodic disturbances associated with local political activity – meetings and marches against unemployment and fights with local fascists.
2 After 1919 the reported size of the crowds involved in 'non-political' disturbances falls, sixty to eighty being a pre-war figure and twenty to thirty post-war. The ratio of reported arrests rises as the size of the crowds falls.
3 The age and sex composition reported also changes, men, women and children figuring in the pre-war reports, while in the 1920s and 1930s the accounts increasingly mention the predominance of male youths. This is also reflected in the details of those arrested, the age distribution progressively narrowing over time to the 14- to 18-year-old band, with a complement of slightly older, often unemployed, lads!
4 The most frequent places of disturbances remain remarkably consistent across the whole period; but in the post-war reports a number of new landmarks of confrontation make their appearance – for example, the Carlton Club, and the Coffee Stall in Essex Road, both of which are described as hang-about centres for youth and the unemployed.
5 In the 1920s and 1930s disturbances were almost exclusively concentrated at weekends and public holidays, whereas in the earlier period they show a slightly

broader distribution through the week and throughout the year, though here again weekends and holidays show a peak concentration.

6 More significant was the fact that the reported occupations of juveniles arrested shows a higher concentration of those in 'street trades' in the later period than in the earlier.

This evidence points both to the changing configuration of the parent cultures and the changing pattern of juvenile employment. Increasingly it was wage-earning and unemployed boys who were left behind on the front lines of street confrontation with the law, as their parents increasingly identified the etiquette of public propriety with the exercise of parental responsibility. But the visibility factor is not enough in itself to explain the concentration of police activity on street-corner youth. The introduction of legislation against street-trading by juveniles, the stricter enforcement of elementary school attendance after the war, separated them conspicuously from their younger brothers and sisters at the same time as their elders and betters retreated from the scene. Second, the creation of new categories of juvenile offence also created greater pressure on the police to enforce them. Third, the polarizations within the local youth constituency between the apprenticeships of the workshop and those of the street was diminishing. Not only was the irregular economy in decline, but the interwar years saw the decline of many of the Finsbury workshop trades, and the migration of skilled labour to the new light industries being set up in West London. Juvenile labour became increasingly concentrated in shop and distributive trades, a small army of messenger boys was taken on by the post office, while the railway continued to employ a considerable number of van boys. Office work in the City claimed many girls from domestic service and laundry work. These jobs were still often dead-end and low-paid, but at least they were *decasualized*, even if the attitude of young workers to them was not.

All of this served to articulate the conditions of juvenile labour more closely to the institution of juvenile delinquency, to make substantive in policing practice the imaginary connection between a dangerous place (the streets of the working-class city) and a dangerous time (youth).

Of course it also gave impetus to those who were busy constructing safe places (youth clubs and organizations) where working-class youth could have safe times (rational recreation). But here it must be noted that Islington was not penetrated nearly so early or so thoroughly by the agencies of religious evangelism and philanthropy, as many other working-class areas (MacLeod 1974). Here, for a long time, the police were the sole agency of urban reform. This factor, coupled with the survival of the irregular street economy, and the presence of a well-organized criminal community, explains why it took the police much longer to establish public propriety in Islington than many other inner cities. The great watershed, which occurred in the 1914-18 period for Islington, undoubtedly occurred in many industrial areas by the 1870s and 80s (Storch 1976).

That this could happen at all is due to the decentralized nature of the apparatus of enforcement; its key particularisms – the logistics of police operations, and the cultures of local resistance – interact to determine the actual tempo of change in different urban contexts. However, if we want to underline the 'law' of this uneven and combined development, we will have to look in more detail at the structural processes which underlie the constraining variables of policing the working-class city.

Relations of force

The picture given so far has been no simple one of urban pacification. We have seen that the limits imposed on policing by working-class resistance were as significant as those imposed on street cultures in the name of public propriety. The proletarian public realm retained its historical individuality as a nexus of institutions and practices, through the very means of its accommodation to the capitalist city.

But what effect did these relations of force have on the internal development of police structures and functions? It seems to me that the British police have become, almost uniquely, a dependent part of a wider apparatus; we might call this the 'educational state system' – the system which educates the subjects of capital about the state, and about their legal conditions of existence as 'individuals' in 'civil society'. It is no coincidence that working-class kids call police 'The Law' because it is from them that they receive their physical and moral education about the place they occupy as legal subjects in class society. Especially where 'father's word is law', it is the policeman whose name is taken in vain as its support. As for those who refuse to learn their lesson, they are notoriously confused about which or whose law they have transgressed – the law of patriarchy or of propriety. For in the institution of public propriety, the two are indeed chronically conflated.

But this in turn has imposed a peculiarly contradictory role on the police themselves. The British bobby is called upon to perform two basic and distinct tasks:

As the moral entrepreneur of public propriety, and by implication arbiter of deviance, he performs a purely expressive function of community welfare and is expected to do so impartially, as a public servant, in contexts occupied solely by what appear to be individual citizens in need or distress. This aspect of the job is necessarily very labour intensive.

As the administrator of a juridical ideology of crime, in which the bourgeoisie has enshrined its version of the rights of capital and the obligations of labour, he performs a repressive function in a policing context where there are two categories of client – the legitimate and the illegitimate possessors of property. This aspect of the job has become increasingly capital intensive.

How these two sides of the job operate in practice is best described by a rank-and-file policeman in a novel he wrote about the force in the 1960s:

it was as though there were two police forces. One was real, the one which caught criminals, and the other one was the one that existed in some high-up's office in the Yard. The real police force was there to catch criminals the best way it knew how; and if you couldn't get them down according to Judges Rules, you got them down in your own way. The real police force worked in and around police stations; the real police force *worked*.

The other one was the one the Press wrote about, the one the taxpayers believed in. It was full of unsung heroes with blue eyes and honest English faces . . . *that* police force helped old ladies across the road, in between spells of taking finger prints and running four-minute miles. That police force gave you a pain in the arse. Not only didn't it exist, it *couldn't*. If it did, the prisons would be empty. And the senior officers knew all about the real police force . . . . But for some reason, once you got up that end of the ladder you started forgetting what it was like. Police duty as it was done became a dirty word. And let some poor sod get caught out in something – whether it was a bit of exaggeration in a magistrate's court, or laying someone else's old woman – and they all raised their clean little hands in horror. 'But this is terrible', they would say, their own dirty skeletons locked out of sight, 'to think a policeman could do a thing like this'. When what they really meant was, 'Some bloody reporter's going to get hold of this and splash it on the front page'. [Brock 1968]

So the combining of expressive and repressive functions seems to lead to a whole series of conflicts within the police force itself, and in its relations to other institutions which police the boundaries of the bourgeois public realm.

Normally a capitalist state develops forms of representative democracy and public accountability, which reproduce the conditions of bourgeois hegemony through a process of active consent. Normally, therefore, its powers of physical coercion are called on as a last resort, and against those who have first been publicly outlawed as legal subjects by a variety of ideological mechanisms. But the police force is in a peculiar position here, as an agency of the state which has to penetrate into the heart of civil society if it is to be effective, which has to win active consent to its presence if it is to do so, but which both directly and immediately represents the state's powers of physical coercion. The situation is critical when it comes to policing the working-class city. For, as we have seen, in those areas which were characterized by a backward, small-scale economy, the police force was charged with introducing elements of urban discipline into a population which had not yet fully experienced industrial discipline. And these districts sustained popular cultures which incorporated quite highly-developed countervailing norms of law and order, which could only be totally eliminated by outright repression. It was thus decisive that police intervention in the life of these areas should be seen as the neutral administration of a rational system of justice, rather than the brutal extension of bourgeois class power; if the police were to be seen as legal subjects, not as class subjects, it was necessary to evolve for these 'difficult' neighbourhoods a policing strategy which would maintain the legitimacy of the force's role, as much to the world outside as within itself, by representing the illusory unity of its functions against the manifest reality of their contradictions.

The routine practices of policing were, therefore, designed to conform to the same principles of formal legal rationality[5] as the judicial system they serviced with 'offenders'. Only this kind of bureaucratic accountability could give the appearance of the police and the judiciary being independent of each other, and both being independent of political pressure and vested interest. So the policeman on the beat was trained to apply standard protocols of surveillance, investigation and arrest to all citizen subjects, irrespective of class, colour or creed; just as the magistrate was supposed to apply universalistic rules of evidence, definitions of crime and punishment, with similar impartiality in the court.

As we have seen in Islington, however, the universality of the legal subject could only be substantiated by systematically violating the due process of law in the manner of its enforcement: which, in turn, undermined the whole enterprise of legitimation. The alternative strategy, observing the full letter of the law, would only generate mass arrests, which would overstretch limited manpower resources and threaten the bureaucratic system of processing offenders. The case of street football and gambling illustrated how concretely the problem arose, and also how the police evolved a method of dealing with it: by a partial suspension of formal legal rationality, turning half a blind eye to the rule book; and by the partial suspension of statutory norms of public order, turning the other half of the blind eye to a good deal of minor infringement. Such a strategy enlarged the autonomy of the rank-and-file police over and against the higher white-collar echelons whose job is to maintain the bureaucratic accountability of the organization as a whole. But equally, the calculated use, or abuse, of discretionary powers produces a highly arbitrary system of policing, which undermines the official posture of the force as neutral arbiters of justice. The force is still confronted with the impossible choice of enforcing law *or* order.

In the event, an answer was found by modifying the operational definition of public order, thus producing mediation from within the police apparatus itself.

The statutory definitions, as we have seen, consisted of universalistic rules of public behaviour applied to isolated economic agents going about their lawful business, which in practice meant going from A to B in the shortest possible time. These norms enter into a whole series of legal regulations which criminalize any other kind of public behaviour – the laws against being a suspected person, loitering with intent, causing an obstruction, behaviour likely to cause a breach of the peace, insulting behaviour, definitions of riot and affray. These rules and regulations are, therefore, especially strategic in the city centre, where the symbolic institutions of power are concentrated and where different social classes – elsewhere residentially segregated – congregate in large numbers. Their function here, then, is to outlaw the social promiscuity of the urban crowd, as well as its potential political thread, by reinforcing its characteristics as an atomized mass.

Now initially, and at the time when large numbers of the so-called 'dangerous and perishing' classes still lived crowded together in close proximity to the citadels of power, the police attempted to apply the same norms of public order to these residential areas as to the central place itself. As the problems of enforcing these norms became apparent, and as the urban poor were evicted from the city centre, the policing strategy changed. The innovations consisted precisely in differentiating between the two urban contexts. While statutory norms were still routinely enforced in the centre, in the new heartlands of the working-class city they were increasingly used only as an emergency measure, to justify the last resort of physical repression. In their place, a system of informal, tacitly negotiated and particularistic definitions of public order were evolved which *accommodated* certain working-class usages of social space and time, and *outlawed* others. What were ratified were those practices which articulated the institutions of patriarchy and public propriety within the class habitat; what were outlawed were those practices of women and children which challenged the monopoly of those institutions over the working-class city and its legitimate usage. The new norms in effect imposed a system of unofficial curfew, informal out-of-bounds, to define what were the wrong people, wrong age, wrong sex, in the wrong place and the wrong time. And 'wrong' was defined in the simultaneous terms of a moral ideology of deviance and the juridical ideology of crime. A kind of guilt-by-association was insinuated into these norms: if you were a legal subject caught following a less than pedestrian line of desire,[6] or a class subject caught out of your legal place, you were not only out of (statutory public) order, but had broken a moral code of respectable public behaviour. The first condition supplied the criminal offence, the second justified arrest. Here are some generic examples which may help illustrate how these norms operate:

(*a*) Two smartly dressed young women are standing outside a Wimpy Bar in mid afternoon talking to each other. All things being equal, they will be assumed by the law, as well as by the general populace, to be two housewives having a gossip while out shopping. However, the same two young women doing exactly the same thing in exactly the same place at midnight will, all things being equal, be assumed to be prostitutes waiting for a pick up.

(*b*) A group of working-class lads walking home down a main thoroughfare late at night, joking and singing, will be more likely to be subject to routine intervention by the law than a similar-sized group of girls, behaving in the same way. If two of the lads leave the main group to stroll through the back streets to get home, they will be twice as likely to get stopped and questioned if they pass through a cluster of middle-class residential streets on their way, than if their route passes exclusively through a working-class district.

(*c*) A group of school-age boys or girls who decide to venture downtown for a look around the city centre one evening are likely to be picked up by the police and taken to the police station for interrogation, whereas if they were behaving in the same way (window shopping, eating bags of crisps) in their own locality, they would be unmolested. In one context they will be regarded as potential delinquents and morally 'at risk', while in the other they are simply normal boys and girls doing an everyday thing. However, if Arsenal win an important home game, and they go up west with a crowd of their mates from the North Bank to celebrate, but in fact spend their time wandering about as above, they will be regarded as extremely well-behaved. They may, on the other hand, also discover that on such an occasion they can get away with public behaviour which, if repeated in their own home areas or in a middle-class suburb, would be regarded by residents as constituting a riot, and by the law as behaviour likely to cause a breach of the peace.

(*d*) Today, a group of young people can play football in most working-class streets without scarcely provoking interference by the police. Fifty years ago, their grandparents, doing the same thing in the same place, were highly likely to incur summary arrest and fines.

Once you have learned the ground rules, there is nothing haphazard or arbitrary about the application of these discretionary norms.

The principles of variation are rigorously determined by the strategic priorities of policing under different sets of circumstances, and those priorities are in turn determined by the need to maintain a balance between the conflicting demands of observing the letter of the law and the organizational maintenance of public order. The new methods set out to impose a principle of negotiation between the external policing of the neighbourhood and its internal systems of social control. More concretely, it was an attempt to forge an alliance between the spokesmen of proletarian patriarchy and propriety and the enforcers of bourgeois law and order. Here, uniquely, the police force and the labour movement perform complementary functions of political socialization – though, from a socialist standpoint, entirely negative ones. For the combined effect is to limit the access of working-class polity, while outlawing as potentially deviant the very 'public realms' they have had to construct to reaffirm some kind of social existence in the face of their disenfranchisement as speaking subjects within the class habitat. But more recently, in a period which has seen a general weakening of the links between sexual and generational relations in the reproduction of labour-power, their massive reinforcement at this superstructural level of 'community relations' has, if anything, served to sharpen working-class perceptions of the situation.

If the alliance at the top has been remarkably successful, the negotiation of informal norms at the grass-roots has been far less smooth. Firstly, because the constant drive towards increased accumulation of capital demands the continual recomposition and relocation of its labour force. Not only is this process resisted, thus unleashing community struggles which go far beyond the confines of public propriety, but it throws up new social forces (for example, immigrant workers) whose material cultures also challenge these constraints. If outsiders are to become established, informal norms must be negotiated anew. The fact that their very presence threatens the delicate equilibrium of existing tolerances means that the police normally respond by falling back on the more or less brutal reimposition of statutory public order when policing these groups.

A degree of immunity from this kind of direct legal repression has been won by the more sedimented sections of the class; but only by surrendering some of the means by which they once policed themselves. And these welfare functions, once confiscated, become the cutting-edge of the police campaign for active consent and public support. In many of the rougher inner-city neighbourhoods, however, and despite everything that municipal reformers can do, a strong countervailing sense of moral and social cohesion has survived. In these conditions, if the local police show one very public face in defence of order and another, more private one, in the enforcement of the law, they are likely to be condemned as two-faced.

Far from disappearing, the contradictions between the two sides of police work have intensified. They continue to undermine each other, while taking on new, more mediated forms. For example, the welfare function only remains credible if its implication for law enforcement (that is, the scrupulously impartial adherence to due process of law) is also observed. But in criminal work the emphasis is inevitably on productivity, increasing the ratio of arrests, and this in turn means bending the rules. This is also a problem for organizational maintenance. The more resources allocated to increasing the efficiency of repressive policing, the more manpower has to be poured into 'community relations' to restabilize the public image of the force. The more technologically sophisticated, and hence impersonal, the systems of surveillance, the more home-beat coppers are needed on the ground. The more manpower is drained here, the more rationalization is needed in policing methods in the other departments. The more this push-me-pull-you process accelerates, the more essential and the more impossible becomes the task of representing the repressive edge as a natural extension of the welfare wedge – the Sweeney as the legitimate offspring of Dixon of Dock Green.

In the post-war period, and especially during the last decade and in the inner city, the situation has come to a head. Increasingly in these areas the police have had to reply on apparatuses outside their control – notably, the mass media – to construct local emergencies which would sanction the reimposition of statutory norms through the systematic violation of the due process of law. If it was so easy to fabricate imaginary scenarios of lawlessness, hooliganism, mob violence and general rampage, we should remember that the survival of distinctive habitats of class subjectivity is necessarily a scandal, as well as a source of secret fascination and fear, in a Welfare State dedicated to equality of opportunity. Whatever social or political force manages to emerge from its invisibility, to break through the cover of routine surveillance and control, is by definition an emergency. And if it is 'bad' news, it is because it is always news from nowhere, a non-sense as well as a *non sequitur* from this vantage point. The restoration of order simply demands that this bad news return back into nowhere as quickly as possible. The separate tempos of police and media intervention thus work in counterpoint to each other, never in simple harmony.[7] If the police were relatively successful in isolating and attacking the new dangerous classes, they had also to pay the price of increased dependency on sources of legitimation in civil society. It was to prove a costly trade-off; for, as their own behaviour came increasingly into the public limelight, so many of the carefully negotiated norms and other special arrangements which constituted time-honoured station practice came suddenly to be redefined as 'corruption' because they did indeed violate principles of neutral administration and due process.

Yet the suppression of these practices could only endanger the organizational maintenance of local forces, already heavily under strength. The only alternative short-cut to getting results consisted in reverting to the more overt techniques of physical intimidation. Either way the image of public service and accountability was damaged, and exposed the force to even greater political pressure from watch-dog groups. Inevitably, the push-me-pull-you process took its toll of the internal command structure of the force. The division of police labour became ever more specialized, and generated tensions between rival departments, each jealously guarding its professional autonomy. But the conflicts that have begun to shake the foundations are not merely institutional: they have distinct class connotations.

We have already noted the latent antagonism between the local beat coppers and their superior officers. The former are naturally concerned to safeguard their discretionary powers which alone allow them to gain intimate working knowledge of neighbourhood underlife, and to successfully perform the delicate balancing act between productivity and acceptability. But however they negotiate their presence in the community, they are still accountable to their superiors. These latter are usually college-trained administrators (Trenchard's Boys) who are pre-occupied with a different set of priorities, above all the need to balance the demands of organizational maintenance with the observance of procedural norms. This is only one instance of a wider conflict between those whose conditions of police work require that they take account of the existence of 'the working-class city', and those whose position of public accountability requires that they do not. So, for example, a basic antagonism quickly developed between station staff, in charge of maintaining negotiated order in their local manor, and the new elite cadres like the Special Patrol Group and Regional Crime Squads, organized on paramilitary lines, whose explicit and peripatetic function was precisely to restore statutory order without regard for any of the factors constraining the operations of the local force.

Increasingly then, a split has tended to develop in the occupational socialization of the police force between its professional ideology and its material cultures. This too has a history (see Pilling 1971).

Even as late as the Edwardian period, especially in industrial areas, policing was still regarded as a normal working-class job. Artisans and skilled men would get a job on the local force when times were hard, and return to their 'real' trade when seasonal or cyclical demand picked up. Police culture was that of a working class temporarily in uniform. But with the growing professionalism of police work, the growing diversification of skills based on mental as well as manual labour, a quite distinctive occupational culture emerged. The force now tended to attract working men whose aspirations, for whatever reason, fell short of their long-term prospects in the labour market. Recruits were mainly married men, often with considerable work experience in civilian life – but their entry into the force signified a far more permanent shift. This was reflected in the fact that police work had come to be seen as a highly deviant occupational choice within the range of working-class job opportunities. Police PROs tried to turn this to good account by promoting a middle-class image of the force as a 'vocation' and a 'career'. But, for the raw recruit, the reality was of course quite otherwise, and so very different working-class paradigms were brought to bear. The trade magazine of the force is still obstinately called *The Job*, and, as its pages stress, it is one of society's dirty jobs and pretty underpaid at that. The ideology of public service, as in other sectors, backfired and produced growing trade-union militancy amongst the rank and file. Paradoxically, this militancy is an effect of the social isolation of the policeman from the mainstream of working-class life. The extent of social closure within this occupational community is indicated by the tendency of police work to become a family tradition – son succeeding father from generation to generation. There are other, no less idiosyncratic, factors at work in recruitment. Chief among them in the post-1945 period is the increasing *juvenilization* of the force. National service in the 1950s was an important feeder here, and so of course was the mounting level of youth unemployment in the 1970s. But cultural factors are equally important. The effect of such mass phenomena as the Teds, the Mods and Rockers, and the Skinheads on those young people who remained within the confines of parent cultures wedded to public propriety, should not be underestimated. In working-class districts where subcultures were strong, ultra-conformists could easily be isolated from the mainstream of local peer-group life. It may be significant then that those young constables I spoke of in Islington,[8] who had all joined the force after 1965, though they gave very disparate and personal reasons for doing so, were almost unanimous in saying that what they liked best about the job, what they had missed previously, was the sense of comradeship – the fact that you had mates you could depend on, who would back you up no matter what. This peer group ideal seemed, by all accounts, most strongly exemplified in the section house where the single lived; here horseplay, petty pilfering and strenuous parties seemed the order of the day. While they displayed deference to the symbolisms of Authority, these working-class youth were quite active in a whole culture of insubordination, with its own quite elaborate rituals of misrule. All this seemed to be officially tolerated, though not encouraged, as a necessary safety valve for young men subject to rigorous discipline at the bottom of the command structure – good for bonding them into an efficient crime-fighting unit. Just as it served as a defence against what was perceived as social ostracism by the local community.

The result had been to narrow the scenario of law and order down to a battle between two rival gangs, both composed of young, single, working-class males, each seeking territorial control over the class habitat – but with this difference, that one mob have the full weight of the state behind them, the other only themselves and their mates to fall back on. The scores they have to settle still revolve around the question 'Who rules?' But they no longer revolve around the material stakes of a class struggle, as it was with the costers in the 1880s. Now the struggle is purely symbolic. Nevertheless, it is one which has all too real a consequence for those who are on the losing side.

It is in fact a battle which the police force cannot afford not to be seen to be winning. And increasingly they have fallen back on the repressive weight of the state as represented by the juvenile penal system in order to hold their own. It is the closed world of 'The Institution', acting at a distance through him, which confers on the beat-copper his secret power in his dealings with the rival mob. Higher police productivity has come to mean not so much higher rates of arrest, or even conviction, but more deterrent levels of judicial sentencing – higher rates of imprisonment. One lad sent down for a short sharp shock in a detention centre, instead of being let off with a fine, came to be seen as a more efficient expenditure of scarce police resources than cautioning a dozen of his mates and visiting his parents. But this solution is not without its problems. It often means artificially escalating the charge and/or fabricating evidence in order to ensure conviction and higher sentence; yet this might mean endangering the posture of formal legal rationality which the force might be anxious to preserve in public settings such as the court. Equally, it might mean a higher proportion of contested cases and jury trials; further, the routine processing of offenders by courts, and with it the bureaucratic equilibrium of justice, would be put under strain. Nor does the problem stop there. As a log jam of cases builds up, so the remand centres would clog up with those awaiting trial. However useful from the policing viewpoint, the deterrent effect of this preliminary taste of institutional life, overcrowding and deteriorating conditions could only lead to unrest amongst both staff and prisoners. As a consequence, local judicial practices have had to be unofficially adjusted to take account of variants in policing strategy. A secondary system of informal norms of sentencing and treatment has evolved; but this does not always reflect police priorities – indeed it may run directly counter to them. Inevitably, the result is to produce widespread discrepancies between different areas of the city and different parts of the country, and vicious anomalies between crime and punishment in individual cases. Hardly the best advertisement for legal universalism.

To sum up, I have tried to suggest that the structural contradictions in policing practice derive from the force's peculiar historical position within the British state. In Gramsci's terms, it was the first branch of the state to exemplify a shift in ruling-class strategy from a war of manoeuvre to a war of fixed position (see Anderson 1977). This pioneering role was forced upon it by the underdeveloped nature of the local state administration in a period of rapid urbanization, and at a time when long-established structures of popular recreation and justice retained powerful material supports. The response of the police to its predicament partially succeeded in imposing the elements of a properly capitalist urban discipline in the name of public propriety, but signally failed to resolve its own contradictions. These have sharpened into chronic conflicts within the force itself, and in its relations to a whole series of environing institutions. The current crisis in the policing of the working-class city has become a crisis of legitimacy for the bourgeois public realm as a whole.

9 Sex discrimination, work and the law

Jeanne Gregory

The Sex Discrimination Act, which came into force in December 1975, provided the model for the new Race Relations Act, passed the following year. Yet the pioneering attempts at combating discrimination through legislation had been confined to racial inequality. The Race Relations Acts of 1965 and 1968 were regarded by liberal reformers as necessary steps in the process of attitude change and for them the 1976 Act represented the culmination of their struggle for effective enforcement powers (Lester and Bindman 1972; Bindman 1976). In regard to sexual inequality the Equal Pay Act 1970, which became operative at the same time as the Sex Discrimination Act, was the only other relevant piece of legislation. The Labour government undoubtedly considers that it has made its stand on behalf of racial minorities and women, and no further major pieces of legislation regarding these groups are contemplated. Unless a Conservative government intervenes to weaken the legislation, these two Acts are likely to constitute the legal ammunition for combating discrimination for some time to come.

In order to evaluate the strengths and weaknesses, the limits and potential of this legal ammunition, I intend to analyse the legislation in terms of three major theoretical issues. First, the existence of this kind of interventionist legislation throws new light on the changing role of the state in capitalist society. Second, both the content of the legislation (specifically, the concept of equality it contains), and the procedural forms devised for its enforcement, are directly relevant to an understanding of the contradictions and limits of bourgeois law. Third, to monitor the fate of this legislation is to expose starkly the sexist and racist features of contemporary Britain and so recognize the continuing significance of 'pre-capitalist' structures and ideology.

The role of the state

Marxist theories of the capitalist state are becoming increasingly sophisticated in response to changing forms of state intervention which do not accord with earlier, simplistic explanations. Thus, when coercive methods of control were more overt, coercive views of state intervention fitted the pattern of events with a reasonable degree of accuracy. However, welfare legislation was not overtly coercive; on the contrary, it was passed largely in response to working-class pressures. Yet these initiatives were co-opted to meet the requirements of capital and the basic structure of inequality remained. Disillusioned socialists came to regard the welfare state as an ideological confidence trick to assure 'a reasonable degree of economic efficiency by the erection of social and political shock absorbers' (Saville 1958). In order to understand these processes, Marxists increasingly concerned themselves with the ideological functions of state institutions (Althusser 1971; Poulantzas 1973; Miliband 1969).

Evidence of divisions of interest *within* the ruling class is not easily accommodated within theories which confine their analysis to the repressive and ideological roles of the state. In recognition of such divisions Barratt-Brown introduced a third concept into the debate and wrote of the 'conformative' role of the state (Barratt-Brown 1971). When he referred to 'conformative' institutions, he meant those which 'contain, incorporate and moderate the conflicts inside capitalist society'. He draws attention to conflicts of interest and to the role of government as controller of the more extreme abuses of power and as mediator in the interests of stability. He refers to the conformative effect of wage bargaining procedures and the 'creeping blanket of consensus politics'. Yet he is also aware of the ambiguous character of conformative institutions: they create new opportunities for pressing demands and so generate a potentially explosive force.

Adopting a similar approach, anti-discrimination legislation can be seen as a response to the demands of oppressed groups for the removal of historical barriers to the achievement of full equality. These claims are compatible with bourgeois notions of justice and economic efficiency. The state therefore assumes a conformative role, using the legislation to control those employers whose practices fall short of acceptable notions of equal opportunity, and to evolve institutional structures for channelling the conflicts. Although the British legislation must be placed within an international context (it is both a weaker version of similar American legislation – the 1964 Civil Rights Act – and a response to European Economic Community articles and directives),[1] it is no accident that it was the brain child of a Labour government. Regarding themselves as representatives of a broad social spectrum, they are confident that legislative tinkering with the system will achieve stability in the general interest. Their task is defined as bringing into line a small number of deviant employers whose unacceptable behaviour threatens the basic consensus.

It is this social democratic ideology that sets the parameters of state intervention. In response to domestic and international pressures, the government has provided ammunition for members of disadvantaged groups to challenge their oppressors. As the conflicts of interest are more deeply rooted than legislators recognize, they have constructed a potential hornets' nest. On the one hand they have raised the expectations of women and racial minorities, who will protest if the ammunition proves ineffectual. On the other hand even weak legislation challenges deeply entrenched customs and attitudes, and will be opposed by employers as an unwarranted interference with market forces and property rights. The apparent neutrality of the government itself is revealed as hollow, both because of the sexist and racist assumptions retained in other legislation,[2] and because, as a major employer of labour, it is not necessarily exempt from scrutiny.[3]

The conformative institutions used by the state to contain these contradictions serve to draw attention away from the basic inequalities created by the economic processes, in particular the utilization of women and racial minorities as a reserve pool of unskilled, low-paid labour. Whereas the impotence of these institutions is more evident when unemployment rises, it does not necessarily follow that the processes of containment will break down. If the lines of battle continue to be drawn within the institutional ideological framework erected by the state, the blame for failure will be deflected. To understand why this is so, it is necessary to examine the nature of bourgeois law in more detail.

The role of law

The clearest Marxist exposition of the relationship between capitalism and law is found in the work of Pashukanis (1978). He equates the legal form with the development of commodity exchange, which reaches its peak in bourgeois society. In a society based on commodity production both the products and persons appear in the process of exchange as abstractions. Under these conditions the abstract legal form is generated: man becomes a bearer of rights and legal fetishism complements commodity fetishism. Political power becomes separated from economic power and the statute form is evolved. Pashukanis was concerned to expose 'the relative and historically limited nature of the fundamental juridical concepts' (1978, p. 34), which bourgeois jurisprudence presented as neutral and *a priori*.

'. . . legal ideology becomes the ideology par excellence, and defending the class interest of the exploiters appears with ever increasing success as the defence of the abstract principle of legal subjectivity' (ibid., p. 45). For Pashukanis there is no such thing as proletarian law. With the overthrow of bourgeois society comes the gradual withering away of law altogether. Writing in post-revolutionary Russia in the 1920s he saw contemporary legal developments in terms of a transitionary period before the full flowering of communism.

Pashukanis was not alone in drawing attention to the gulf between formal freedoms and the realities of economic power in capitalist society. In discussing the content of contracts between workers and employers, Weber comments: '[The rules] create the framework for valid agreements officially available to all. Actually they are accessible only to the owners of property and thus in effect support their very autonomy and power positions' (Rheinstein 1966). Unlike Pashukanis, however, Weber believed that the centralized bureaucratic controls of socialist societies were also potentially coercive. Despite his recognition of the persistence of substantive inequalities, he considered that formal legal rationality represented the most highly developed form of modern Western capitalism. Using the nineteenth-century German legal code as the basis for an ideal type of formal legality, he foresaw the declining importance of substantive considerations and procedures, and the construction of a gapless system of abstract rules.

In assessing the current relevance of Pashukanis and Weber, it is important to take account of the historical context within which they formulated their ideas. However, this alone does not solve the issues raised by their theories. Although certain developments in the content and form of capitalist law would seem to be contrary to theoretical prediction, they could be regarded as futile or misguided efforts to overcome the contradictions inherent within capitalism. Alternatively, they could be seen as far-reaching adaptations, indicative of an embryonic form of law not reflected in the theoretical accounts.

Thus, in opposition to Weber's expectations, substantive justice continues to play an important role in advanced capitalist societies. It is unrealistic to dismiss this as a cultural lag, arguing that the full development of formal legal rationality is hampered in certain countries by the heritage of the common law tradition. Rather, substantive inequalities are given recognition in legislation which attempts to transcend the limits of formal equality. Underprivileged groups or priority areas are identified and ways of providing special assistance are devised. New administrative forms are evolved to give effect to the legislation; administrative tribunals are proclaimed for their informality and for their use of 'lay' members, who apply their experience of everyday life to the cases before them, rather than narrowly considering a set of formal rules. That is, the tribunals are deliberately 'tilted' (Reich 1966) in order that substantive considerations can be given priority.

Marx recognized that in order to take account of substantive differences between individuals, 'right instead of being equal would have to be unequal' (in Pashukanis 1978, p. 20). This is precisely what substantive justice attempts to do, but without abandoning fundamental notions of individualized justice and equality before the law. As Mitchell (1976) puts it: 'The mind of liberal and social democratic man soars into the skies with his belief in equality only to find that it must return chained, like the falcon, to the wrist whence it came.' Weber was aware of these tensions but considered that formal legality was the pinnacle of bourgeois achievement. In opposition to this viewpoint, Kinsey (1978) argues that:

> codification and rational formalism in legal method represents a low point in the development of bourgeois legality . . . . It is precisely the flexibility and pragmatism embodied in the common law of England which allows the maintenance of the appearance of justice.

Anti-discrimination legislation undoubtedly reflects such pragmatism, both in the content of the new laws and in the procedural forms devised for enforcement. However, it is by no means certain that the appearance of justice can be maintained. Notions of formal and substantive justice coexist uneasily in the Acts and the informal 'tilted' procedures pursue an uncertain course. Although the institutions used to enforce the legislation serve a conformative function by providing official avenues for the expression of conflict, their failure might serve to draw attention to the very injustices they were established to rectify. We may yet see a retreat to formal legality and a reassessment of Weberian theory.

Similar considerations apply to the apparent oversights in the work of Pashukanis. Thus it could be argued that far reaching changes in adminstrative law within capitalist societies serve to undermine his basic thesis on bourgeois law. Such administrative developments as he observed taking place in post-revolutionary Russia he interpreted in terms of the withering away of law in the period of socialist transition. He therefore cannot help us to understand the significance of these developments *within* capitalism (see Korsch's critique in Pashukanis 1978, pp. 189-95). Administrative law has been defined as 'the law relating to the organization, composition, functions and procedures of public authorities and special statutory tribunals' (de Smith 1975). The twentieth century has witnessed a rapid growth in the number of such authorities and tribunals in advanced capitalist societies. As their powers and duties span an increasingly wide range of social activity, it is imperative to consider the implications of this growth for theories of bourgeois law.

One interpretation of these developments is found in the corporatist theory of law. Starting from the assumption that state institutions benefit the interests of society as a whole, corporatism is more concerned with finding the most effective organizational solution to a specific problem, rather than with legal rights and safeguards. It is therefore 'antinomian': its full realization would 'mean the end of the rule of law as traditionally known' (Winkler 1975). The mushrooming of Quasi-Autonomous Governmental Organizations (Quangos) fits well with corporatist accounts. Such organizations can be set up in whatever sphere the government wishes to make (or be seen to make) an intervention. The discretionary powers of such bodies enable them to determine the pace and direction of action; they can respond both more selectively and with greater flexibility to policy requirements. The government retains control through appointments and finance and yet any hostility is deflected onto the organization.

An assessment of corporatist theory can be made on two levels: first, to what extent it correctly interprets current trends and second, what are the advantages of administrative over judicial processes? In relation to the first question, administrative expansion has by no means occurred unchecked. Studies of administrative law devote considerable attention to an analysis of legal safeguards to the possible abuse of administrative powers (see, for example, Wade 1971; Robson 1928; Griffith and Street 1966; de Smith 1973; Jowell 1975). Although the judiciary sometimes appear reluctant to overturn the 'reasonable' exercise of administrative discretion,[4] they have on other occasions readily assumed the mantle of legal protector. From Lord Hewart to Lord Denning, judges have sought to clip the wings of interventionist policy-makers, who devised strategies to avoid legal scrutiny (Hewart 1929; Gould 1970); yet although they regard themselves as championing individual liberties against the might of the state machine, this should not be confused with protecting working-class interests. When Lord Denning rebuked the attorney-general with the words of Thomas Fuller: 'Be you ever so high, the law is above you', the Master of the Rolls was supporting the freedom of a member of an extreme right-wing organization to further its racist and anti-union activities.[5] Similarly, the recent judgments against the Secretary of State for Education in the Tameside case[6] and against the Department of Trade in the Laker Airways case[7] are hardly victories for the working class. Judicial attitudes towards Quangos are epitomized in the recent comments made by Lord Denning concerning the 'immense powers' of the Equal Opportunities Commission and the Commission for Racial Equality: 'These are inquisitional powers of a kind never before known to the law.' The Commissions can compel employers to release information even if they thereby 'incriminate themselves'. Lord Denning evidently considers it his duty to correct the balance by protecting employers who find themselves the subject of litigation in sex or race discrimination cases from the embarrassment of having to disclose confidential documents.[8]

If the legal controls on corporatist impulses can have such reactionary consequences, it would seem to follow that administrative processes offer potential advantages over the judicial approach. Ganz (1967) argues that 'the interests of the individual may be as effectively protected by a purely administrative process as by legal rules . . . the official may act more humanely'. These sentiments are echoed by Titmuss (1971) in relation to welfare rights. He emphasizes the advantages of a scheme which allows for 'flexible responses to human needs and to an immense variety of complex individual circumstances' and argues that this can be achieved more easily through the use of administrative discretion than through a fully judicialized rights-based system.

Both Ganz and Titmuss stress the advantage of a movement from law to an 'administration of things' (Ganz 1967, p.106), but fail to recognize the limitations on such a movement when it takes place within capitalism. The findings of an American study (Nonet 1969) provide a useful illustration of these limitations. Nonet traces the changing philosophy of an American agency set up to administer workmen's compensation legislation. He shows how the welfare outlook of the agency gradually evaporated as a result of hostility from the employers, who were less philanthropic than expected, and as a result of increased union activity on behalf of its members. Based on a consensual world view, agency policy failed because of the realities of industrial conflict. The evidence clearly indicates that the injured workmen made fewer gains in the hands of a well-meaning paternalistic commission than under a fully judicialized system where advocates could bring test cases and develop a body of case law.

A similar change in philosophy is occurring within the Supplementary Benefits Commission in this country. Significantly, Donnison, the present chairman of the SBC, has admitted that the paternalism of his predecessor Titmuss is no longer workable. He offers a mixed bag of explanations: the increasing number and range of recipients of benefit, 'staff shortages, sharper class conflicts [and] a punitive scrounger-bashing press' (Donnison 1977). Undoubtedly the increasing membership of claimants' unions and other welfare rights groups would agree with him.

The anti-discrimination legislation contains provision for both litigation and administrative action. The latter would seem to offer the more appropriate mechanisms for launching a comprehensive and systematic attack on sexual and racial disadvantages, but given the constraints imposed by a capitalist system, the mechanisms may fail to operate. As Marx argues, 'right can never be higher than the economic structure of society and its cultural development conditioned thereby' (quoted in Pashukanis 1978, p. 20).

Sexism and racism

Sociological discussions of class rarely include a consideration of sexual and racial inequalities.[9] As a consequence, an important dimension is missing which may crucially affect the validity of the arguments. For example, Marshall (1970) traces the history of the struggle in Britain to achieve civil, political and social rights, without considering the extent to which women lagged behind in these achievements.[10] If he had been less chauvinistic, he might also have been less complacent about the degree to which citizenship was replacing class in post-war, welfare-state Britain.

Marxists are equally guilty of such omissions. To discuss social conflicts in terms other than class struggle would be seen as adopting the pluralist categories of bourgeois sociology. Marxists tend to concentrate on those aspects of capitalism which distinguished it from other social formations. The work of Pashukanis (1978) exemplifies these tendencies. He refers to the principle of freedom and equality as 'a concretely effective principle which is embodied in bourgeois society from the moment it emerges from and destroys feudal-patriarchal society'. He writes of 'the dissolution of the patriarchal family, and its transformation into a contractual family'. Because his central concern is the relationship between commodity exchange and the emergence of legal rights, he exaggerates the degree to which capitalism made a complete break with all that had preceded it. He assumes that social groups not directly involved in commodity exchange nevertheless become legal subjects through the general application of bourgeois legality. He overlooks both the continuing significance of pre-capitalist structures within capitalist society, and the extent to which bourgeois society continues to generate 'expelled' populations of its own (Mathieson 1974).

The contemporary position of women and ethnic minorities cannot be understood without reference to pre-capitalist social formations. Although capitalism has rejected an economic and social system based on slavery, the historical legacy of slavery provides the key to understanding present-day racial oppression. In regard to women, it is the failure of capitalism to break with patriarchal forms of social relationship which accounts for female oppression. In some respects therefore, the subjection of women is less visible than that of racial minorities. Explanations of racial inferiority in terms of biological or anthropological theories are academically less respectable than similar accounts of female inferiority. Although outside academic circles, beliefs in racial inferiority undoubtedly persist, there may be some hesitation in expressing such opinions. With regard to women, it is still socially acceptable to hold the view that 'woman's place is in the home' and to treat legislation relating to female equality with amusement. Friedan's account (1977) of the hysterical laughter with which American congressmen greeted the proposal to include women in Title 7 of the Civil Rights Act 1964 underlines this attitude.

The destruction of obstacles to female equality does not involve the simple removal of the remaining vestiges of feudal structures and attitudes. Rather, 'Women's subordination under capitalism lies in the articulation between patriarchal relations and capitalist development' (Bland *et al.*, 1978). The patriarchal family not only survives under capitalism but performs a useful role within it. The separation of the economy from the family while retaining the pre-capitalist sexual divisions of labour 'gave a new meaning to male supremacy' (Zaretsky 1976). Women continue to perform their traditional mothering and home-making function, while providing a useful reserve labour force when required. Ethnic minorities are also used as a reserve supply of labour, performing the unskilled, low-paid tasks that white male workers reject. Like the women, they can be used to depress wage levels; although when no longer required, they are more likely to make financial demands on the welfare state. Women usually return to their position within the family as economically dependent wives or daughters.[11]

Viewed solely in terms of the processes of commodity exchange, the racial and sexual composition of the labour force is irrelevant. Legislation which aims to increase the efficiency of the labour market by reducing the operation of 'irrational' factors would therefore seem to be not only perfectly compatible with capitalism but actually serve to strengthen it. Anti-discrimination policies are invariably 'sold' to the business world on this basis. It is only when we begin to explore those aspects of capitalist societies that cannot be interpreted solely in terms of commodity exchange that the limits to this process of 'rationalization' can be fully grasped.

Kamenka and Ehr-Soon Tay (1975) suggest that much radical critique, including the women's liberation movement, is most effective against the remaining *Gemeinschaft* structures within capitalist societies. Inevitably, there is a tendency for such radicalism to frame its demands in terms of *Gesellschaft* values, and concentrate on expanding the scope of individual rights. As Arthur says of Pashukanis, his great contribution was to show that 'the revolutionary overthrow of capitalist forms of social organisation cannot be grasped in terms of a quantitative extension of existing rights' (Pashukanis 1978, p. 10). Because women and racial minority groups lag so far behind in basic freedoms, Marxists often dismiss them as a kind of rearguard, whose demands detract from and slow down the main revolutionary impetus. Yet only if we understand the inter-penetration of *Gemeinschaft* and *Gesellschaft* structures within capitalism will we be able to exploit the resulting contradictions.

Pashukanis's concern is the abolition of the legal form and of legal ideology altogether, but he admits that the prerequisite for this is 'a society in which the contradiction between individual and social interests has broken down' (ibid., p. 104). Anti-discrimination laws would of course no longer be necessary in a society in which sexism and racism, along with other social divisions, ceased to exist. Meanwhile, oppressed groups will presumably attempt to push bourgeois law to its limit and demand their rights, without necessarily accepting that as the final goal. By monitoring the successes and failures of such attempts, we can increase our understanding of contemporary capitalism.

The legislation

The concept of equality

Before discussing the two main anti-discrimination laws, it is worthwhile to consider briefly the achievement of the Equal Pay Act, as this piece of legislation highlights the limitations of formal equality.

The Equal Pay Act, passed in 1970, came into force at the end of 1975, giving employers five years in which to adjust their pay policies to meet the requirements of the Act.[12] It states that a woman is entitled to equal pay if she is employed on like work or broadly similar work with a man in the same employment or on work that has been rated as of equivalent value to a man's job under a job evaluation scheme. Some blatant cases of discrimination have been successfully tackled as a result of the Equal Pay Act, but the fact that women's average earnings remain at 64 per cent of those for men (and in money terms the gap is actually widening: see New Earnings Survey 1978) indicates the timidity of this piece of legal ammunition in relation to the complex problem it was supposed to tackle. Many employers, with the connivance of the unions, used the five-year breathing space to avoid overlapping male and female jobs, and so prevent the 'like work' clause from being evoked.

The 'like work' clause expresses the intention of the legislators to offer women only formal equality with men, ignoring the substantive inequalities which nullify the clause. The problem of low pay in traditionally female forms of employment is ignored, together with the exploitation of part-time workers, the majority of whom are women. Even where the 'like work' clause is successfully used, the employer can still argue that there is a material difference, other than the difference in sex, which justifies the pay differential. It is terms like 'broadly similar' and 'material difference' which have allowed tribunals to accept pedantic distinctions in order to dismiss equal pay applications. Thus one woman lost her case because she had *more* responsibility than the man with whom she compared herself.[13] The work of male cleaners has been considered more arduous, and therefore worthy of higher payment, than than of female cleaners.[14] A housemother in a school for handicapped children was refused equal pay with the housefather, significantly enough on the grounds that the roles they performed were largely those of a mother and a father in ordinary life.[15] The Employment Appeal Tribunal has occasionally reprimanded industrial tribunals for their more blatantly sexist decisions, but in general, the legal hurdles that must be surmounted in order to win an equal pay case indicate that even this modest law represents a challenge to common-sense understandings of male and female differences.

In comparison with the Equal Pay Act, the Sex Discrimination Act is a more sophisticated piece of legislation. Like the Race Relations Act 1976,[16] it recognizes the limits of formal equality and attempts to tackle the roots of discrimination and compensate for the effects of past discrimination. In particular, two novel features of the legislation represent a tentative movement towards establishing a measure of substantive equality. First, it is no longer necessary for the applicant to prove an intention to discriminate. If the woman (or member of a racial minority group) can show that the employer's requirement or condition is such that the proportion of women (racial group members) who can comply with it is considerably smaller than the proportion of men (racial majority group members) who can comply, and that it is to her (his) detriment, then there is a case to be answered. It is then up to the employer to show that the requirement or condition is justifiable in terms of business necessity. No employer is asked to jeopardize the profitability of his enterprise, but he may be required to subject traditional modes of operation to rational scrutiny to reduce the possible occurrence of 'indirect discrimination'. For example, Belinda Price successfully argued that fewer women were able to comply with the Civil Service rule that applicants for direct entry to the Executive Officer grade must be in the age group 17½ to 28 years. The Civil Service Commissioners have been asked to reconsider their employment policies by 1980.[17]

Second, employers and training bodies are permitted to offer special training facilities to women or ethnic minorities in areas of employment from which they have traditionally been excluded. It is unlikely that these discretionary powers will be widely used when general unemployment rates are high; those who do wish to make use of the powers have to tread cautiously. For example, enlightened employers such as the London Borough of Camden find that they can operate training schemes for minority group employees once they have appointed them, but they cannot discriminate in their favour in order to ensure the initial appointments. Similarly, the Equal Opportunities Commission reprimanded the Open University for operating an illegal quota in favour of women.[18] Neither the principle of indirect discrimination nor the provision of special training schemes is likely to make much impact on the position of disadvantaged groups. Those who have a stake in maintaining the status quo complain of reverse discrimination as soon as any policy threatens to become effective. Affirmative action programmes are illegal in this country; it is the experience of America, where anti-discrimination policies are more aggressive, which demonstrates most vividly the contradictions which flow from determined and systematic attempts to transcend the limits of formal equality. The Bakke decision, in which a white male successfully challenged his rejection from a medical school which operated a quota system in favour of negroes, has left American affirmative action programmes in some confusion (*The Times*, 29 June 1978).

Any attempt to recognize the interests of particular groups within a prevailing ideology of competitive individualism will have divisive consequences. This is apparent even in relation to the cautious provisions of the British legislation, as the case of Mrs Steel demonstrates.[19] Mrs Steel, who had worked for the Post Office for sixteen years, lost her bid for a 'walk' in favour of a young man who became a postman in 1973. He was considered senior to her because she only became a permanent postwoman in 1975 when the Post Office accepted women into the permanent grades in response to the Sex Discrimination Act. After three tribunal hearings she won her claim for back-dated seniority. The consequence of this decision will be to lengthen the seniority queue for the men, as the women are slotted into their rightful positions. The ambivalent attitude of male trade unionists towards the legislation is not surprising.

The judicial arm of enforcement

The sections of the legislation relating to employment are enforceable through industrial tribunals, with the right of appeal by either party on a point of law to the Employment Appeal Tribunal, and from there to the Court of Appeal, and possibly to the House of Lords. Although the procedure begins with the informal, tilted tribunals, they must observe the precedents set by the superior courts whenever the latter are involved. Industrial tribunals are regarded as a cheap, rapid and easily accessible method of dealing with disputes. From the point of view of potential applicants in sex and race discrimination cases, however, there are several formidable obstacles. First, although the legislation recognizes group discrimination there is no group procedure. Similar cases against one employer are sometimes heard together, but tribunals dispense individualized justice to those appearing before them. When Ann Hutchinson won her case against Electrolux, the firm moved her to different work in an attempt to avoid raising the wages of the women performing the same tasks.[20] Individual litigation is inappropriate and cumbersome in relation to group oppression. Lustgarten (1978, pp. 178-205) points out that 'virtually every suit under the American civil rights laws is brought as a class action'.[21]

A second major obstacle is that in contrast to unfair dismissal cases, the burden of proof in discrimination cases rests with the applicant. This frequently involves proving the superiority of one's skills or qualifications over all other candidates for the job or the promotion. Not many members of oppressed groups have sufficient self confidence to sustain such arguments in the face of opposition.[22] It requires stamina and single-mindedness, the firm conviction that an important principle is at stake, to persist in an application against such odds. An applicant risks victimization, or may be 'bought off' by an employer seeking to avoid the expense and publicity of a court case. If the emotional stress and hostility cause the applicant to leave his/her job and drop the case, the tribunal loses jurisdiction and cannot proceed.[23]

A third hurdle to successful enforcement is the difficulty of gaining access to information necessary to present an argument. Employers are not only in a better position to purchase legal assistance, they also retain control of confidential reports and other relevant documents. The outcome of two recent cases (see note 8) has reinforced this power imbalance. In the first case a woman was not selected for interview for promotion; in the second case a coloured man was not successful in an application for transfer. They both asked to see the confidential reports on their fellow workers who apparently received more favourable treatment. In both cases, the Employment Appeal Tribunal ordered disclosure of the relevant documents, holding that it was clearly necessary in order that justice be done, adding that it was unlikely ever to be easy for an applicant to discharge the burden of proving discrimination. Although the 'expert' members of the appeal tribunal were presumably applying their knowledge of industrial relations in reaching their decisions, the Court of Appeal saw fit to reverse the judgment. Apparently oblivious of the American Public Information Act, the judges were fearful of the disturbance and unrest that might result if confidential reports were disclosed; L.J. Browne was particularly horrified with the notion that someone refused a bank overdraft could compel the bank to disclose confidential documents relating to other customers.

A fourth weakness arises from the choice of industrial tribunals to enforce anti-discrimination laws. Apart from the legally qualified chairman, industrial tribunals have two lay members, representing 'the two sides of industry' and making use of their knowledge of industrial relations to reach decisions. In relation to unfair dismissal procedure, which constitutes the bulk of the caseload of industrial tribunals, the system may prove relatively satisfactory in containing and individualizing conflicts. It is highly inappropriate for enforcing legislation which sets out to disturb the traditional pattern of industrial relations. Lustgarten considers that it is unlikely that the tribunal members 'will be sympathetic to claims that longstanding and widely agreed customs and practices must be jettisoned because of their impact on non-whites and women'.[24] He gives examples of industrial practices that will inevitably hamper attempts by new groups to break into areas of employment from which they have traditionally been excluded; these include the use of friendship networks for filling vacancies, giving preference to workers with union cards or previous experience and the 'last in, first out' principle for redundancies.

Courts are generally most reluctant to interfere with the discretion of the employer. As he is paying the wages, they respect his right to choose the criteria for assessing the value of his employees. Two important equal pay cases before the Court of Appeal were decided against the applicants on the basis of this kind of argument. In the first case the court accepted the management's right to reward employees on the basis of a personalized, subjective assessment scheme which it was impossible to challenge.[25] In the second case the court placed considerable weight on the opinion of the applicant's head of department that full-time teaching experience of less than three years was superior to eight years part-time teaching experience.[26] These decisions are in keeping with the employer's general right to control and discipline his workers. The woman who complained of sex discrimination when she was dismissed for wearing trousers lost her case. The Employment Appeal Tribunal held that an employer is entitled to a large measure of discretion in controlling the image of his establishment, including the appearance of staff.[27]

Finally, the superior courts are impatient with what they regard as trivial matters. When Lord Denning reversed a decision of the Employment Appeal Tribunal and declared against the man who complained that the women were allowed to leave work five minutes earlier than the men,[28] he did so on three counts. First, he held that the 'natural' differences of sex must be regarded even in the interpretation of an Act of Parliament. Second, he argued that arrangements made in the interests of safety and good administration are not infringements of the law even though they may be more favourable to one sex. Thirdly, he added that even if he were wrong on the first two counts he would apply the *de minimis* principle; that is, he considered the matter too trivial to warrant legal intervention. His first two arguments are a wilful disregard for the law, as the drafter of the legislation, F. Bennion, pointed out in an angry letter to *The Times* (15 July 1977). His third argument clearly indicates that he does not consider there to be an issue of principle at stake.

The administrative arm of enforcement

Although some of the barriers to successful litigation could be removed (Coussins 1977), many severe limitations on this method of enforcing anti-discrimination laws would remain. In recognition of some of these problems the legislation also set up administrative bodies, the Equal Opportunities Commission (EOC) and the Commission for Racial Equality (CRE). Rather than relying on individual complainants to come forward, the commissions are given the task of working towards the elimination of discrimination and promoting equality of opportunity generally. To achieve this end, they are permitted to undertake formal investigations, to demand oral and written evidence and serve a non-discrimination notice on the employer if they find evidence of discrimination. These are weapons with which the Commissions can systematically seek out and destroy the main sources of discrimination. The EOC has undertaken only two investigations. The only completed one, into the Tameside eleven-plus selection arrangements, found no case of discrimination against girls. The Electrolux investigation has been going on for two years without any sign of reaching a conclusion. The CRE has been considerably more active and has some thirty investigations under way, but their experience suggests that the 'immense powers' that worry Lord Denning are not so formidable. Formal investigations and non-discrimination notices are subjected to legal restrictions designed to safeguard employers' rights. The CRE are in the process of issuing their first non-discrimination notices. The first one was against a Birmingham night club who immediately announced that they had no intention of changing their policies. The outcome of such conflicts will be crucial for the future of the legislation. Experience suggests that the Commission may find itself isolated, with the court taking a sympathetic attitude towards the employers 'bullied' by the mighty Quango.

The EOC chairman expresses her dilemma in these terms:

> The EOC has all the time to walk a tight-rope between the demands of the long-standing campaigners for women's equality . . . and the majority of the population who are fearful . . . of busybodying. [EOC press notice, 8 February 1979]

The long-standing campaigners are not represented on the EOC, although it increasingly takes over the role of official spokesman for their viewpoint (Byrne and Lovenduski 1978). Both Commissions are composed of the usual political, industrial and geographical mix which accords with the government's view of the range of legitimate interests that require representation. This is the recipe for successful containment, not revolutionary change.

Conclusion

The state has made a moral commitment to combating discrimination because neutrality is no longer possible but it is a weak moral commitment. The state is vulnerable because it cannot avoid intervention but at the same time it dare not intervene effectively. Its own legal institutions and ideology can be used against it to expose these contradictions. As women and racial minorities lag so far behind in the achievement of basic bourgeois rights, strategies should include seeking the maximum possible benefits from the legislation and pressing for an extension of its more radical features. The two Commissions can be supported whenever they adopt aggressive positive policies but challenged when they misuse their discretionary powers.[29] The legal and administrative institutions of the state will perform their conformative role too complacently if they are allowed to retain the initiative without such conflicts. At the same time, it is important to disperse the cloud of mystification surrounding the legislation, so that it is clearly recognized as part of the processes of containment. It is on the statute book in order to protect, not threaten, the fundamental structures of capitalist society, and therefore cannot by itself constitute the vehicle for achieving a non-racist, non-sexist society.

10 Popular justice, dual power and socialist strategy

Boaventura de Sousa Santos

It is almost a commonplace to say that there is no Marxist theory *of* law, though it is less commonly acknowledged that there are a few Marxist theories *against* law, the most famous one being Pashukanis'. The reason usually invoked for this theoretical deficit has been that neither Marx nor Engels devoted more than scattered and sketchy (non-systematic) references to the question of law in capitalist society. It seems to me, however, that in view of the mutual implications of theoretical and strategic issues in Marxism, the *material* reason of this theoretical deficit has to be found in the fact that neither of the dominant strategies in the working-class movement up until now has necessitated a Marxist theory of law. Leaving aside for the moment the problems related to the distinction between reform and revolution, we can *grosso modo* identify two main strategies: the revolutionary (insurrectionary) strategy, the most coherent and global formulation of which is Lenin's, was the official line of the Third International particularly until 1934/35 (the beginning of the Popular Front period); the reformist strategy, for which Eduard Bernstein provided the most eloquent theoretical reconstruction, corresponded to the practice of the parties of the Second International till its collapse in 1914 and became the official line of the socialist movement after the split of the working-class movement between the socialists and the communists in 1922-3.

The revolutionary strategy aims at destroying the capitalist state by means of a global confrontation that may include violence, substituting for it the dictatorship of the proletariat, a new state form created in the struggle by the working class and adequate to the performance of the tasks of the transitional period before communism. Law does not play any important role within this strategy. As an instrument of capitalist domination bourgeois law has to be fought against as much as the bourgeois state. Indeed the third condition of admission to the Communist International stated that 'the communists can have no confidence in bourgeois law'. In view of this there is no need to theorize in detail the possible use of legality by the working class; on the contrary, the Marxist theory of law, if one is produced at all, must reveal the negativity of law *vis-à-vis* the revolutionary movement. In this sense the Marxist theory of law becomes a Marxist theory against law. The best example is Pashukanis's general theory of law, no matter how crucial his insights may be for the elaboration of a Marxist theory of law adequate to our current strategic needs.

Unlike the revolutionary strategy, the reformist strategy is based on the extensive use of law, since the gradual transformation of the capitalist state into a socialist state is to be achieved by means of social reforms brought about within the established constitutional framework. But the use of law presupposes a sophisticated Marxist theory of law only if and when the gradual transformation of the state is conceived of as a gradual destruction of the capitalist state form and the gradual emergence of a new socialist state form. However, the reformist strategy in practice has tended to *forget* its strategic goal – i.e. the transformation and destruction of the capitalist state – concentrating rather on social reforms, which in the end have, in fact, stabilized the capitalist state. In view of this practice, the use of law, far from presupposing a Marxist theory of law, is most adequately guided by the bourgeois theories of law which, with their vast, rich, and sophisticated body of legal thought, always reproduce the capitalist state. The impasse of the Marxist theory of law is best illustrated by the work of Karl Renner. Renner's Marxist critique of the law of property ends up in the apologetic view of the state stabilizing changes in the capitalist law of property at the beginning of the twentieth century.

To my mind a sophisticated Marxist theory of law is only needed by a working-class strategy based on the supercession of the reform/revolution dichotomy as historically known. This implies the non-bourgeois use of bourgeois legality and the creation and expansion of instances of alternative socialist legality. Though embryonic, hesitant, and reversible, there are signs of a strategic reorientation in this direction throughout Europe, both West and East, since the early 1960s. Such reorientation is related to three main factors. First, the profound changes in the process of capitalist accumulation and in the structure of the capitalist state after the Second World War. Second, the horrifying experience of fascism and the consequent relegitimation of the democratic rule in general. Third, the ever more visible degenerative features of state socialism in the USSR and the states under its influence and the consequent re-evaluation of the rather ambiguous role of the USSR in the European working-class movement since the foundation of the Third International, particularly after Stalin's takeover.

The theoretical foundation for such strategic reorientation in the field of law and the state must be based upon three preliminary tasks. First, to eliminate some time-honoured pseudo-theoretical constructs such as the topographic metaphor (base/superstructure) and replace it by a more analytical, more consciously materialistic model of determination, which will also have to be more sensitive to strategy and tactics. (In this connection Wright (1978) offers some potentially fruitful lines of theoretical progress.) Second, it must accept the challenge to re-read, re-think, and re-evaluate the period of the European working-class movement between 1890 and 1923, more or less the period of the Second International and the founding years of the Third International, in the course of which the most profound, rich, open-ended debate within Marxism took place. The names of four people emerge, amongst others, as of crucial importance for our theoretical undertakings, particularly in their least well-known (rarely translated?) works. I mean Karl Kautsky, Karl Korsch, Rosa Luxemburg and Eduard Bernstein; especially the last two. It may be surprising, even shocking that these two names are thus brought together, given the widely known fact that they belonged to opposite wings of the German social democracy. Eighty years later, however, we must read and evaluate them in view of our struggles, not theirs. Besides, no matter how much did actually separate them, they did share some important views: the intimate link between democracy and socialist struggle (starting inside the working-class party) and the global democratization of social and political life in socialist society.

Finally, the third preliminary task consists in reanalysing concrete revolutionary struggles, some of which are of the insurrectionary type, and in considering the empirical concepts emerging from them in view of their possible use, in transformed versions and under very different conditions, in future struggles. In this essay I will concentrate on this last task, using as an example the experiences of dual power in some modern revolutions from the Russian revolution in 1917 to the Portuguese revolution in 1974-5. I will start by commenting on Lenin's and Trotsky's conceptualizations of dual power. I will then explore some possible lines of theoretical reconstruction of the concept of dual power with specific focus on law and judicial action. Finally I will refer to some strategic and tactical uses of dual power in law and justice, both in revolutionary and non-revolutionary situations.

The discussion of dual power in Lenin and Trotsky

For Lenin dual power is 'the striking feature' of the Russian revolution: 'it is the main peculiarity of our revolution, a peculiarity urgently requiring the most thoughtful analysis' (1960). It consists

> in the fact that side by side with the Provisional Government, the government of the *bourgeoisie*, there has developed *another* government, weak and embryonic as yet, but undoubtedly and actually existing and growing government – the Soviets of Workers' and Soldiers' Deputies.

To the question of the class composition of this other government, Lenin answers that 'it consists of the proletariat and the peasantry (clad in army uniform)'. As to the political nature of this government Lenin goes on to say:

> It is a revolutionary dictatorship, i.e., a power based on outright revolutionary seizure, on the direct initiative of the masses from below and *not on a law* enacted by a centralized state power. It is an entirely different power from that generally existing in parliamentary bourgeois-democratic republics of the usual type still prevailing in the advanced countries of Europe and America. This circumstance is often forgotten, often not given enough thought, yet it is the crux of the matter. *This* power is of *the same type* as the Paris Commune of 1871. Its fundamental characteristics are:
>
> 1) The source of power is not a law previously discussed and enacted by parliament, but the direct initiative of the people from below, in their localities – outright 'seizure', to use a current expression;
> 2) The direct arming of the whole people in place of the police and the army, which are institutions separated from the people and set against the people;

order in the state under such a power is maintained by the armed workers and peasants *themselves*, by the armed people *itself*;

3) Officials and bureaucrats are either similarly replaced by the direct rule of the people themselves or at least placed under special control; they not only become elected officials, but are also *subject to recall* at the first demand of the people; they are reduced to the position of single agents; from a privileged group occupying 'posts' remunerated on a high 'bourgeois' scale, they become workers of a special 'branch' and remunerated at a salary *not exceeding* that of a competent worker. [Lenin 1960, p. 50]

Writing in April, Lenin acknowledges that the soviets are an embryonic and incipient proletarian state form. Moreover, owing to the influence of petit-bourgeois elements (Mensheviks and Social Revolutionaries) in the soviets, the latter, having entered into an agreement to support the Provisional Government, are in fact 'voluntarily surrendering its own supremacy to the bourgeoisie'. These extremely peculiar circumstances of the Russian revolution, 'unparalleled in history', have led to the '*interlocking of two dictatorships*: the dictatorship of the bourgeoisie and the dictatorship of the proletariat and the peasantry'. But

there is not the slightest doubt that such an 'interlocking' cannot last long. Two powers cannot exist in a state. One of them is bound to disappear . . . . The dual power merely expresses a *transitional* phase in the development of the revolution, when it has gone farther than the ordinary bourgeois-democratic revolution, but has *not yet reached* a 'pure' dictatorship of the proletariat and the peasantry. [Lenin 1960a, pp. 58-9]

Trotsky's characterization of dual power is simultaneously broader and more optimistic. Unlike Lenin, Trotsky (1963, p. 101) sees the situation of dual power as a 'distinct condition of social crisis, by no means peculiar to the Russian revolution of 1917, although there most clearly marked out'. After specifying that there is no question of dual power where the ruling class power is divided between two of its factions such as the German Junkers and the bourgeoisie (whether in the Hohenzollern form or the republic), Trotsky adds that the dual power

does not presuppose – generally speaking, indeed, it excludes – the possibility of a division of the power into two equal halves or indeed any formal equilibrium of forces whatever. It is not a constitutional, but a revolutionary fact. It implies that a destruction of the social equilibrium has already split the state superstructure. It arises where the hostile classes are already each relying upon essentially incompatible governmental organization – the one outlived, the other in process of formation – which jostle against each other at every step in the sphere of government. The amount of power which falls to each of these struggling classes in such a situation is determined by the correlation of forces in the course of the struggle.

The situation of dual power may lead to a civil war, in which case the duality of power assumes a territorial expression and thus becomes even more visible. 'But before the competing classes and parties will go to that extreme . . . they may feel compelled for quite a long time to endure, and even to sanction a two power system.' Trotsky then illustrates the situation of dual power with references to the English, French, German, and Russian revolutions. As to the Russian revolution the peculiarity of its dual power lies in that, contrary to the previous revolutions, 'we see the official democracy consciously and intentionally creating a two power system, dodging with all its might the transfer of power into its own hands'. Thus dual power starts in a concealed form and comes to the surface only when the bolsheviks displace the compromisers at the head of the soviet. Trotsky concludes that

> in the immeasurably greater maturity of the Russian proletariat in comparison with the town masses of the older revolutions, lies the basic peculiarity of the Russian revolution. This first led to the paradox of a half-spectral double government, and afterwards prevented the real one from being resolved in favour of the bourgeoisie.

The differences between Trotsky and Lenin on the question of dual power may probably be traced back to the different contexts of their writing: on the one side, a political statement written in 1917 and on the spot; on the other side, an historical analysis written between 1930 and 1932 in Prinkipo island. In any case their writings have much in common and reveal the following general features of dual power:

1 It occurs in a revolutionary crisis, in a situation of intense class struggle in which the question of the radical transformation of society becomes a 'practical', 'realistic', political question;
2 there is a plurality of centres of political power arising from contradictions between competing classes and not from divisions within any of the classes in the struggle;
3 the source of legitimacy of the emerging (proletarian) class power is not law issued by a centralized government but rather 'revolutionary legality' or, as Lenin puts it, 'outright revolutionary seizure on direct initiative of the masses from below'. This initiative may be so 'direct' that it may even surprise the 'professional revolutionaries' for, as Lenin (1960, p. 50) candidly confesses, 'we must know, for instance, how to supplement and amend our old Bolshevik "formulas" for, as it proved, they were sound in general, but their concrete realization turned out to be different. *Nobody* hitherto thought, or could have thought, of dual power'.
4 the differences in social support and institutional development between the two polar powers may be more or less notorious and are always changing;
5 the powers in conflict find themselves in a situation of global confrontation or, at least, they tend to such a situation, since in the initial stages insufficient class consciousness or other factors may lead the emerging power to compromises and concessions;
6 the two powers represent not only contradictory class interests, but also contradictory state forms, a parliamentary democracy versus a Paris Commune type of government;
7 the situation of dual power is always an unstable one, because the division of power it entails tends to be resolved in favour of one of the classes in the struggle.

Trotsky's conversion of dual power into a universal dimension of a revolutionary situation has contributed to a fuller understanding of other twentieth century revolutions: in Germany 1917-23 (Broué 1971), in Spain 1936-9 (Broué and Témime 1972) and in various countries in Latin America (Zavaleta 1974). It is now imperative that we revise the concept of dual power so as to enrich its analytical content and adapt it to the strategic prospects of socialist revolution in Europe today. With this in mind I propose now to discuss the issue of dual power in the context of the Portuguese revolution 1974-5.

Popular justice in the context of dual powerlessness in Portugal

This is not the place to give a full account of the Portuguese revolution. It is even highly probable that the historians of the future will deny the status of a true revolution to the Portuguese events of 1974-5 as they have done with the German revolution of November 1918 (Broué 1971).

The Portuguese revolution began as a military revolt led by a sizeable group of democratic and anti-fascist young officers, who were eager to put an end to the colonial war. In relation to the political project at home the programme of the Movement of the Armed Forces (MFA) was straightforward in spite of its generalities: immediate destruction of the fascist features of the state apparatus; elections for a constitutional assembly where parliamentary democracy would be restored; political pluralism and autonomy of working-class organizations; an anti-monopolist economic policy aiming at a more equitable distribution of wealth. Concerning the colonial question, however, the programme was rather ambiguous. It called for a political settlement in a large Portuguese space. Such ambiguity was the inevitable consequence of the fact that the young officers had felt compelled to compromise with Spinola who, excepting Costa Gomes, was the only general who had had conflicts with Caetano's regime. To compromise was then considered important, not only to minimize the possibility of resistance by some military units loyal to the old regime, but also to avoid any attempt at a unilateral declaration of independence by the white population in the colonies, particularly in Angola.

Spinola clearly represented the interests of monopoly capital while the young officers of the MFA were granted from the start a tremendous popular support by the working class and large sectors of the petit-bourgeoisie. This popular mobilization (economic *and political* strikes broke out throughout the country) was instrumental in bringing about Spinola's total defeat, as well as the neutralization of the rightist elements inside the MFA and the political radicalization of its more leftist elements. This fact plus the firm rejection by the leading liberation movements of any Spinola-type solution for the colonial question were the main preconditions for what would become the most remarkable decolonization process of modern times – a decolonization process almost totally free from neocolonialist features.

The qualitative changes in the political process took place after March 1975 when Portuguese society underwent a revolutionary crisis: extensive nationalization of the industry; total nationalization of the banking and insurance system; land seizures in Alentejo; house occupations in large cities; workers' councils; self-management in industrial and commercial enterprises abandoned by their former owners; co-operatives in industry, commerce, and agriculture; neighbourhood associations; people's clinics; and cultural dynamization in the most backward parts of the country. None of these measures, taken individually, challenged the capitalist foundations of society or the class nature of state power. However, all these measures taken together – along with the internal dynamics of working-class mobilization and of popular initiative, the generalized paralysis of the state apparatus and the developing conflict within the armed forces – did indeed bring about a revolutionary crisis. But on no occasion was there a situation of dual power conceived of as a situation of 'global confrontation' between 'two dictatorships'. Although a full analysis of this fact is still to be made it seems to me that one of the major causative factors lies in the very nature of the events that led to the revolutionary crisis. It all started as a *military* revolt, that is, a revolt from above, originating within the state apparatus itself. The aim was to destroy the fascist state power but indeed only the most explicitly fascist features of the state were destroyed, such as the political police, political courts and prisons, the one-party system, and paramilitary fascist militias. The state apparatus was otherwise kept intact, with its fifty-year heritage of authoritarian ideology, recruitment, training, and practice. Though under popular pressure there were some purges of personnel in public administration and industry, they were rather limited in number, often opportunistic and, in some crucial sectors of the state apparatus, such as the administration of justice, virtually non-existent. In any case, purges were always restricted to personnel and never reached the structures of the state power. As to the two branches of the repressive state apparatus – the police (PSP and GNR) and the armed forces – the situation was even more striking. Since the police offered no resistance to the young officers of the MFA, there was no need to dismantle or even restructure the organization; only the top officers were replaced. As to the armed forces, there is no question but that they were shaken to their roots; but precisely because the revolt originated in their ranks and the political process was kept under military leadership, the armed forces felt globally re-legitimized and postponed any profound internal restructuring. This explains, among other things, why the soldiers' committees appeared very late in the process and without internal dynamics.

In sum, the state apparatus, once cleansed of its distinctly fascist features, did not collapse. It rather suffered a generalized paralysis. Because the political events had started inside it, it was 'relatively easy' to bring about the paralysis of the bourgeois state power. In this sense there was no bourgeois rule. But neither, and for similar reasons, was there a proletarian rule. In this connection the role played by the big working-class parties (PS and PCP) must be briefly mentioned. Having gained considerable influence in the state apparatus and inside the armed forces after March 1975, the PCP, the only political organization worth the name, looked rather suspiciously on the spontaneous mobilization and creative organizations of the working class, both at the point of production and at the point of reproduction. Under the mystifying argument that the enemy had already been destroyed by the nationalization of monopoly capital and that the sector of the MFA then in power would, if supported, carry out the class interests of the proletariat, the PCP always favoured policies inside the state apparatus and rejected as adventuristic the idea of revolutionary legality and of popular power. The socialist party, of recent formation and heterogeneous composition, resented the influence of the communists in the state apparatus and rejected as authoritarian any political form but parliamentary democracy. Drawing its support from the bourgeoisie, sectors of the petit-bourgeoisie and of the working class, who resented the power politics and the arrogance of the communists, the socialist party soon became the opposition party *par excellence*. As in Germany in 1918, the socialists became the leading party in a broad coalition of bourgeois and conservative political forces which, as the recent developments reveal, subsequently managed to subalternize them.

It may be said that the same process that had quite rapidly obtained the suspension or neutralization of bourgeois rule, had at the same time prevented proletarian rule from emerging in its own name. This was less a situation of dual power than a situation of dual powerlessness, as I would characterize it; a situation which was resolved in favour of bourgeois rule in November 1975. The Portuguese revolution shows, indeed, as one of its striking features, that the bourgeois state may undergo a generalized paralysis for an extended period of time without coming to a collapse. On the contrary, it remains intact as a kind of reserve state only to be reactivated if and as soon as the relations of forces change in its favour.

Within the global situation of dual powerlessness I have just described, restricted forms of dual power emerged in specific areas of social life and in specific sectors of the state apparatus. One of such situations of dual power took place in the judicial apparatus and assumed the form of popular justice. I have elsewhere described and analysed in detail the major instances of popular justice in Portugal between March and November 1975. The most publicized case, though not the most characteristic one, was the Diogo case. José Diogo, a rural worker in Alentejo, was accused of having murdered a big landowner, his former *patrão* and for many years president of the municipality. In view of the increasing popular solidarity for Diogo the case was transferred from the local court to the Lisbon court, since 'the emotional climate around the case', in the state attorney's words, did not allow for an 'independent and orderly' administration of justice. From the Lisbon court, and for the same reasons, the case was again transferred, this time to Tomar, a small town some 100 kilometres north of Lisbon. A big political rally was held there on the day of the trial, and close to one thousand people jammed the area in front of the court-house. For reasons that were not clear, Diogo was not brought to the court, and the 'official' trial was postponed. Thereupon José Diogo was tried, on the steps of the state court-house, by a self-appointed popular jury of industrial and rural workers. After many people spoke up, particularly amongst the rural workers, denouncing the despotic rule of large landowners in Alentejo as well as the oppressive conditions under which the rural proletariat were forced to live, the *latifundiário* was 'posthumously condemned' by the jury 'for having oppressed and exploited' the people of Alentejo; at the same time, after considering the extreme conditions under which José Diogo had acted, the same jury acquitted him; his action, however, being an individual action, could not be considered, nor justified, as a revolutionary action. This was a highly confused situation: José Diogo, though in preventive detention, could not be brought to court; on the other hand, against previous rulings, bail was granted and raised in a few hours.

Most of the other popular courts dealt with housing problems. The best known of these cases was the Maria Rodrigues case. Maria Rodrigues was illegally occupying a house. Suit was brought against her by her landlady and she was to be tried in November 1975. The secretariat of the revolutionary residents' commissions, acting in her name, boycotted the trial and organized a popular jury composed of twenty-eight delegates of several residents' commissions. This popular jury met in the inner courtyard of the state court-house and, after long hours of discussion on the housing question, Maria Rodrigues was granted the right to stay in the house she had occupied. Vigilance committees were then organized to prevent any attempt at eviction by the police.

All these cases are very embryonic, poorly-organized forms of popular justice, hence of dual power in the judicial area. Nevertheless they point to a proletarian revolutionary legality and legal form. The normative boundaries of the cases are transformed so that the class content of the dispute – always mystified by bourgeois legality – becomes apparent. The object of the dispute is thus immensely expanded and the gap – characteristic of bourgeois legal process – between the 'real' dispute and the processed dispute is eliminated. Moreover, the class relations in the dispute are inverted. The popular jury, organized on the basis of class position rather than abstract citizenship, assumes itself as the justice of the oppressed classes; accordingly, the defendant in the state court becomes the plaintiff in the popular court and vice versa. The effect of isolation – also characteristic of bourgeois justice – disappears since both parties come to court not as abstract individuals but rather as class members. The trial form is retained but not only the jury structure is changed but also the rules defining the relevant issues are completely subverted. The actions of José Diogo and Maria Rodrigues are contextualized in the history of class struggle in Alentejo and in urban ghettos respectively, and are evaluated differently in the light of their different meaning in that struggle. There is no strict distinction between substantive and procedural issues; the question of the fairness of the trial is mediated by the recognition that the dispute as brought to court is the tip of the iceberg, a small detail of a much broader class struggle in which the class enemy can never be presumed not guilty. There is neither a professional monopolization of the legal process nor technical expropriation of legal language and discourse.

Since these restricted instances of dual power, as many others in other areas of social life (industry, education, prisons, etc.), were taking place in a situation of global dual powerlessness, they were always fragmentary actions and as such they could not be reproduced in a cumulative way. As there was no unified revolutionary strategy to bring about proletarian rule in its own name, the dual power initiatives could not grow into a global confrontation with bourgeois state power. State power was paralysed but virtually undivided. This explains why the state judicial apparatus never lost control of either the Diogo or Rodrigues cases. Indeed, after 25 November, 1975, when the conditions for active bourgeois rule were restored, the two cases were tried and both defendants were found guilty. And though I will not go into that here, it is highly debatable whether the specific instances of popular justice in the specific conditions of the Portuguese revolution played a positive or a negative role.

Another alternative legality: squatter settlements in Rio

The cases of popular justice in the Portuguese revolution make a two-fold contribution to revolutionary strategy. First, they show that in order to eliminate the historical aberrations involving the idea of popular justice, the latter must be conceptualized as dual power in the judicial function, as working-class justice versus bourgeois-class justice. Second, they illustrate one of the possible ways in which the concept of dual power must be transformed in order to increase its analytical and strategic value. Once the specific conditions of the revolutionary crisis do not permit a global confrontation with the old state power, it may be possible and correct to create restricted or sectionalized forms of dual power to operate in specific areas of social life or in specific sectors of state action.

It is, however, possible to think of other ways in which the concept of dual power may be transformed to fit the complex diversity and dynamics of the socialist struggle in our time. In the cases presented so far the dual power takes place in a revolutionary crisis and, though in a sectionalized version, it embodies a situation in which antagonistic powers confront each other, that is, a situation of inter-class conflict. It is conceivable, however, to use the concept of dual power – in a weakened but nonetheless valuable form – in non-revolutionary situations, embodying complementary or parallel, rather than confrontational, powers and in which, on the surface at least, intra-class conflicts are dealt with. I will try to demonstrate such a possibility – restricted for the present purposes to dual power in law and justice – by referring to the judicial functions performed by residents' associations in squatter settlements throughout Latin America and elsewhere, and presenting as an example the case of the residents' association in a squatter settlement in Rio (Brazil), which I have studied extensively.

Pasargada, as in my study I call this *favela*, is a large old squatter settlement in Rio. The land which the founders of the settlement first occupied in the early 1930s was at the time privately owned and is now state property. For some years the community has been electing a residents' association (RA) formally in charge of representing the community interests before the various state agencies, particularly in relation to public services and facilities, and of promoting peaceful interaction inside the *favela*. My research, however, has revealed that beyond these functions – which are of course poorly performed, given the over-exploitation of the masses, the repressive legislation and the fascist political rule in today's Brazil – the residents' association has gradually become a legal forum, an instrument of dispute prevention and dispute settlement inside Pasargada. In this capacity the RA performs two kinds of functions: ratification of legal relationships and settlement of disputes arising from them. The legal relationships usually originate in contracts (sales, leases, etc.) involving property and property rights to land, shacks, houses and parts of houses and shacks, but may also consist of relationships of a public-law type involving the rights of the community as a whole *vis-à-vis* its individual members.

When, for instance, residents want to draft a contract they may come to the RA to see the *presidente*. Usually they are accompanied by relatives, friends or neighbours, some of whom will serve as witnesses. The parties explain their intentions to the *presidente*, who raises questions about the nature of the contract and its object until he is satisfied. Then the contract is written down and filed. The RA's intervention, which I call ratification, is a very subtle and complex process by means of which the legal relationship between the parties is provided with an autonomous source of security. When a dispute breaks out between two neighbours, the RA may be called upon to settle it, in which case a process is set in motion leading to the discussion of the case by the parties and neighbours in a hearing presided over by the *presidente*.

I have analysed in detail the normative and rhetorical structures of these legal processes, which I have called Pasargada law, and which cover a very intense and complex legal interaction outside the state legal system. In Pasargada, the state legal system is called the asphalt law. Pasargada law is obviously valid only inside the community, since from the point of view of state legality all the transactions based upon land illegally occupied have no legal validity. Pasargada's normative structure is thus based on the *inversion of the basic norm (grundnorm)* of property by means of which the legal status of Pasargada land is consequently inverted: from illegal occupation into legal possession. Once this inversion takes place the property norms of the asphalt law can be selectively borrowed by Pasargada law and applied inside the community. Indeed the principle of private property and the legal consequences it entails are as respected in Pasargada law as in Brazilian official law. Legal discourse in Pasargada relies on a very rich and elaborate legal rhetoric and I would suggest that the studies of legal rhetoric in Western philosophy, particularly in German legal philosophy, have a great deal to say to Pasargadian legal reasoning. Comparing Pasargada legal reasoning with the prevalent legal reasoning in modern capitalist state justice it can probably be shown that in a given legal apparatus the wealth of legal rhetoric tends to increase as the amount of coercive powers decreases, and vice-versa. And indeed Pasargada law is a very embryonic and precarious form of legality and the RA coexists with other power centres in the community. It is also a very accessible, participatory, and non-professionalized legal setting. The distinction between procedural and substantive questions is not rigidly established and mediation is the dominant model of dispute settlement.

However precarious, Pasargada law represents an alternative legality to the bourgeois state legality and, as such, it also represents the exercise of an alternative form of power, however weak. Since Pasargada law does not claim validity or enforcement outside the community and merely aims at solving intra-class conflicts, the two legal powers are not in confrontation. They are rather parallel or even complementary. In this weakened form the concept of dual power could, I suggest, be applied to the unequal relation between Pasargada law and asphalt law. The objection might be raised that this is an illegitimate extension of the concept of dual power since Pasargada law merely prolongs the state law and is probably highly functional for the latter's overall objectives of domination. Though I partially grant that, I would like to counter-argue with three remarks.

First, by producing an alternative legality, Pasargada law attempts to neutralize or to counteract the fact that in capitalist societies (at least in peripheral ones) the working classes have no access, as proprietors, to social relations based on property, because their rights are declared to be illegal by the official legal system. It should be borne in mind that though in terms of their surface structure the conflicts dealt with by Pasargada law are created, discussed, and solved as intra-class conflicts, in terms of their deep structure, however, they are reflexive expressions of a much broader inter-class conflict. And this duality is ever present in Pasargada law, since the security of legal relations is a guarantee of the internal development of the community. Indeed the greater the internal development of the community the lesser the likelihood that the bourgeois interests in urban land speculation will pressure the state to remove the community to the outskirts of the city.

Second, Pasargada law centres around a community-based *elected* organization, the Residents' Association. Despite the limitations of the electoral process, Pasargada law thus offers an alternative democratic administration of justice, all the more remarkable because it takes place at the fringes of a fascist state. It performs, if no other, an educative function and potentially at least may contribute to raise the class consciousness of the urban working class living in squatter settlements.

Third, Pasargada law is not part of a revolutionary strategy nor does it take place in a revolutionary situation. On the contrary it operates under very difficult conditions of struggle. And in view of such conditions it may be argued that a complementary or parallel dual power is the necessary prehistory of a confrontational dual power.

Conclusion

I have explored in this essay some possible ways of expanding the concept of dual power with specific reference to the judicial functions of the state apparatus. I do not claim to have been exhaustive. On the contrary, I am fully aware that between the two extreme instances analysed here – popular courts and Pasargada law – there are an infinite number of intermediate cases. As an example I would only mention the neighbourhood courts organized in Santiago squatter settlements during the Allende government and with his support. Considering the reciprocal implications of theoretical and strategic questions in Marxism, the conceptual work must take into account the ever changing conditions of socialist struggle in Europe today, both West and East, both in central and peripherial countries. Whenever the global overthrow of the class state is out of the question a realistic socialist strategy must start from the redefinition of the state itself. The state's non-monolithic and contradictory structure must be studied in detail; the modes of determination that are specific to each of its sectors must be closely analysed; strategies of dual power must then be organized in those sectors where conditions are most favourable.

This strategic orientation does not presuppose the rejection of bourgeois democratic legality and parliamentary democracy wherever they exist. It rather presupposes the possibility of a non-bourgeois use of bourgeois democratic legal and political forms. In the present conditions in South Europe, particularly in Portugal, it seems that it is up to the working class to defend bourgeois democratic legality and parliamentary democracy and to put these bourgeois forms to a non-bourgeois use. Such use involves an unequal struggle but given the contradictory nature of those forms such inequality is itself dynamic and a source of new conditions of struggle. The strategic objective is to raise the contradictions in specific sectors of state action to the point at which bourgeois legal and political forms and instruments become un-reproductive of class domination beyond the limits of controllable dysfunctionality. This is a strategy of maximum risk, as any revolutionary strategy should be.

11 The theory of the state, class struggle and the rule of law[1]

Sol Picciotto

The problem of the rule of law has a powerful political and intellectual fascination. It provides a focus for a range of crucial questions about the nature and relationship of power and order in society. Behind the day-to-day political sloganizing on law and order we find elaborated philosophical and social scientific positions of diverse kinds. In Britain, the recent radical Toryism of Thatcher and Joseph rests, it seems, on the rather less new intellectual positions of F.A. Hayek, the equivalent in legal and constitutional theory of monetarism in economics (Centre for Policy Studies, 1976). Hayek can certainly take the credit for having captured the slogan of the 'rule of law' for the libertarian right. More recently we have seen E.P. Thompson urging forward the forces of the libertarian, perhaps even Marxist, left to regain the banner.

What is more, it seems to be agreed on most sides that this resurgence of debate about law has deep social and economic roots. It clearly takes place within a more general crisis of the state, in the context of a period of economic crisis which became apparent in the 1970s. This has brought into question not only the adequacy of the state's performance of its functions in relation to the economy, but more fundamental questions as to the very form of the state and its limits. To take two major examples: there has been considerable public discussion, in many countries, of the question of terrorism, and of whether the state can continue to act legally and democratically in the face of it; and the trend towards 'corporatism' has also received world-wide debate, also in relation to the question of the survival of the rule of law.

However, it would be mistaken to see such issues in terms of the impact of an external economic crisis upon a formerly stable social order. Rather, the crisis involves a deepening and generalization of underlying tensions which made themselves felt in the various social conflicts that gathered momentum during the years of post-war economic expansion, and which can be seen to be part of a general class movement. While there was still an adequate basis for continued capitalist expansion these conflicts could be swallowed up in one way or another in the process of capital accumulation. The crisis is seen to break out when the contradictions of that process of accumulation become so acute that a new basis for accumulation can only be established after a general social restructuring. The crisis must therefore be seen as being that very social restructuring process (see generally,

Holloway and Picciotto 1977).

The call for the rule of law in such a social crisis expresses either a demand for the application of coercion in social relations, or for the control of such coercion through the 'due process' of law. The coercion is legitimized by being wielded through the state and in the form of law. It is surprising how seldom the debate about law gets beyond this initial ambiguous dichotomy of coercion/legitimacy. It is this ambiguity that enables the rule of law to be used as a slogan which is effectively a call for repression, and also to be attacked as such. Stuart Hall and others have recently contributed an exhaustive account of the ways in which the call for law and order has been used in the recent period in Britain in orchestrating an increasingly repressive response to the crisis (Hall *et al.* 1978). At the same time, the rule of law can be used as an appeal for 'the imposing of effective inhibitions upon power and the defence of the citizen from power's all-intrusive claims' (Thompson 1975, p. 266). Thompson makes the argument that in order to obtain the consent of the ruled, the ruling class is obliged to resort to legitimizing forms such as law, and thereby is obliged either to act justly or be exposed as having fallen short of the standards of justice thus established (see, for example, ibid., p. 263). Perry Anderson has pointed to the Gramscian elements in this argument (1977, p. 7). Stuart Hall and his collaborators work within a theoretical framework explicitly derived from Gramsci. Anderson's own detailed study of Gramsci clearly shows the limitations of the approach to the theory of the state based on the notion of a 'balance between coercion and consent'. Anderson himself concedes that 'the analytic issues with which Gramsci was most concerned in fact need to be reconceptualised within a new order of categories, beyond his binary landmarks' (ibid., p. 26), and that 'the relationship between the two terms [consent and coercion] cannot be grasped by their mere conjunction or addition' (ibid., p. 41). Anderson's own argument, however, scarcely escapes this binary conjunction: he sees bourgeois-democratic power as 'simultaneously and indivisibly *dominated by culture* and *determined by coercion*' (ibid., p. 42). This relegates the confrontation with the coercion of the state to the final insurrectionary situation and puts on the immediate agenda a compromise with bourgeois democracy, which seems to leave out of account any view of the coercive nature of bourgeois-democratic legality. In the case of Thompson, his neo-Gramscian lapses may perhaps be attributed to his overpowering urge to find any stick with which to assault the abstractions of the neo-Marxist structuralists: unfortunately the nearest weapon looks very like a structuralist concept. The main bulk of his own historical work on the other hand makes a great contribution to the theorization of the specific way in which the development of law mediated and contributed to the development of capitalist relations of production (see, for example, Thompson 1976).

A moment's reflection should indeed be enough to convince us that the analysis of law and state power by the mere combination of the contradictory ideas of consent and coercion does not help to explain *what form* of coercion is involved, nor *how* the consent is obtained. We need a different starting-point if we are to try to understand the specific way in which law mediates class relations.

Legal relations and social relations

It is characteristic above all of law and the legal system, probably more than of any other social institution or part of the state apparatus, that it appears to be essentially neutral, an empty vessel that can be filled with whatever content society chooses. So any attempt to understand law as a social relation of class, or power in any sense, must first explain this appearance of neutrality.

Quite clearly it cannot be satisfactorily explained as nothing more than a 'mere mask', an ideological hypocrisy which conceals the reality of class power (although there is a considerable amount of ideological pretence and hypocrisy about the law). It is equally inadequate to see the law simply as an instrument or apparatus manipulated by the ruling class. While obviously factors such as the cultural and ideological background of judges are very relevant, it is inadequate to attribute the class character of a social institution simply to the social origins of those who control it. Most Marxists would agree that revolutionary change entails the transformation of the very character of social institutions such as the state and the legal system, and not simply the replacement of the personnel which operates them. The main limitation of both these approaches (the 'instrumental' and the 'mere mask' or ideological) is that they do not provide a perspective of the class relations embodied in the law itself, but tend to accept the *externality* of class to law. This therefore reinforces the picture of law as a neutral and historically unchanging state apparatus.

The characteristic neutrality of law is generally attributed to its autonomy within capitalist society. In capitalism, social relations are not directly relations of power or force: they appear as the relations of free and equal individuals. In pre-capitalist societies social relations took the form of some sort of social hierarchy, and the government of such a society could consist of commands passed through the hierarchy. Alternatively, in some societies solidaristic groups were able to take decisions regarding social order according to some kind of basic collective process, which however would take account of the different status of groups such as elders, women, etc. In either of these models, the legal and political order of the society is not separate from its social and economic structure. It is under capitalism that a legal order emerges which appears as autonomous. It should be emphasized that this kind of analysis, so far, is by no means confined to the explicitly Marxist approaches, but is fairly common to many social scientific analyses of law. The real issue which divides different approaches is the nature and conditions of the autonomization of law.

We may first of all distinguish what I will call the 'sociological' conceptualization of the autonomy of law. Such an approach is based essentially on the analysis of a sphere of social relations separate from what is designated the 'economic' sphere of production. This results in the abstract analysis of social relations isolated from their roots in production, from the relationship of human society to nature through production. We may take as an example one of the more sophisticated of recent sociological theorists of law, R.M. Unger. In his formulation, legal autonomy is specified as having four different aspects: substantive, institutional, methodological and occupational autonomy. This 'legal order' Unger sees as having 'emerged with modern European liberal society' (1976, pp. 52-4). He states the historical conditions of emergence of such a legal order as being (1) a pluralistic social order, and (2) a dominant natural law ideology (ibid., p. 66 ff.). He categorizes liberal society, and distinguishes it from the tribal and the aristocratic, in terms of the nature and relationships of the social groupings in each. It can be seen quite clearly that he is concerned to analyse social relations in a way that has no explicit relation whatever to production, in the broad sense, to the 'material conditions of life'. Unger does relate his abstract schema to analyses of specific historical examples, as a means of illustrating, testing or refining the initial model. For him, theoretical models are 'ideals as well as descriptions' (ibid., p. 267); but his combination of abstract ideal types and historical descriptions fails to grasp history as an actual process of social change through struggle.

For Marxist approaches, the essential question is to trace the nature of the relationship between law and the 'material conditions of life'. In order to grasp the specific characteristics of order and domination embodied in the form of legal relations in any particular society and epoch, it must be related to the nature and historical development of the relations of production. Very much hangs upon the conceptualization of the 'relations of production'. Lukács has recently re-emphasized that Marx's starting-point is the 'sum total of relations of production'.

> His conclusion, that 'It is not the consciousness of men that determines their being but on the contrary their social being that determines their consciousness', does not reduce the world of consciousness with its forms and contents directly to the economic structure, but rather relates it to the totality of social existence. The determination of consciousness by social being is thus meant in a quite general sense. It is only vulgar materialism (from the period of the Second International through to the Stalin period and its consequences) that made this into a unilateral and direct causal relationship between the economy, or even particular aspects of it, and ideology. [Lukács 1978, p. 32]

Lukács goes on to explain in detail how Marx's dialectical method enables him to mount a sustained critique of bourgeois political economy, which cuts itself off from reality since it has no way of relating the working of the abstract laws of the autonomous sphere of economics to the totality of social existence.

Many of the theories of the Marxist renaissance have sought to escape the vulgar materialist heritage pointed to by Lukács. This has not been a movement simply in ideas. The attempts to recapture a living Marxist theory also stem from the experience of many of the social struggles of the 1960s and 1970s, in which it became clear that class struggle was not confined to the narrow sphere of work. Racial and sexual oppression, struggles over issues broad and narrow, from housing to imperialist exploitation, all called for an analysis which could relate them to the dynamics of capitalism as a total system, yet did not reduce them to mere epiphenomena incidental to the 'real' struggle at the 'point of production'.

It is in this context that we must see the popularity of theories which emphasize the 'relative autonomy' of legal relations, as well as the state, ideology and much else, from capitalist accumulation.

> Hence, even in a social formation over-determined by the laws of motion of capitalist production, the conditions for that production – or what has come to be called *social reproduction* – are often sustained in the apparently 'unproductive' spheres of civil society and the state; and in so far as the classes, fundamentally constituted in the productive relation, also contend over this process of 'social reproduction', the class struggle is present in all the domains of civil society and the state. [Hall *et al.* 1978, p. 202]

In this kind of view the notion of relations of production is limited to the narrow sphere of the direct production of commodities, which Marx called the *immediate process of production*. Yet it runs quite counter to Marx's strong emphasis on the analysis of 'the capitalist process of production . . . seen as a total, connected process, i.e. a process of reproduction' (1976, p. 724). In fact, the explicit distinction made in formulations such as the one quoted above between 'social reproduction' and the 'productive relation' reveals quite clearly the limitations of the neo-Marxist structuralist approaches, whose foremost exponent in the field of the theory of the state has been Poulantzas.

In these theories, in fact, relations of production are seen not as social but as technical or economic. They are 'determinant in the last instance'; class relations are seen as 'rooted' in them, but as actually *constituted* as distributional relations, in a sphere of 'civil society' which is inserted *between* the essentially 'economic' sphere of production and the state (see Clarke 1977). This enables Poulantzas to develop a 'regional' theory of the state which is essentially 'politicist', without however avoiding the ultimate reductionism of economism (see Holloway and Picciotto 1977, 1978). He points the way to the development of an equally abstract theory of law. Since, for him, legal relations are seen as *external* to the relations of production, there is no way in which their contradictory development can be grasped as part of the actual historical development of the capitalist mode of production. Some basic characteristics of bourgeois law can be derived *a priori*: 'The roots of its [capitalist law's] specific features (abstraction, universality, formalism) . . . have to be sought in the social division of labour and the relations of production' (Poulantzas 1978, p. 86). But since this cannot be traced as an actual historical process, it remains a bare abstraction.

An understanding of how law and a legal system which are economically neutral and seem to operate with an independent rationality can nevertheless have a class character cannot therefore start from the notion of 'relative autonomy'. In *Capital* Marx speaks of the need for a scientific analysis of the 'forms of human life' (1976, ch. 1, section 4). This scientific analysis is vital in order to grasp the class nature of social forms in any society, but especially so in capitalist society, since under capitalism the main characteristic of class domination is that it is mediated through commodity exchange. Hence the social character of particular social institutions or forms is concealed by the fetishism of the commodity. Thus the form of appearance of social relations (the forms in which they actually appear) conceals their social character and therefore their content. For example, profit conceals the social nature of the surplus product under capitalism and its source in labour, which under capitalism has the specific class character of surplus-value.

However, Marx emphasizes that while the elucidation of the social content of these forms is necessary in order to understand them, a revolutionary perspective requires a method that can grasp the historical and therefore transitory character of both form and content. Thus he points out that classical political economy had already understood the content of profit as value with its source in labour, but having 'never once asked the question why this content has assumed that particular form' it failed to grasp its historic character (1976, p. 174). The question why is therefore important for Marx because the scientific analysis of social forms is not a merely logical exercise, but a matter of 'reflection *post festum*' on an actual process of history. It is not the case that people bring the products of their labour into relation with each other as values because they see these objects as embodying human labour, but the reverse. There was an actual historical process by which commodity production became dominant (which is still a continuing though ever more contradictory process). It is the actual equation of products in exchange that produces values and thus the equation of human labour. This is the essential materialist basis of the Marxist concept of form, as opposed to the idealism of Hegel, in which 'the genesis and mutation of form is only within the power of the mind' (Sohn-Rethel 1978, p. 17). Hence a Marxist analysis of a particular social form cannot be a purely logical derivation. John Holloway and I have pointed out in relation to the theory of the state the inadequacy of any theory which attempts a simple logical 'derivation' of the state from the capital relation, in whatever way the latter is conceived or understood (Holloway and Picciotto 1977, p. 85; 1978, p. 27).

This point may be illustrated by reference to Balbus's essay (1977). Balbus begins explicitly from the 'logic of capital' and states that he derives the 'logic of the legal form' as a 'homology between the commodity form and the legal form'. Thus the legal form tends to be presented as merely a mystifying fetishism, which mystifies simply because it appears as autonomous, yet one that is internally coherent and without internal contradictions or tendency to crisis. Change is only introduced from outside, by reference to the 'transformation from competitive, laissez-faire capitalism to monopoly, state-regulated capitalism', which 'has resulted in a partial transformation of the content of the homology between economic and political exchange' (1977, p. 586). However, in his closing paragraph he emphasizes that this method of demonstrating structural homologies is only a starting-point, since 'the demonstration of structural or synchronic homologies is not intended as a substitute for an analysis of *praxis* which would serve to reunite structure and history, synchrony and diachrony'. This indicates at least an awareness of the dangers of Hegelian idealism in his method.

A major contribution to the theorization of law as a social form in the development of capitalist production relations was made by the Bolshevik jurist Pashukanis, whose work has recently been revived in discussions in the West (Pashukanis 1978; Arthur 1976). No one is clearer than he that 'Marxist theory considers every social form historically. Consequently it sets itself the task of elucidating those historically given material conditions which brought this or that category into being' (1978, p. 111). However, the limitations of Pashukanis's analysis, in my view, stem from the fact that he confines himself to the analysis of the historical unfolding of the capitalist mode of production at the most general level, namely the full development of commodity production. But commodity production does not become fully developed until labour-power itself also becomes a commodity – that is, when capitalism dominates the social reproduction forces. Although Marx begins with the commodity, the money-form and the general formula for capital, M–C–M, he very soon introduces the unique commodity, labour-power, and goes on to develop his analysis of the expanded reproduction of capital on that basis. This Pashukanis does not do. This does not negate his whole enterprise, since the juridical process which is his main concern does, in its bourgeois form, serve to mediate and confine social relations merely as relations of circulation. So the analysis at the general level of commodity production tells us quite a lot about the forms developed by bourgeois law.

Analysing the development of legal forms

At this point it may be helpful to summarize the argument so far. Since there has been much abstract talk of structure and form, it may help to clarify the argument about the relationship between legal and economic relations to think of it in the context of the key example of the wage–labour relation and the employment contract. (The choice of this example also has disadvantages, notably that it has an obvious economic side whereas other legal relations may not.) The individual, subjective relationship of a particular worker and employer is a microcosm of a social relationship. Legal autonomy means that the law establishes a framework for the regulation of that relationship according to established procedures and an independent set of legal rules. A simple 'instrumentalist' class view would emphasize the class origins of the judges, lawyers and legislators who create and apply the law, and would conclude that they would consequently tend to favour employers, implying that the same system could produce a more fair or just result if controlled by people with a different class background. While clearly there are 'good' and 'bad' judges, this can only be a small part of an explanation of the class nature of law. A neo-Marxist structuralist theory would presumably emphasize that although the economic nature of the wage–labour relation is determinant in the last instance, it is constituted or reproduced as a legal relation in the sphere of civil society. The dynamics of this legal relation must be analysed in their 'relative autonomy', but the roots of its specific features can be traced to the relations of production. The problem is to explain how the 'relatively autonomous' legal logic and procedure can succeed in reinforcing and maintaining the wage–labour relation in a way that is functional for capital.

Form analysis emphasizes that legal relations must be grasped as *part* of social relations as a totality, and their historical development theorized as part of the changes in the social relations of production resulting from the unfolding contradictions and underlying tendencies of the dominant mode of production. However, people's actual relationships in capitalist society are not immediately social: due to the domination of commodity production, social relations are mediated by the exchange of commodities. They therefore appear as fetishized forms: that is, they actually take place in forms which conceal their class nature. People are brought together as 'employees', 'consumers', 'neighbours' because they buy and sell objects (including their own labour-power, which is a rather unique commodity). These are partial and fragmentary relationships, which are reproduced by the underlying process of capitalist accumulation, seen as a contradictory and crisis-ridden process of expanded social reproduction through class struggle. At its most general level, class struggle is the struggle to penetrate and transcend those forms, to restore the humanity to a fetishized society.

The most basic aspect of the fetishization of social relations under capitalism is the separation of the economic and the political and the autonomization of the state (see generally Holloway and Picciotto 1977). Historically this took place on the basis of primary or primitive accumulation of capital by merchants' capital, at a time when the direct relation of exploitation was not yet capitalist wage labour. Thus the first moment of the capitalist state is to *establish and guarantee exchange* as the mediation of production and consumption. This involves the creation and maintenance of individuals as *economic and legal subjects*, the bearers of reified property rights. Thus, as Pashukanis rightly emphasizes, the basic legal category is the legal subject as the bearer of rights and duties (1978, sec. 4). This individual legal subjectivity is enshrined and maintained by legal procedures. A 'right' in bourgeois legal form does not create but fragments class solidarity.

This has been the repeated lesson of many struggles, not least over the last few years in Britain. While the left campaigned successfully against the repressive Tory Industrial Relations Act, it has been largely disarmed by the extensive juridification of the employment relationship by measures enacted by a Labour government on TUC advice. These, by extending legal rights on a large scale ('rights' to compensation on redundancy, against 'unfair' dismissal, to 'equal pay for equal work', etc.) have done much to defuse the collective struggles and strength that brought them about. Substantive gains are achieved through collective struggles building up class solidarity: the channelling of such struggles into the form of claims of bourgeois legal right breaks up that movement towards solidarity, through the operation of legal procedures which recognize only the individual subject of rights and duties. Of course we have learned and must go on struggling to overcome this: in criminal prosecutions through collective defence strategies and solidarity groups; through solidarity tactics in the courtroom or tribunal to try to build a human warmth against the dead hand of legal etiquette and courtroom discipline; in mass campaigns for the assertion or take-up of rights. But these merely enable us to probe the limits of bourgeois law as a social form. To transcend those limits, even to the smallest extent, requires the political perspective of a movement aiming at the total transformation of social relations. This involves a determination to struggle within but also through and beyond those legal forms, or around and in spite of them. It requires, for instance, a determination such as that of the Trico women strikers to organize collectively and continue a campaign of which individual 'cases' are only a part, and in which court judgments, win or lose, affect but do not deflect the strategy. It is particularly difficult to build this kind of campaign around claims of legal rights, even where mass claims are made, because an aggregation of individual claims does not amount to a movement. Thus, for example, campaigns on housing can be undermined by the different legal status of squatters, private tenants, council tenants and owner-occupiers; struggles over factory closures or dismissals can be undermined by the differential rights of individuals to redundancy pay.

Correlative to the legal subject as the individual subject of rights is the principle of individual personal responsibility, which is established as the cornerstone of criminal law. Now, it should be emphasized that the historical struggles for the establishment of the individual as subject of rights, and also as personally responsible for his or her own actions (and nobody else's) were progressive struggles. A right encapsulated in bourgeois legal form is certainly better than no right at all, and individual personal responsibility is certainly better than arbitrary punishment. The point is that under capitalism social 'rights' take this form when enshrined in law, and a struggle for social justice must aim to transcend the limitations of this form if it is to succeed. Nor does it mean that the legal form of 'rights' should be ignored as totally illusory, since that is the form into which social relations are actually reproduced: the task is to surpass it.

As we have indicated, the individual legal subject is essentially the bearer of commodities, the owner of economic assets producing a revenue. Hence the bulk of law is concerned with property. Even aside from substantive law, this characteristic is embedded in the nature of legal procedures. Civil procedure takes the basic form of a private claim by an individual (or aggregation of individuals) which is basically a claim for damages quantified in money. This means that as a procedural requirement, any interest to be thought of in legal terms must be expressed as a commodity. Legally protected interests boil down to the individual's person or property. But even rights in respect of the person are reified: the physical person is considered as an income-producing asset (so it is cheaper to injure a poor person than a rich one); the only non-physical personal interest recognized by English law is 'reputation'. Hence all kinds of needs or demands are forced into the commodity form when put forward as legal rights – for example, proposals to control the extent of corporate and state surveillance tend to be discussed in terms of the right of the individual to 'privacy'. The anomalies it causes may be papered over to some extent by legal devices, but the contradiction runs deep.

Enforcement of legal rules comes to take the form of referral to a process of adjudication, the 'trial' of a 'case'. Again, it is important to emphasize that it was a historical process that produced the form of trial that today seems in its basics to be the essence of rationality. For instance, in English law it was only during the seventeenth century that the accused gained the right to call witnesses, and not until late in the nineteenth century to give evidence in his or her own defence. This of course was part of the process of abstraction of the trial, from being an inquiry by persons involved with an issue by the use of magical or religious ordeal or ritual, to the adversarial contest between competing subjects of right based on formal conventions as to proof of fact and judgment of law. It is in the context of this kind of analysis that we should consider, for instance, the development of the jury, from a pre-capitalist institution of local justice to an abstract mechanism for 'finding the facts' as presented before them and allowed by the rules of evidence and on the basis of the law as ruled by the judge. To try to make of this an instrument for anything that could move towards popular justice would need much more than to ensure that the jury is 'randomly selected' (whatever that may mean; see NCCL 1979): for a start it needs an effort to turn that randomly selected group of stony-faced individuals into an actual collection of human beings, whose job is to look at a human problem. However great an improvement this form of trial is on trial by ordeal, this should not prevent us from trying to grasp its bourgeois characteristics and its limitations.

As has already been mentioned, the development of these basic characteristics of the legal form was part of the historical process of autonomization of the state, which predated the establishment of the capitalist mode of production on the fully adequate basis of 'free' wage labour. This also involved the centralization within society of the power to apply legitimate physical force and its vesting in the state as the abstract representative of social power, that is, class power. The consequent creation of absolutist sovereignties was only slowly, and through struggle, tempered by the whole process of depersonalizing that centralized power: this was the importance of the constitutionalist struggles waged by the bourgeoisie for the 'rule of law'. At the same time, since this was the period of primitive capitalist accumulation, this 'rule of law' exhibited startling contradictions, and this continues to be the case in any society where the moment of primitive accumulation still figures significantly (though overlain by the subsequent development of the movement of capital). Social relations are not yet dominated by the 'equal exchange' characteristic of the 'dull compulsion of economic relations', but by the extensive use of direct compulsion, systematic privilege or bribery, coercive creation of property rights and labour forces, etc. To counter this, the establishment of the legal subject as bearer of rights and duties, the establishment of reified property rights and abstract judicial processes, involves the spectacular demonstration of the supremacy of abstract Law, through the insistence on stern formalism, theatricality, the combination of strict justice with benign mercy, etc. (see generally Hay, in Hay *et al.* 1975).

The establishment of the capitalist mode of production on the basis of 'free' wage labour lays the basis for the liberal moment of the capitalist state. Once the formal subordination of labour to capital is established – that is, the objective and subjective conditions of labour (means of production and means of subsistence) confront labour as capital monopolized by the buyer of labour-power – the worker enters into wage labour on the basis of the 'dull compulsion of economic relations' alone, and not on the basis of any political or social coercion. Production now dominates exchange, which then becomes the sphere of realization in which commodity-capital becomes money-capital and must be returned to the sphere of production in the shortest possible time. The state must now establish the conditions for circulation by guaranteeing and maintaining the *equivalence* of exchange and the reproduction of social relations on the basis of free and equal exchange in the sphere of circulation. But when social relations are viewed from the point of view of *production*, this equality of exchange is seen to be illusory:

> The constant sale and purchase of labour-power is the form; the content is the constant appropriation by the capitalist, without equivalence, of a portion of the labour of others which has already been objectified, and his repeated exchange of this labour for a greater quantity of the living labour of others. [Marx 1976, p. 730]

Hence liberal state forms, which develop to facilitate the free play of 'market' forces on the basis of the equal treatment of free citizens, have at their heart the relation of production that constantly creates inequality and ultimately crisis, in the state form as well as in economic relations.

In the sphere of legal relations, the moment of liberalization involves the movement to *generality of application* of law. As Neumann points out (1957, p. 28), this involves three elements: 'the law must be general in its formulation, its generality must be specific, and it must not be retroactive'. Specificity and non-retroactivity are necessary in order to provide certainty so that individuals may plan their private transactions within the framework of the law. Law therefore provides a predictability which enables individual exchanges to take place. However, this analysis, which is close to a Weberian one, fails to catch the dynamics of the process and its contradictions. There is a constant *tension* between the need for generality of application and the need for precision in formulation, which can be traced back to the contradiction between the *formal* equality of exchanges and their actual content. Liberal legal procedures are continually riven by this contradiction. This contradiction continually emerges *within* legal forms themselves, and not simply as an *external* contradiction between the abstract and formal equality of law and the inequalities of economic relations.

Liberal state forms try to rely on the self-reproduction of social relations. The availability of recourse to law aims to facilitate circulation by preventing breakdown in individual transactions: the parties themselves must carry through or reconstitute the terms of disputed transactions in anticipation of the probable outcome of recourse to the available procedure. The reference of such transactions for judicial adjudication very gradually leads to the elaboration of principles of obligation and liability based on generality of application : 'reasonableness', 'foreseeability', 'consideration', etc. But simultaneously with the development and propagation of this liberal 'rule of law' we see its progressive breakdown and recuperation. The reference of social conflict situations to courts cannot be left to individuals, but is supplemented with the growth of bodies of state officials who can selectively initiate state intervention to impose exchange equivalence. It is significant that this occurs first in the field of 'social welfare', that is in relation to the terms of sale of labour-power, since it is here that, once free of all fetters, the rapaciousness of capital is felt. As we have already pointed out, it is above all the commodity labour-power that cannot be adequately produced on the basis of 'equal' exchange alone (see Aumeruddy *et al.* 1978). It is class struggle that forces on capital even the most basic conditions for social reproduction; and while this simultaneously forces the development of more adequate legal and state forms, at the same time they can only contain the underlying contradictions of capital, at a higher and more acutely contradictory level of development.

Once the bourgeoisie has established its decisive control of parliament, the liberal conflict between generality of application and specificity is increasingly contained by the enactment of specific codes of legislation (Neumann 1957, p. 39). As Neumann points out, this does not develop until after the bourgeoisie has decisively gained control of Parliament. (That this control was not established without an important struggle is shown, for example, in Foster's account [1974, ch. 3] of the fight by the radicals of Oldham to control elections, even based on a limited franchise.) To the extent that this control enables the substantive content of law to be legitimized by its origin in a political institution, the role of judges can be reduced to what Neumann calls the 'phonograph' approach, 'applying the law as it is'. This denial to even judges of any part in making law is part of a general denial of any lawmaking or legitimizing capacity to any force outside parliament. Any deliberate challenge to this exclusive legitimizing authority is met with denunciations of extreme fervour – 'kangaroo courts', 'who is running the country?', etc. But it is also noticeable that where such a challenge manages to develop a significant momentum, there can be pressure to back down so that 'the law should not be brought into disrepute' (for example, of course, the dockers' strike in Britain which finally killed the Tory Industrial Relations Act).

The contradiction between generality of application and specificity is a feature of the liberal rule of law that creates the most mystification. The belief that the law is or should be precise is one that runs very deep; yet so is the equally strong contrary pressure for 'freedom under the law' – the power of the individual to arrange his or her own affairs without 'interference' from specific orders or directions. This contradiction creates a kind of 'porosity' in the juridical law enforcement process, a latitude or leeway of indeterminacy which essentially gives scope for the exercise of social or economic power. Anyone who has tried to define a policeman's legal power of arrest, or experienced the ways in which the legal 'porosity' is exploited in practice will understand this point. It creates the framework for the exercise of the specific form of state power which at the beginning of this essay I pointed out was so badly grasped by the dichotomy of coercion/consent.

The activities of 'law enforcement' officials are structured by this form of generally applicable laws retroactively applied to individual conduct. This mediation of the 'application' of laws is also carried out of course above all by the 'professionals', the lawyers. This raises all the familiar problems of 'access' to the law –

the cost, social and cultural barriers, etc. Seen in this light, the pressure to make the law equally accessible to all is simply a desperate attempt to maintain the credibility of the liberal myths. However, this is not to say that it is not important to *demystify* law, especially to *deprofessionalize* it. Here again we can note the lessons of the past few years of militancy around the law in Britain, and the sharp dichotomy between the line of 'law for the poor' or 'you too have rights' (see, for example, Hodge 1974) and the struggles to work towards a demystification (for example, Release 1978).

It is usual to 'periodize' classical liberalism as corresponding to the heyday of competitive capitalism, usually thought of in terms of Britain in the period roughly 1840 to 1875. Yet in English law liberalization had hardly begun by 1875. This is partly explained by the particular relation in Britain between the juridical process and other parts of the state. It is more important however to try to grasp the periodization in terms of the dynamic movement of the development of the capitalist relations of production, rather than in terms of static 'ideal types'. The formal subjection of labour to capital, as we have seen, lays the basis for the liberal moment, which continues to be a significant element in the social reproduction process dominated by the valorization of capital. But as the capitalist mode of production develops further, new contradictions and new social forms come to the fore, which involve a reformulation of the social structure. From the last decade of the nineteenth century, the increasing domination of monopoly capitalism brings to the fore the complex of contradictions analysed by Marx as the tendency for the rate of profit to fall and its counter-tendencies. These contradictions can no longer be overcome simply by maintaining exchange equivalence in the sphere of circulation, but require increasingly direct intervention to redress imbalances, to create the possibilities of an equivalent exchange, to create the conditions for valorization. This is the response of capital to the increased growth of production on a social scale, the socialization of production.

These underlying tendencies lead through crisis and struggle to the restructuring of the state apparatus, which has meant in the twentieth century the modification of the legal apparatus and its supplementation by new forms. The general codes of the liberal form of law have become the overblown regulatory systems which increasingly require an elaborate bureaucratic apparatus. The old contradiction between generality of application and specificity becomes the conflict between legal certainty and administrative discretion. Compare for instance the general commercial law codes of the nineteenth century, for instance on Sale of Goods, with the modern detailed specification by regulation of what must go into a sausage, etc., etc. The undermining of generality leads to the establishment of specific bureaucratic apparatuses to regulate different areas of social conflict where 'market' principles of allocation break down. The general jurisdiction of courts of law is supplemented by the establishment of specific tribunals, which can work more closely with the bureaucratic apparatus. Formal 'judicial review' of these tribunals serves to maintain the fiction that the universality of law and observance of procedural 'natural justice' are not affected, but this is an increasingly hollow myth.

Even the central areas of private law are increasingly undermined by the need to contain the increasing socialization of the means of production. Thus the principle of individual responsibility and liability, which we have seen is a key concept procedurally as well as ideologically, becomes increasingly undermined, for example by the growth of private and state insurance. Even the institutions of private property are undermined and often reformulated as in shareholder ownership of companies; mortgage, hire-purchase, even leasehold are adapted to give the institutions of finance capital effective control over property legally 'owned' by the purchaser or tenant. The struggle to maintain a role for traditional juridical processes is rent by the contradiction of either on the one hand upholding the increasingly hollow myths of the liberal 'rule of law', or on the other attempting to reform them. For instance the pressure to revitalize the judiciary must attempt to legitimize judicial activism by some kind of view of the judge as 'policymaker' (on the US pattern); but this undermines the established credibility of the delicate balance between parliament and judiciary and opens up the terrible prospect of extraparliamentary lawmaking.

Thus we see that the restructuring of the state apparatus which is part of the general crisis of capitalism creates pressures to break through the limits of the existing forms; yet at the same time, since it is through the state that increasingly the restructuring must take place, state forms themselves become the focus of struggle. The strategy for a working-class movement must be, not to uphold the impossible ideals of the liberal forms of state and the 'rule of law', but to insist on the necessity that it be transcended, in forms which challenge the dominance of capitalist social relations.

Notes

1 Left idealism, reformism and beyond

The following comrades made useful and welcome criticism of the original draft of this article: Freddi Cooke, Glynis Cousin, Bob Fine, Mike Fitzgerald, Victoria Greenwood, Richard Kinsey, Nigel South and Ian Taylor.

1 See Greenwood and Young (1976 and 1979) for a discussion of reformist legislation in the areas of abortion, prostitution, homosexuality and drug use. Taylor (forthcoming) discusses the Labour Party and reformism in the areas of crime and delinquency since the Second World War.

2 See Young (1975) and the introduction to Pearce (1976) for a discussion of the fashion in which the vulgar materialism of criminological positivism was inverted in the 1960s to form the basis of an idealist critique, namely, labelling theory.

3 In the mid 1970s, parallel to left idealism, emerged feminist idealism which involves a very similar series of assumptions. For instance, the discussion of rape involves a conflation of concepts (rape and all heterosexual intercourse), a simple ahistorical causality (patriarchy gives rise to rape) and a belief in a hidden figure which tends towards ubiquity.

4 For an historical example of left idealism see the descriptions of crime in nineteenth-century French workers' newspapers cited in Foucault (1977, pp. 286-92).

5 To be more precise, Lockean contract theory.

6 The most extreme example of this is Gordon (1971) who among other left idealists denies the deterrent effect of prison because of its similarity to life outside.

7 At first sight, it might be supposed that the left-idealist notion of the endemic nature of ruling-class crime contradicts the notion of law as a direct expression of ruling-class interests. But on the contrary: violation by the bourgeoisie of their own rules clearly demonstrates the thesis of the cynical reality behind the universalistic mystification of law.

8 There are precious few comparative examples within advanced capitalist societies; this is why Clinard's book (1978) on Switzerland and Sweden is such a blockbuster. For Switzerland, an eminently capitalist society, with an extremely high immigrant population, inequalities of wealth and a high rate of guns in private hands, has a very low rate of crime. The only comparisons

usually made are with 'socialist' societies where the 'low' rate of crime is seen as a continuing corollary of the capitalism causes crime thesis (for example, Schwendinger and Schwendinger 1975, p. 25).

9 As Corrigan (1977) wittily points out, left functionalism, if it were to follow its own logic, would have to argue that, given that welfare is a ruling-class control device, instead of fighting the cuts in the welfare state, it would be better to welcome them!

10 As Westergaard and Resler point out in a parallel discussion on the causes of poverty (1975, p. 19), such a focus on marginal aetiology detracts from seeing social problems as a product of fundamental imbalances within the total society.

11 The division within reformist thought is between the normal and the determined and this differentiation generates separate social categories: for example, youth, women, men, the aged are each granted a different degree of rationality, crime is contrasted with mental illness, the political criminal is clearly separated out from the 'common' criminal, the sick delinquent distinguished from the youthful experimenter. Once this is achieved the correct mode of intervention is determined by the nature of the categorization. For a discussion of this see Greenwood and Young (1979).

12 This involves a fight on two points: (*a*) against the incorrect use of positivist and classicist measures, that is, against inappropriate treatment and punishment; (*b*) against conservativism (that is, against deterrent measures which violate the classicist principles of bourgeois rights). Reformism, then, is primarily concerned with correctionalism; what form of state intervention will be most effective in controlling crime and deviancy.

Idealism, in contrast, will not admit the determination of an individual's action outside of that accruing from coercion or as a product of mystification. Positivist theory is the arch enemy, in which a peculiar and distinctive form of critique recurs, namely moral futurism: determinist theories are criticized as misguided because they do not grant people the freedom that they *ought* to have. Human freedon is constantly sullied by the machinations of the control apparatus; the fashion in which people's material reality impinges upon them outside of the impact of the overt agencies of control is neglected.

13 This is not, of course, to suggest that this process can be explained in terms of purposive intent on the part of the ruling class (although no doubt some element of this occurs) nor that the institutions involved are 'explained' by their functional input to the system.

14 I have deliberately phrased this exercise on a level of simplicity and without historical specificity. At the very least one should note the presence in modern societies of intermediate layers between the working class and the unemployed, for example, women, youth at school, etc.

15 Of course, crime is not the only object involving ideological inversion. Other problems, such as strikes, fare similarly: strikes are a problem of capitalism rather than that capitalism causes the problem of strikes.

16 The homology between commodity fetishism and legal fetishism is established by means of semiological analysis. As a result the only political practice which

Balbus finds time for is that of 'decoding' which he affirms is none the less 'no mere academic exercise' (1977, p. 585).

17 Fitzgerald and Sim (1979) give an illuminating breakdown of the petty nature of the crimes for which most people are imprisoned.

2 Law and class

I wish to give special thanks to Simon Clarke for his usual comradely assistance. My thanks also to Jock Young, Richard Kinsey, Sol Picciotto, John Lea, Carole Brigden and Inge Krijnen.

1 Labelling theory and other 'subjectivist' critiques of deviance declare the labelling of deviants as an alienated and irrational form of power. But they do not locate the historical basis of this form of power, and thus tend to present it as a universal form whose history lies only in the changing nature of the class which wields it or of the functions to which it is put. See my articles on labelling theory (1977) and on Sartre and the Panopticon (1977a).

2 See, for example, Melossi (1976a).

3 It is in response to the eternization of form to be found in both these tendencies that Michel Foucault (1977) has emphasized the historical character of what he calls the 'power–knowledge continuum'. Thus he analyses 'disciplinary power' as one that represents the 'dark side' of juridic equality and political democracy, and which emerged at the close of the eighteenth century. The fundamental problem which Foucault has run into, however, is his inability to relate this historical transformation of power to the underlying social relations embodied in them. In other words, Foucault, too, falls into a kind of historical formalism of his own; it was expressed originally in his surrendering any attempt to comprehend changes in the 'power–knowledge continuum' by means of the theory of 'historical discontinuity' (the 'break' or 'caesura' in forms of power can be described, but it cannot be explained). More recently, Foucault's inadequate attempt to relate the growth of the disciplinary form to the technical development of forces of production is a step in the right direction, but does not succeed. The only explanation offered for this technical development is the growth of the 'disciplines' themselves. The social roots of a change in power relations turns out, in his analysis, to be their effect. Once again, in a more sophisticated and historically conscious version, Foucault fails to relate forms of power to their content. See my forthcoming critique of Foucault in *Capital and Class* and Dews (1979), who relates Foncault to the *nouvelle philosophie* movement.

3 Despotism and legality

My thanks go to the editorial collective of this book, participants in the CSE Law Group and the NDC, but especially to Isabel Roberts.

1 Renner's work rests upon a framework of ideas common to Austro-Marxism but largely taken for granted by Renner himself. The available literature in English is small but I have found the following particularly useful: Gulick (1948), Bottomore and Goode (1978), Kolakowski (1969), especially ch. 5; Korsch's introduction to Pashukanis, extracted in Pashukanis (1978); Colletti (1972); and Buttinger (1954).

Otto Kahn Freund's introduction to Renner (1949) is useful in so far as it points to some of the problems met in the application of the more substantive aspects of Renner's thesis to the English common law, but it is of little help in reaching a theoretical understanding of the work. There are many works in German but two are of particular interest: Leser (1968), and Hannak (1965).

2 cf. Colletti (1972), ch. 1 *passim*, and also T.B. Bottomore's introduction to Bottomore and Goode (1978).

3 Note Pashukanis's critique (1978, pp. 124-30) of Renner and in particular the following general comment:

> . . . the theories mentioned do not provide any criteria whatever for a genuine sociological interpretation of the individualistic categories of bourgeois law, which they criticise, not from the point of view of the proletarian conception of socialism, but from the standpoint of the dictatorship of finance capital. The social significance of these doctrines is that they justify the modern imperialist state and its methods, particularly those employed in the last War.

4 For brief but informative analyses of the neo-Kantian epistemology of Austro-Marxism see Colletti (1972), ch. 1, and Lichtheim (1961), pp. 303-6.

5 See, for example, Hume (1793), pt 1 *passim*, and Smith (1976a), book 3. For commentaries upon this point see Halévy (1972) pt 1; Winch (1978); and Annette (ch. 4 in this volume).

6 This is a heavily worked area but two recent works deserve especial notice: Pearson (1979) and Ignatieff (1978), especially ch. 2.

7 From the middle of the nineteenth century onwards bourgeois legal theorists were to designate this the 'shift from status to contract'. Probably the most influential was Maine's *Ancient Law* (1861).

8 It is interesting to note that exactly the same questions and arguments were posed in contemporary legal theory. For a particularly good example see Bagehot (1956), ch. 1.

4 Bentham's fear of hobgoblins

1 The number of Jeremy Bentham's writings is enormous. There is a large amount still in manuscript form, much of which is difficult to decipher. Bentham also often puts important theoretical considerations of the nature of law in long footnotes. References to the *The Works of Jeremy Bentham*, ed. John Bowring, 11 vols (1838-43) – which are often unreliable – will be cited as *Works*. References to manuscripts in the Bentham Collection, University College, London, will be cited as BC MSS. References to individual works in

the new definitive edition in progress, *The Collected Works of Jeremy Bentham*, ed. J.H. Burns, will be cited according to the title of the volume.

2 Some older works on Bentham that are useful are: Ogden (1932), Mack (1962), Halévy (1972) and Himmelfarb (1972-3). Some recent interpretations are: Long (1977), Rosenblume (1978) and Steintrager (1977).

3 For a discussion of the distinction between the role of law within the sphere of circulation and law within the sphere of production see Pashukanis (1978). In ch. 5, 'Law and the state', Pashukanis incorrectly sees the discipline of the factory in terms of 'feudal authority'. Foucault and Melossi correctly see the discipline of the 'social factory' as a modern development within capitalist special relations of production. See also Renner (1949).

4 For a discussion of the significance of poverty for social discipline see Scull (1977), Pasquino (1978) and Procacci (1978). These two articles are influenced by Michel Foucault and are about the formation of disciplinary 'discourses'. I am indebted to Mike Sonenscher for his unpublished critique of these two articles. Polanyi (1957) is still important.

5 See Bendix (1963), Pollard (1965), Thompson (1967), Tronti (1977) and Lazonik (1978).

5 Discipline and capitalist development

1 The discussion that follows is in large part an attempt to respond to and develop critically some of the themes raised by Melossi.

2 There are, of course, numerous exceptions throughout the history of capitalist development. Migrant worker barracks in South Africa and immigrant worker hostels in Western Europe are contemporary examples of such exceptions.

3 It is of course necessary to be aware that Bentham's *architecture* was not adopted as a general model for prison design. However, this in no way detracts from the importance of the principle of inspection and surveillance embodied in the concept of the Panopticon.

4 For a discussion of the historical importance of prison labour see Rusche and Kirchheimer (1964).

6 Institutions of social control and capitalist organization of work

1 [See also the chart on page 81. *Translator.*]

2 It is perhaps superfluous to underline the fact that this discussion of Foucault is a *Marxist use* of a work that does not consider itself to be Marxist. For this reason I have designated Foucault, perhaps inappropriately, as an *idealist* because any sense of 'determination in the last instance' by the relations of production, characteristic of Marxism, is absent from the foundations of his work.

3 For a general discussion on this oscillation between resocialization and terrorization since the middle of the last century see Rusche and Kirchheimer (1964) and Melossi and Pavarini (forthcoming). Certainly the tendency in recent years of

several prison systems to augment their productive character through the use of prison labour has not been the least reason for the increasing diffusion of class consciousness throughout the prison system and the consequent struggle for the equalization of prison conditions with those prevailing externally as regards labour. The longest struggles on these questions have probably taken place in the United States.

4 In the United States both the modern police system and the diffusion of practical assistance as a practice among the masses results from the events of the 1920s and 1930s (cf. Cooper *et al.* 1975; Piven and Cloward 1972).

5 On the developmental tendencies of social control since the war in Italy see Seppelli and Abozzo (2973).

6 [The '150 hours' campaign initiated and won by the engineering workers in 1972, after a long campaign, involves the right to use 150 hours of work-time annually for study purposes. For an account in English see Boddington (1978). *Translator*.]

7 The texts referred to in note 3 show the police apparatus and social surveillance as they emerged and increased impressively in the United States. Sergio Bologna (1973) has attempted to link these to the concept of a new order of capitalist power based on the expulsion from the factory of the 'working class ejected from the work process' and the development of a new level of planning of the ghetto intended as a massive population destined to be permanently without work. See also Melossi (1976c).

7 'Decarceration' and the fiscal crisis

1 See Bakal (1973) for a discussion of some problems of implementation of these programmes in relation to youth in Massachussetts. See also Ohlin (1973).

2 Rusche and Kirchheimer (1964) appear extremely influential in the formation of Scull's approach. They also reject humanitarianism as a basis for explaining changing practices of control. Instead they link these changes to changes in the labour market. Commentary on their work has been supplied by Melossi (1978) and Jankovic (1977). Foucault (1977) provides a critique of humanitarianism from a different perspective.

3 Particularly in the area of industrial relations. Also see Hall *et al.* (1978) for a discussion of this process and its consequences in relation to mugging.

4 See Miller (1974) for a useful discussion of the role of prison labour.

5 The growth in crime in the post-war period appears to be faster at the 'soft' end of the continuum. Many offenders who have been convicted of indictable offences during this period would have, in many cases, been acquitted in previous periods (see Pitts 1979). The implications for Scull's thesis are, of course, extremely important.

6 Gough primarily criticizes O'Connor for his 'underconsumption' theory of the crises and for his general conception of the 'crises' being reduced to a crisis of the state. Both these writers are part of a wider debate which Scull seems to be unaware of. See important contributions to this debate from Bullock and Yaffe

1975), Fine and Harris (1976).

7 Gough argues that the term 'crisis' is more appropriate to the British and Italian economies and that the remainder of advanced capitalist societies are better characterized as being in 'recession'.

8 Greenberg (1975) suggests that some forms of state community control are significantly cheaper than incarceration but that some could, if implemented properly, end up by being more costly.

9 Greenberg (1977), in a survey of emerging results from a variety of community correctional schemes, found, as one might expect, that these strategies of control have not reduced the rate of recidivism.

10 This is a general tendency in all 'left functionalist' accounts, which see the class struggle as a function of the structure. See Clarke (1977). For a discussion of the limits of state intervention see Holloway and Picciotto (1977).

11 One of the few useful inquiries in the vein is Hall *et al.* (1978).

12 The rate of receptions into prisons and borstals has doubled between 1940 and 1970 increasing from 30,000 to 60,000 (HMSO 1971). See Pitts (1979) for a discussion specifically in relation to youth.

13 'Decriminalization' is an exaggeration in the sense that it has invariably taken the form of semi-decriminalization. For a discussion see Greenwood and Young (1979).

14 Although the number of historical studies carried out in the labelling or interactionist perspective has been limited, the work by Platt (1969) and Erikson (1966) has much in common with Scull's own approach.

15 Scull's criticisms of Rothman are set out in detail elsewhere. See Scull (1977*a*).

16 For discussions of the relation between Marxism and social science see Goldman (1972) and Swingewood (1975).

17 Rosdolsky (1977) provides an excellent commentary on Marx's painstaking analysis of the primacy of the commodity as the starting point for the analysis of the capitalist mode of production.

18 Parsons, Durkheim and Weber are all involved in explicit or implicit debates with Marx. See Swingewood (1975) for further discussion of these critiques.

19 See van den Haag (1975) and J. Wilson (1977) for an exposition of this position. For a review see Platt and Takagi (1977).

20 Mitford (1974, p. 286) writes, 'To my surprise, Wanden Hocker told me that he thought the figure (80 per cent) was too low and that in his opinion 90 per cent of the people in prison do not belong there'.

21 See Stedman-Jones (1977) for a useful critique of the notion of 'social control' and other 'functionalist'-orientated terminology.

8 Policing the working-class city

1 Anderson (1977) argues this; his article is also a good introduction to the whole post-Gramscian debate on state and civil society.

2 See Storch (1976) for an empiricist reading of Victorian policing.

3 All historical material refers to the London borough of Islington. This research

was carried out under the auspisces of a grant from the Leverhulme Trust. It consisted of an analysis of local newspaper reports from 1875 to 1935 and of oral testimony collected from residents who grew up in Islington between the world wars. I am grateful to Lucy Bland for collecting much of this material, and also to the staff of the Islington library service for their help. The Islington Bus Company is collecting oral testimony on the political history of Islington during the inter-war period, and I am grateful to Neil Martinson for enabling me to consult that material.

4 See Walters (1975), an autobiographical account of working-class life in Islington between the wars. It gives a very good picture from the point of view of a spokesman of public propriety who lived in 'notorious' Popham Street.

5 For a full discussion of this concept see Balbus (1973).

6 A comment on the ironic fact that urban planners use the term 'line of desire' to indicate the direction of maximum pedestrian flow between fixed points, for example from tube station to office, or from home to shops.

7 The objective effect of so-called 'moral panics' is therefore one of *reassurance* that the bourgeois public realm is alive and well and has triumphed once again over adversity. This aspect is ignored by Cohen (1973).

8 I gathered this information through participant observation while a youth worker in Islington between 1971 and 1974.

9 Sex discrimination, work and the law

1 On sexual equality see EEC Treaty article no. 119 and EEC directive nos. 75/117 and 76/207.

2 Immigration laws are the most blatant example of racist legislation. In regard to sexism, such areas as nationality, pensions, taxation and social security are excluded from the scope of the Sex Discrimination Act. In addition, there are more subtle ways in which legal provisions operate to oppress women (see Wilson 1977; Sachs and Wilson 1978).

3 Industrial tribunal cases frequently involve state institutions as respondents, for example local authorities, the Civil Service Commissioners, the Post Office and even the Commission for Racial Equality.

4 For example, *Punton* v. *Ministry of Pensions* [1964] 1 All ER 448; *Stringer* v. *Ministry of Housing and Local Government* [1970] 1 WLR 1281; *R.* v. *Metropolitan Police Commissioner* ex parte *Blackburn* [1973] 1 All ER 324.

5 *Gouriet* v. *Union of Post Office Workers* [1977] 2 WLR 310.

6 *Secretary of State for Education and Science* v. *Tameside Metropolitan Borough Council* [1976] 3 WLR 641.

7 *Laker Airways Ltd* v. *Department of Trade* [1977] 2 WLR 234. In general see also Griffiths (1977).

8 *SRC* v. *Nassé* and *Leyland Cars Ltd* v. *Vyas* [1978] 3 WLR 754.

9 In theoretical discussion minority groups are rarely mentioned, women almost never. In the empirical works women figure only as wives. See, for example, Dahrendorf (1963); Ossowski (1963); Bottomore (1965); Bendix and Lipset

(1967) – there is a brief reference to women and disadvantaged ethnic groups by Goode on p. 601; Goldthorpe (1969); Parkin (1971). Exceptions include Westergaard and Resler (1975) who have a chapter on women, and Beteille (1969) with chapters on racial inequality. Stratification studies are not alone in these omissions – see Oakley (1974) on the concealment of women throughout sociology. Racial minorities receive attention as a 'social problem'.

10 It could be argued that in 1945 the position of ethnic minorities in this country was not essential to his general argument, but women represented half of the 'citizens' to whom he was referring!

11 Only a completely ruthless immigration policy can achieve a similar parsimony. The Germans are more 'efficient' than the British in this respect, although British immigration controls are tightening. The recent use of virginity tests on Asian women and immigrants is a grotesque example of the double humiliation of minority group women.

12 Equal Pay Act 1970, ch. 41, which became Schedule 1 of the Sex Discrimination Act 1975, ch. 65. See also Coussins (1976).

13 *Waddington* v. *Leicester Council for Voluntary Services* [1977] IRLR 32. See also Coussins (2976).

14 *O'Connor* v. *Alpha Cleaning Services*, case no. 5560/76, and *Greendale* v. *Jarman and Flint Ltd.*

15 *Fildes* v. *Gwent County Council*, case no. 12125/76. See also Coussins (1976).

16 Race Relations Act, ch. 74. This paper focuses mainly on the employment provisions of the two Acts, although the legislation also covers discrimination in the provision of goods, facilities and services, enforced through the county courts.

17 *Price* v. *Civil Service Commission and Civil Service National Whitley Council (Staff Side) No. 2.* The tribunal was unable to grant relief to Price herself: 'One could not allow the applicant to have her application considered without allowing the same facility to all persons . . . over the age of 28. The consequences of that would be very serious.'

18 See Coussins (1977). This occurred because a man complained of reverse discrimination and because the Open University had not made an application for exemption under the legislation. It would be difficult to argue that all their courses provided training in areas from which women had been excluded.

19 *Steel* v. *The Post Office No. 2* [1978] IRLR 198.

20 *Hutchinson* v. *Electrolux Ltd* [1976] IRLR 289 and *Electrolux Ltd* v. *Hutchinson* [1976] IRLR 410. See also Coote (1977).

21 Lustgarten regards the British legislation as a legal transplant from America. Its weaknesses result from the transplantation of the concepts without the concomitant procedural devices.

22 Many discrimination cases bear an uncanny resemblance to rape trials. The evidence is presented in such a way that the applicant is often on the defensive.

23 Statistics provided by ACAS show that in 1977 45 per cent of all cases under the Race Relations Act and 31 per cent of equal pay cases were withdrawn

before the tribunal hearing. These figures exclude cases that were settled privately or successfully conciliated. Only 15 per cent of race cases and 7 per cent of equal pay cases were cleared up by conciliation, compared with 33 per cent of unfair dismissal cases.

24 Lustgarten would favour the formation of discrimination tribunals composed of persons with experience of 'the reality of discrimination and less institutionally connected with the entrenched forces of industrial life' (1978, p. 205). Such tribunals undoubtedly would provide a more sympathetic forum for discrimination cases, although progress would be hampered by the attitudes of the superior courts.

25 *National Vulcan Engineering* v. *Wade* [1978] IRLR 225.

26 The Employment Appeal Tribunal dismissed Pointon's appeal against the tribunal decision to reject her original claim (*M. Pointon* v. *The University of Sussex* [1977] IRLR 294) and the courts of appeal upheld that decision on 6 December 1978.

27 *M. Schmidt* v. *Austicks Bookshops Ltd* [1977] IRLR 360. See also the unfair dismissal case in which the Employment Appeal Tribunal supported the decision of an employer who dismissed an employee for wearing a 'Lesbians Unite' badge: *Boychuk* v. *Symons Holdings Ltd* [1977] IRLR 395.

28 *Automotive Products Ltd* v. *F. Peake* [1977] IRLR 365.

29 Paradoxically, this will involve using similar judicial procedures to those available to racist and sexist employers objecting to an intervention by one of the Commissions. It is in fact more difficult to challenge a *refusal* to intervene because of the wide discretionary powers of the Commissions. However, there is one case in which the EOC changed its mind and withdrew financial assistance shortly before the hearing. This decision is to be challenged in the High Court. See Coote (1978).

11 The theory of the state, class struggle and the rule of law

1 Earlier drafts of this paper were given at meetings of the CSE Law and the State Group and the Coventry Local Group, and I would like to thank members of those groups for comradely criticism. Special thanks also to John Holloway and Heidi Gerstenberger. This paper was also delivered at the British Sociological Association Conference at the University of Warwick in April 1979.

Bibliography

Ainlay, J. (1975-6), 'The new criminology and critical criminology', *Telos*, no. 26

Althusser, L. (1971), 'Ideology and ideological state apparatuses', in L. Althusser, *Lenin and Philosophy*, New Left Books

Anderson, P. (1977), 'The antinomies of Gramsci', *New Left Review*, no. 100

Annette, J. (1978), 'Bentham as a radical philosopher: the materialist analysis of language and law', unpublished chapter of an extended work on Bentham's social and political theory

Arthur, C. (1976), 'Towards a materialist theory of law', *Critique*, no. 7, pp. 31-46

Aumeruddy, A., Lautier, B., and Tortajada, R.J. (1978), 'Labour-power and the state', *Capital and Class*, no. 6, pp. 42-66

Bagehot, W. (1956), *Physics and Politics*, Beacon Press

Bakal, Y. (ed.) (1973), *Closing Correctional Institutions: New Strategies for Youth Services*, Lexington Books

Baker, K. (1975), *Condorcet: from Natural Philosophy to Social Mathematics*, University of Chicago Press

Balbus, I. (1973), *Dialectics of Legal Repression*, Russell Sage Foundation

Balbus, I. (1977), 'Commodity form and legal form: an essay on the "relative autonomy" of law', *Law and Society Review*, vol. 11, no. 3, pp. 571-88

Barratt Brown, M. (1971), 'The welfare state in Britain', *Socialist Register*

Bendix, R. (1963), *Work and Authority in Industry*, New York: John Wiley

Bendix, R., and Lipset, S.M. (eds.) (1967), *Class, Status and Power*, Routledge & Kegan Paul

Bentham, J. (1938-43), *Works*, ed. John Bowring, 11 vols., Willis

Bentham, J. (1962), *Panopticon*

Bentham, J. (1970), *An Introduction to the Principles of Morals and Legislation*, eds. J.H. Burns and H.L.A. Hart, Athlone Press

Bentham, J. (in progress), *The Collected Works of Jeremy Bentham*, ed. J.H. Burns

Beteille, A. (ed.) (1969), *Social Inequality*, Penguin

Bindman, G. (1976), 'The law and discrimination: third thoughts', *British Journal of Law and Society*, vol. 3, no. 1

Blackstone, W. (1973-5), *Commentaries on the Laws of England* 12th ed., vol. 2, Oxford

Bland, L., Brunsdon, C., Hobson, D., and Winship, J. (1978), 'Women "inside and outside" the relations of production', *Women Take Issue*, Centre for Contemporary Cultural Studies, and Hutchinson

Boddington, S. (1978), 'Italy: new approaches to worker education, *Builletin of the Institute of Workers' Control*, no. 37

Bologna, S. (1972), 'Composizione di classe e teoria del partito', *Operai e Stato*, Milan

Bologna, S. (1973), 'Questioni di metodo per l'analisi del piano chimico', *Quaderni Piacentini*, no. 48/9

Bonger, N. (1969), *Criminality and Economic Conditions*, Indiana University Press

Bottomore, T.B. (1965), *Classes in Modern Society*, Allen & Unwin

Bottomore, T.B., and Goode, P. (1978), *Austro-Marxism*, Clarendon Press

Braveman, H. (1974), *Labor and Monopoly Capitalism*, New York: Monthly Review Press

Brock, E. (1968), *The Little White God*, Allen & Unwin

Broué, P. (1971), *Revolution en allemagne 1917-23*, ed. de Minuit

Broué, P., and Témime, E. (1972), *The Revolution and the Civil War in Spain*, Faber

Buci-Glucksman, C. (1976), *Gramsci e Lo Stato*, Rome

Bullock, P., and Yaffe, D. (1975), 'Inflation, the crisis and the post-war book', *Revolutionary Communist*, no. 3/4, pp. 5-37

Byrne, P., and Lovenduski, J. (1978), 'Sex, equality and the law', *British Journal of Law and Society*, vol. 5, no. 2

Cacciari, M. (1972), *Introduction to Georges Lukács Kommunismus 1920/21*, Padua

Centre for Policy Studies (1968), *Bibliography of Freedom*

Clarke, S. (1977), 'Marxism, sociology and Poulantzas's theory of the state', *Capital and Class*, no. 2, pp. 1-31

Clinard, M. (1978), *Cities with Little Crime*, Cambridge University Press

Coates, A.W. (ed.) (1971), *The Classical Economists and Economic Policy*, Methuen

Cockburn, C. (1977), *The Local State: Management of Cities and People*, Pluto Press

Cohen, S. (1973), *Folk Devils and Moral Panics*, Paladin

Cohen, S. (1977), 'Prisons and the future of control systems', in M. Fitzgerald *et. al.* (1977)

Colletti, L. (1972), *From Rousseau to Lenin*, New Left Books

Cooper, L., *et al.* (1975), *The Iron Fist and the Velvet Glove*, Centre for the Study of Crime and Social Justice

Coote, A. (1977), 'The women who won't be frozen out', *Guardian*, 22 February

Coote, A. (1978), 'Equality and the curse of the Quango', *New Statesman*, vol. 96 (1 December)

Corrigan, P. (1977), 'The welfare state as an arena of class struggle', *Marxism Today*, vol. 21, pp. 87-93

Coussins, J. (1976), *The Equality Report*, National Council for Civil Liberties

Coussins, J. (1977), *Amending the Equal Pay Act and Sex Discrimination Act*, National Council for Civil Liberties

Crime and Social Justice Collective (1977), 'The management of police killings', *Crime and Social Justice*, no. 8, pp. 34-43

Cross, R. (1971, *Punishment, Prison and the Public*, Stevens & Sons

Dahrendorf, R. (1963), *Class and Class Conflict in Industrial Society*, Routledge & Kegan Paul

de Smith, S.A. (1973), *Judicial Review of Administrative Action*, Stevens & Sons

de Smith, S.A. (1975), *Constitutional and Administrative Law*, Penguin

de Sousa Santos, B. (1976), 'Law and revolution in Portugal: the experience of popular justice after the 25th April 1974', paper given at Fourth Conference of the European Group for the Study of Deviancy and Social Control, Vienna

de Sousa Santos, B. (1977), 'The law of the oppressed', *Law and Society Review*, no. 12, pp. 5-126

Dews, P. (1979), 'The nouvelle philosophie and Foucault', *Economy and Society*, vol. 8, no. 2

Ditton, J. (1977), 'Perks, pilferage and the fiddle: the historical structure of invisible wages', *Theory and Society*, no. 4, pp. 39-71

Donnison, D. (1977), 'Against discretion', *New Society* (15 September)

Downes, D., and Rock, P. (1979), *Deviant Interpretations*, Martin Robertson

Durkheim, E. (1964), *The Division of Labour in Society*, New York: Free Press

Durkheim, E. (1966), *The Rules of Sociological Method*, New York: Free Press

Edelman, B. (1979), *Ownership of the Image*, Routledge & Kegan Paul

Empey, L.T. (1973), 'Juvenile justice reform: diversion, due process and deinstitutionalization', in L. Ohlin (ed.) (1973)

Engels, F. (1962), *Anti-Duhring*, Lawrence & Wishart

Engels, F. (1968), 'Introduction to Marx's critique of the Gotha Programme', in K. Marx and F. Engels (1968)

Engels, F. (1968a), 'Origins of the family, private property and the State', in K. Marx and F. Engels (1968)

Engels, F. (1968b), 'Introduction to the civil war in France', in K. Marx and F. Engels (1968)

Engels, F. (1968c), 'A propos of working-class political action', in K. Marx and F. Engels (1968)

Erikson, K. (1966), *Wayward Puritans: A Study of the Sociology of Deviance*, New York: Wiley

Evans, R. (1971), 'Bentham's Panopticon: an incident in the social history of architecture', *Architectural Association Quarterly*, vol. 3

Ferri Bravo, L. (1972), 'Il "new deal" e il nuovo assetto delle istituzione capitalistiche', *Operai e Stato*, Milan

Fine, B. (1977), 'Labelling theory: the sociological critique of deviance', *Economy and Society*, vol. 6, no. 2

Fine, B. (1977a), 'Objectification and the contradictions of bourgeois power: Sartre and the modern prison', *Economy and Society*, vol. 6, no. 4

Fine, B. (1979), 'The theory and politics of Michel Foucault', *Capital and Class*, no. 9

Fine, B. and Harris, L. (1976), 'Controversial issues in Marxist economic theory', *Socialist Register*, pp 141-78

Fitzgerald, B., and Sim, J. (1979), *British Prisons*, Blackwell

Fitzgerald, M. *et al.* (1977), *Welfare in Action*, Routledge & Kegan Paul

Foster, J. (1974), *Class Struggle and the Industrial Revolution,* Weidenfeld & Nicolson

Foucault, M. (1977), *Discipline and Punish*, Allen Lane

Friedan, B. (1977), *It Changed my Life*, Dell

Fry, G.K. (1979), *The Growth of Govenment*, Frank Cass

Ganz, G. (1967), 'The control of industry by administrative process', *Public Law*, pp. 93-106

Goldman, L. (1972), 'Is there a Marxist sociology?', *Radical Philosophy*, no. 2

Goldthorpe. J., *et al*. (1969), *The Affluent Worker*, Cambridge University Press

Gordon, D. (1971), 'Class and the economics of crime', *Review of Radical Economics*, vol. 3, no. 3, pp. 51-72

Gough, I. (1975), 'State expenditure in advanced capitalism', *New Left Review*, no. 92

Gould, B. (1970), 'Anisminic and jurisdictional review', *Public Law*, no. 358

Gramsci, A. (1973), *Selections from the Prison Notebooks*, Lawrence & Wishart

Greenberg, D. (1975), 'Problems in community corrections', *Issues in Criminology*, vol. 10, no. 1

Greenberg, D. (ed.) (1977), 'The correctional effects of corrections: a survey of evaluations', *Corrections and Punishment*, Page Publications

Greenberg, D., and Stender, F. (1972), 'The prison as a lawless agency', *Buffalo Law Review*, pp. 799-838

Greenwood, V., and Young, J. (1976), *Abortion in Demand*, Pluto Press

Greenwood, V., and Young, J. (1979), 'Ghettos of freedom: the nature of reformist legislation', in *Permissiveness and Control*, ed. National Deviancy Conference, Macmillan

Griffith, J. (1977). *The Politics of the Judiciary*, Fontana/Collins

Griffith, J., and Street, H. (1966), *Principles of Administrative Law*, Pitman

Gulick, C.A. (1948), *Austria from Habsburg to Hitler*, University of California Press

Halevy, E, (1972), *The Growth of Philosophic Radicalism*, Faber

Hall, S., Critchley, C., Jefferson, A., Clarke, S., and Roberts, B. (1978), *Policing the Crisis: Mugging, the State, Law and Order*, Macmillan

Hannak, J. (1965), *Karl Renner und seine Zeit*, Vienna

Hawkins, K. (1975), 'Alternatives to imprisonment', in S. McConville (ed.), *The Use*

of Imprisonment, Routledge & Kegan Paul
Hay, D., Linebaugh, P., and Thompson, E.P. (1975), *Albion's Fatal Tree*, Allen Lane
HMSO (1969), *People in Prison*
HMSO (1971), *The Work of the Prison Department*
Hewart, Lord (1929), *The New Despotism*, Benn
Hilton, G.W. (1960), *The Truck System*, Heffer
Himmelfarb, G. (1970), 'The haunted house of Jeremy Bentham', in *Victorian Minds*, New York
Himmelfarb, G. (1970a), 'Bentham's utopia: the National Charity Company', *Journal of British Studies*, col. 10
Himmelfarb, G. (1972-3), 'On Reading Bentham seriously', in *Studies on Burke and his Times*, vol. 14, Cassell
Hodge, H. (1974), *Legal Rights*, Arrow
Holdsworth, W. (1952), *A History of English Law*, Methuen
Holloway, J., and Picciotto, S. (1977), 'Capital, crisis and the state', *Capital and Class*, no. 2, pp. 76-101
Holloway, J., and Picciotto, S. (1978), *State and Capital: A Marxist Debate*, Edward Arnold
Hume, D. (1793), *Essays and Treatises on Several Subjects*, vol. 1, Edinburgh
Hume, L.J. (1967), 'Jeremy Bentham and the nineteenth century revolution in government', *Historical Journal*, vol. 10
Hutchinson, T.W. (1956), 'Bentham as an economist', *Economic Journal*, vol. 66

Ignatieff, M. (1978), *A Just Measure of Pain*, Macmillan

Jacoby, R. (1975), *Social Amnesia*, Boston: Beacon Press
Jankovic, I. (1977), 'Labour market and imprisonment', *Crime and Social Justice,* no. 8, pp. 17-31
Johnson, R. (1970), 'Educational policy and social control in early Victorian England', *Past and Present*, no. 49
Jowell, J. (1975), *Law and Bureaucracy*, Dunell

Kamenka, E., and Ehr-Soon Tay, A. (1975), 'Beyond bourgeois individualism: the contemporary crisis in law and legal ideology', in E. Kamenka and R.S. Neale, *Feudalism, Capitalism and Beyond*, Edward Arnold
Kinsey, R. (1978), 'Marxism and the law', *British Journal of Law and Society*, vol. 5, no. 2
Kinsey, R. (forthcoming), 'Karl Renner, Austro-Marxism and the law'
Kolakowski, L. (1969), *The Alienation of Reason*, Anchor

Lazonik, W. (1978), 'The subjection of labour to capital; the rise of the capitalist system', *Review of Radical Political Economics*, vol. 10
Lefebvre, H. (1968), *The Sociology of Marx*, Allen Lane
Lenin, V.I. (1960), 'The dual power', in V.I. Lenin, *Selected Works*, 3 vols.,

Moscow: Progress Publishers, vol. 2, pp. 50-2

Lenin, V.I. (1960a), 'Tasks of the proletariat in our revolution', in V.I. Lenin, *Selected Works*, Moscow, Progress Publishers, vol. 2 pp. 53-68

Lenin, V.I. (1973), *The State and Revolution*, Peking: Foreign Language Press

Lerman, P. (1975), *Community Treatment and Social Control*, University of Chicago Press

Leser, N. (1968), *Zwischen Reformismus und Bolshewismus*, Vienna

Lester, A., and Bindman, G. 1972), *Race and Law*, Penguin

Lichtheim, G. (1961), *Marxism*, Routledge & Kegan Paul

Linebaugh, P. (1976), 'Karl Marx, the theft of wood, and working class composition', *Crime and Social Justice*, no. 6, pp. 5-16

Linebaugh, P., and Thompson, E.P. (1972), 'Eighteenth century crime, popular movements and social control', *Bulletin for the Study of Labour History*, vol. 25

Locke, J. (1970), *Two Treatises of Government*, ed. Peter Laslett, Cambridge University Press

Long, D. (1977), *Bentham on Liberty*, Toronto: University of Toronto Press

Lukács, G. (1971), *History and Class Consciousness*, Merlin Press

Lukács, G. (1978), 'Marx's basic ontological principles', pt 1, ch. 4, in his *Towards the Ontology of Social Being*, Merlin Press

Lustgarten, L. (1978), 'The new meaning of discrimination', *Public Law*

Luxemburg, R. (1969), *Social Reform or Revolution?*, Pathfinder

Mack, M.P. (1962), *Jeremy Bentham: An Odyssey of Ideas 1748-1792*, Heinemann

MacLeod, H. (1974), *Religion and Class in the Victorian City,* Croom Helm

Maine, H. (1961), *Ancient Law*, London

Marshall, T.H. (1975), *Social Policy*, rev. ed., Hutchinson

Marx, K. (1968), *Theories of Surplus Value*, pt 2, Lawrence & Wishart

Marx, K. (1968a), 'Civil war in France', in K. Marx and F. Engels (1968)

Marx, K. (1968b), 'Critique of the Gotha Programme', in K. Marx and F. Engels (1968)

Marx, K. (1970), *Capital,* Lawrence & Wishart

Marx. K. (1975), 'The critique of Hegel's philosophy of right', *Marx – Early Writings*, Penguin

Marx, K. (1976), *Capital*, vol. 1, Penguin

Marx, K. (1976a), *The Poverty of Philosophy*, Moscow: Progress Publishers

Mark, K., and Engels, F. (1968), *Selected Works in One Volume*, Lawrence & Wishart

Marx, K., and Engels, F. (1976), *Collected Works*, vol. 5, Lawrence & Wishart

Mathieson, T. (1974), *The Politics of Abolition*, Martin Robertson

Mayhew, H. (1851), *London Labour and London Poor*, vol. 1, George Woodfall

Mayo, M. (1975), 'Community development: a radical alternative', in R. Bailey and M. Brake (eds.), *Radical Social Work*, Edward Arnold

Melossi, D. (1975), 'Criminologia e Marxismo', *La Questione Criminale*, vol. 1, no. 2

Melossi, D. (1976), 'Institutions of social control and the capitalist organization of work', *La Questione Criminale*, no. 2/3, Anno 2, trans. John Lea, Middlesex Polytechnic

Melossi, D. (1976a) 'The penal question in Capital', *Crime and Social Justice*, no. 5, pp. 26-33

Melossi, D. (1976b), 'Il Lavora', *Carcere e Societa*, Venice

Melossi, D. (1978), 'Review article: Rusche and Kirchheimer, punishment and social structure', *Crime and Social Justice*, no. 9, pp. 73-85

Melossi, D., and Pavarini, M. (forthcoming), *Prison and Factory*, Macmillan

Mepham, J. (1974), 'Theory of ideology in Capital', *Cultural Studies,* no. 6, University of Birmingham: Centre for Contemporary Cultural Studies

Miliband, R. (1969), *The State in Capitalist Society*, Weidenfeld & Nicolson

Miller, M. (1974), 'At hard labour: rediscovering the nineteenth century prison', *Issues in Criminology*, no. 9

Mitchell, J. (1976), 'Women and equality', in J. Mitchell and A. Oakley (eds.), *The Rights and Wrongs of Women*, Penguin

Mitford, J. (1974), *The American Prison Business*, Allen & Unwin

National Council for Civil Liberties (NCCL) (1979), *Justice Deserted: the Subversion of the Jury*, ed. H. Harman and J. Griffith

Negt, O., and Klug, A. (1973), *Oeffentlichkent und Erfahrung,* Frankfurt: Suhrkamp

Negt, O., and Kluge, A. (1975), *New German Critique*, no. 4

Neumann, F. (1957), *The Democratic and the Authoritarian State*, Collier-Macmillan

New Earnings Survey (1978), Department of Employment

Nonet, P. (1969), *Administrative Justice*, New York

Oakley, A. (1974) *The Sociology of Housework*, Martin Robertson

O'Connor, J. (1973), *The Fiscal Crisis of the State*, New York: St Martin's Press

Ogden, C.K.(1932), *Bentham's Theory of Fictions*, Routledge & Kegan Paul

Ohlin, L. (ed.) (1973), *Prisoners in America*, New York: Prentice-Hall

Ossowski, S. (1963), *Class and Class Structure in the Social Consciousness*, Routledge & Kegan Paul

Outer Circle Policy Unit (1978), *Policing the Hidden Economy*, OCPU

Panzieri, R. (1976), *Lotte Operai e Nello Sviluppo Capitalistico*, Turin

Park, R.F., and Burgess, E.W. (1927), *Introduction to the Science of Sociology*, Chicago

Parkin, F. (1971), *Class, Inequality and Political Order*, Paladin

Pashukanis, E.B. (1978), *Law and Marxism: A General Theory*, Ink Links

Pasquino, P. (1978), 'Theatrum politicum: the genealogy of capital, police and the state of property', *Ideology and Consciousness*, no. 4

Pearce, F. (1976), *Crimes of the Powerful*, Pluto Press

Pearson, G. (1979), 'Resistance to the machine', *Sociology of Science Handbook*

Pilling, C. (1971), 'Police and working class community', unpublished PhD thesis, Cambridge University

Pitts, J. (1979), 'Changes in the control, prevention and anticipation and surveillance of youthful disorder and delinquency', Middlesex Polytechnic, mimeo

Piven, R., and Cloward, R. (1972), *Regulating the Poor*, New York: Vintage Books; London: A.B.D.

Platt, A. (1969), *The Child Savers: The Invention of Delinquency*, University of Chicago Press

Platt, T. (1978), 'Street crime: a view from the left', *Crime and Social Justice*, no. 9, pp. 26-34

Platt, T. and Takagi, P. (1977), 'Intellectuals for law and order: a critique of the new "realists" ', *Crime and Social Justice*, no. 8, pp. 1-16

Polanyi, K. (1957), *The Great Transformation*, Boston: Beacon Press

Pollard, S. (1965), *The Genesis of Modern Management*, Edward Arnold

Posner, R. (1976), 'Blackstone and Bentham', *Journal of Law and Economics*

Poulantzas, N. (1973), *Political Power and Social Classes*, New Left Books

Poulantzas, N. (1978), *State, Power and Socialism*, New Left Books

Poynter, J.R. (1969) *Society and Pauperism*, Routledge & Kegan Paul

The President's Commission on Law Enforcement and Administration of Justice (1967), *The Challenge: A Crime in a Free Society*, Washington: US Government Printing Office

Procacci, G. (1978), 'Social economy and the government of poverty', *Ideology and Consciousness*, no. 4

Quinney, R. (1977), *Class, State and Crime*, New York: McKay

Radzinowicz, Sir L. (1948-68), *A History of the English Criminal Law and its Administration from 1750*, 4 vols., Stevens

Radzinowicz, L., and King, J. (1977), *The Growth of Crime*, Hamilton

Reich, C. (1966), 'The law of the planned society', *Yale Law Journal*, vol. 75, no. 7, pp. 1161-72

Release (1978), *Trouble with the Law: The Release Bust Book*, Pluto Press

Renner, K. (1949), *The Institutions of Private Law and Their Social Functions*, ed. O. Kahn-Freund, Routledge & Kegan Paul

Rheinstein, M. (1966), 'Max Weber on law', in *Economy and Society*, Harvard University Press

Robbins, L. (1952), *The Theory of Economic Policy in English Classical Political Economy*, Macmillan

Robson, A. (1928), *Justice and Administrative Law*, Macmillan

Rosdolsky, R. (1977), *The Making of Marx's Capital*, Pluto Press

Rose, M.E. (ed.) (1971), *The English Poor Law 1780-1930*, David & Charles

Rosenblume, N.L. (1978), *Bentham's Theory of the Modern State*, Harvard University Press

Rothman, D. (1971), *The Discovery of the Asylum*, Boston: Little, Brown

Rusche, G. (1978), 'Labour market and penal sanction', *Crime and Social Justice* no. 10, pp. 9-16

Rusche, G., and Kirchheimer, O. (1964), *Punishment and Social Structure*, Russell & Russell

Rushing, W. (1969), 'Two patterns in the relationships between social class and mental hospitalization', *American Sociological Review*, pp. 533-41

Sachs, A., and Wilson, J.H. (1978), *Sexism and the Law*, Martin Robertson

Samuels, W. (1966), *The Classical Theory of Economic Policy*, Toronto

Saville, J. (1958), 'The welfare state: an industrial approach', *The New Reasoner*, vol. 3

Schwendinger, H., and Schwendinger, J. (1974), 'Rape myths', *Crime and Social Justice*, no. 2

Schwendinger, H., and Schwendinger, J. (1975), 'Defenders of order or guardians of human rights', in I. Taylor, P. Walton and J. Young, (eds.), *Critical Criminology*, Routledge & Kegan Paul

Scull, A. (1977), *Decarceration*, New Jersey: Prentice-Hall

Scull, A. (1977a), 'Madness and segregative control: the rise of the insane asylum', *Social Problems*, vol. 24, no. 3

Selwyn, N.M. (1976), *Selwyn's Law of Employment*, Butterworths

Seppelli, T. and Abozzo, G. (1973), 'Stato della ricerca sul controllo sociale e sulla devianza', *Italia nel secondo dopoguerra*, Perugia

Shaw, M. (1975), 'The coming crisis in radical sociology', in R. Blackburn (ed.), *Ideology and Social Science*, Fontana

Smith, A. (1976), *The Theory of Moral Sentiments*, eds. D.D. Raphael, and A.L. Macfie, Oxford University Press

Smith, A. (1976a), *The Wealth of Nations*, Oxford University Press

Smith, A. (1978), *Lectures on Jurisprudence*, eds. R. Meek, D.D. Raphael, and P. Stein, Oxford University Press

Sohn-Rethel, A. (1978), *Intellectual and Manual Labour: A Critique of Epistemology*, Macmillan

Spitzer, S. (1975), 'Towards a Marxian theory of deviance', *Social Probelms*, no. 22, pp. 638-51

Stalin, J. (1973), *The Essential Stalin*, ed. B. Franklin, Croom Helm

Stark, W. (ed.) (1952-4), *Jeremy Bentham's Economic Writings*, 3 vols., Allen & Unwin

Stedman-Jones, G. (1971), *Outcast in London*, Oxford

Stedman-Jones, G. (1977), 'Class expression versus social control', *History Workshop*, vol. 4

Stein, P. (1970), 'Law and society in eighteenth century Scottish thought', in N.T. Phillipson and R. Mitchison, *Scotland in the Age of Improvement*, Edinburgh University Press

Steinert, H. (1976), 'On the development of penal policy', unpublished paper given at Fourth Conference of the European Group for the Study of Deviance and

Social Control, Vienna

Steintrager, J. (1977), *Bentham*, Allen & Unwin

Storch, R. (1976), 'The police as domestic missionaries', *Social History*, no. 4

Sutherland, E. (1949), *White Collar Crime*, Dryden Press

Swingewood, A. (1975), *Marx and Modern Social Theory*, Macmillan

Takagi, P. (1974), 'A garrison state in a "democratic" society', *Crime and Social Justice*, no. 1

Taylor, I. (forthcoming), *Crime at the End of the Welfare State*, Macmillan

Therborn, G. (1977), 'Capital and suffrage', *New Left Review*, no. 103

Thomas, J., and Williams, T. (1977), 'Change and conflict in the evolution of prison systems: old dilemmas, emergent problems and future strategies', *International Journal of Criminology and Penology*, no. 5

Thompson, E.P. (1963), *The Making of the English Working Class*, Penguin

Thompson, E.P. (1967), 'Time, work discipline and industrial capitalism', *Past and Present*, no. 38

Thompson, E.P. (1975), *Whigs and Hunters*, Allen Lane

Thompson, E.P. (1976), 'The grind of inheritance: a comment', in J. Thirsk and E.P. Thompson (eds.), *Family and Inheritance: Rural Society in Western Europe 1200-1800*, Cambridge University Press

Thompson, E.P. (1978), introduction to *The Review of Security of the State*, vol. 1, eds. State Research Collective, Julian Friedmann Books

Thompson, E.P. (1978a), *The Poverty of Theory*, Merlin

Titmuss, R.M. (1971), 'Welfare "rights", law and discretion', *Political Quarterly*, vol. 42, no. 2

Townsend, J. (1786), *A Dissertation on the Poor Laws*, London

Tronti, M. (1977), *Ouvriers Capital*, Paris; Christian Bourgeois Editeur

Trotsky, L. (1963), *Basic Writings*, ed. I. Howe, New York: Random House

Trotsky, L. (1969), 'Fascism, Stalinism and the United Front', *International Socialism*, no. 38/39, pp. 2-70

Trotsky, L. (1972), *Terrorism and Communism*, Ann Arbor, Michigan: University of Michigan Press

Trubeck, D. (1977), 'Complexity and contradiction in the legal order', *Law and Society Review*, no. 3, pp. 529-69

Unger, R.M. (1976), *Law in Modern Society*, Free Press, Collier-Macmillan

van den Haag, (1975), *Punishing Criminals*, New York: Basic Books

Wade, H.R.W. (1971), *Administrative Law*, Clarendon Press

Walters, H. (1975), *The Street*, Centreprise Publishing Project

West, E.G. (1975), *Education and the Industrial Revolution*, Batsford

Westergaard, J., and Resler, H. (1975), *Class in a Capitalist Society*, Heinemann

Wilson, E. (1977), *Women and the Welfare State*, Tavistock

Wilson, J. (1977), *Thinking About Crime*, New York: Vintage Books

Winch, D. (1978), *Adam Smith's Politics*, Cambridge University Press

Winkler, J.T. (1975), 'Law, state and economy: the 1975 Industry Act in context', *British Journal of Law and Society*, vol. 2, no. 2

Wood, E. (1978), 'C.B. Macpherson: liberalism and the task of socialist political theory', in R. Miliband and J. Savile (eds.), *The Socialist Register*, Merlin Press

Wright, E.O. (1973), *The Politics of Punishment*, New York: Harper & Row

Wright, E.O. (1978), *Class, Crisis and the State,* New Left Books

Young, J. (1975), 'Working Class Criminology', in I. Taylor, P. Walton and J. Young (eds.), *Critical Criminology*, Routledge & Kegan Paul

Young, M., and Wilmott, P. (1962), *Family and Kinship in East London*, Penguin

Zaretsky, E. (1976), *Capitalism, the family and personal life*, Pluto Press

Zavaleta, R. (1974), *El Poder Dual en American Latina*, Mexico: Mercado, Siglo Veintiuno Editores

Notes on contributors

Jock Young is currently Reader in Sociology at Middlesex Polytechnic. He has written many articles and written and contributed to several books, some of which include *The Drugtakers* (Paladin 1971), *Critical Criminology* (Routledge & Kegan Paul 1975), *The New Criminology* (Routledge & Kegan Paul 1973) and, with Stan Cohen, *Manufacture of News* (Constable 1973). He is a founder member of the National Deviancy Conference.

Bob Fine was born in 1945, gained a degree in Sociology at the University of Oxford and taught at the City University of New York from 1970 to 1973. He is a co-editor of *Capital and Class* and has written several articles on deviancy and the modern state. He is currently Lecturer in Sociology at the University of Warwick.

Richard Kinsey was born in 1944 and gained two degrees – in Law and in Sociology and Psychology – from the University of Leeds. He has written a number of articles on law and is the editor of *La Questione Criminale*. Since 1973 he has been Lecturer in the Sociology of Law in the Department of Jurisprudence, University of Edinburgh.

John Annette was born in 1950, gained a BA from Fordham University, New York, and a Diploma from the Sorbonne University, Paris. His current research is in the area of political economy and jurisprudence in the eighteenth century and he is involved in the Conference of Socialist Economists. He is currently Assistant Lecturer in History at Middlesex Polytechnic.

John Lea was born in 1944 and studied Economics and Sociology at the London School of Economics, gaining an MSc in 1969. His research interests include changing forms of social control in contemporary industrial societies and he is a contributor to *Permissiveness and Consent* (Macmillan 1979). He is currently Senior Lecturer in Sociology at Middlesex Polytechnic.

Dario Melossi, born in 1948, is the author of several articles on Marxist approaches to the criminal and penal questions. He is a member of the editorial board of *La Questione Criminale* and is currently Assistant in the Faculty of Law, University of Bologna. Together with Massimo Pavarini, he is the author of *Prison and Factory* (Macmillan, forthcoming).

Roger Matthews was born in 1948. He gained a BA in Social Science at Middlesex Polytechnic and an MA at the University of Sussex in 1974. He is interested in prostitution and social structure, and is currently Lecturer in Sociology at Middlesex Polytechnic.

Phil Cohen was born in 1944 and educated at Queens' College, Cambridge. He set up Street Aid in 1970 and since then has been a youth and community worker and has conducted research into the culture and history of working-class youth. His publications include, with David Robins, *Knuckle Sandwich* (Penguin 1978), and a forthcoming book, *Stopping the Wheels*.

Jeanne Gregory was born in 1941. She gained a BA at Bedford College and an M Sc from the London School of Economics in 1968. Her research interests include the enforcement of sex discrimination legislation. She is currently Senior Lecturer in Sociology at Middlesex Polytechnic.

Boaventura de Sousa Santos graduated from Coimbra Law School in 1963. He studied criminal law and philosophy of law for some years in West Germany and he earned a doctorate at Yale Law School in 1973. His main research interests are in the sociology of law and the theory of the state. He is currently Professor of Sociology at the School of Economics, University of Coimbra, Portugal.

Sol Picciotto was Lecturer in Law at University College, Dar es Salaam from 1964 to 1968 and he is currently Lecturer in Law at the University of Warwick. He is the author of several articles and books, mainly analysing the relationship between law and the state. He was a member of the Editorial Committee of *Capital and Class* from 1976 to 1978. He is a founder member of the Conference of Socialist Economists.